The Evolution of a New Industry

INNOVATION AND TECHNOLOGY IN THE WORLD ECONOMY
Martin Kenney, Editor

University of California, Davis/Berkeley, Roundtable on the International Economy
Other titles in the series:

The Evolution of a New Industry

A Genealogical Approach

Israel Drori, Shmuel Ellis, and Zur Shapira

Stanford Business Books,
An Imprint of Stanford
University Press
Stanford, California

Stanford University Press
Stanford, California

Special discounts for bulk quantities of Stanford Business Books are available to corporations, professional associations, and other organizations. For details and discount information, contact the special sales department of Stanford University Press. Tel: (650) 736-1782, Fax: (650) 736-1784

Printed in the United States of America on acid-free, archival-quality paper

Library of Congress Cataloging-in-Publication Data

Drori, Israel, author.
   The evolution of a new industry : a genealogical approach / Israel Drori, Shmuel Ellis, and Zur Shapira.
      pages cm
   Includes bibliographical references and index.
   ISBN 978-0-8047-7270-9 (cloth : alk. paper)
   1. High technology industries—Israel—History.   I. Elis, Shemu'el, author.   II. Shapira, Zur, author.   III. Title.
   HC415.25.Z9D76 2012
   338.4'76095694—dc23

                                                                                    2012016316

Typeset by Newgen in 10/15 Minion

Contents

Illustrations

Figures

Preface and Acknowledgments

Israel has a vital high-tech industry that has been the growth engine of the Israeli economy for more than 30 years. The industry is characterized by a distinct entrepreneurial culture, which stems from two interrelated factors: legacy and necessity. That is, it is characterized by a legacy of ingenuity, innovation, and improvisation, and a need to build a new nation and ensure its survival. The search for reasons for the success of the high-tech industry has led many to believe that there is a virtue in natural-resource poverty if it leads to engaging in deep transformation of people and nation. Starting from scratch in nation building has also led some to believe that one could run a social experiment to engineer both society and economy. It is as if "the liability of newness" is turned on its head; deficiencies turn into advantages.

The search for reasons for the Israeli high-tech industry's success must also account for its entrepreneurial culture, which is characterized by a highly motivated, skilled, and innovative workforce that has benefited from substantial government financial and institutional support for R&D and venture creation. For example, most of the world technology leaders, such as IBM, Intel, Microsoft, and Motorola, have R&D centers in Israel. The high-tech industry also benefits from a strong venture capital industry, which is any new industry's "lifeblood." Moreover, there are more Israeli technology companies traded on the NASDAQ than there are in any other country outside North America. Thus, the depth and magnitude of the Israeli high-tech industry has provided the bedrock for the foundation of its growing start-up activity.

The hype concerning Internet prospects in Israel is echoed by the *Red Herring*'s statement:

> It used to be that when you arrived in Israel and stepped off the plane, you were greeted by bright-eyed Zionists ready to share their rugged, pioneering idealism. Now when you step off a plane, you are immediately greeted by a gargantuan

sculpture of a cell phone. ("Welcome to the New Zionist Dream. Welcome to Silicon Wadi," *Red Herring*, September 2000)

The path of recent Israeli history is a story of transformation and adaptation. This is why we decided to take on the endeavor of writing this book, which presents a historical analysis of and insight into the evolution of an entrepreneurial, innovative sector in Israel. We focus on the information technology and communication (ITC) sector, and when we explore its evolution, we find that it is embedded in the country's historical legacy as depicted by its ability to achieve impressive take-off because of a focus on the global market.

We follow a genealogical framework to analyze the sector's growth that acknowledges the major role of initial social, political, and economic conditions in determining the sector's evolution. We argue that two interdependent elements—social structure on the one hand and institutional support on the other—enabled the evolution of the Israeli high-tech industry to succeed. These characteristics allowed the ITC sector to exploit the new global opportunities that opened up to those who assumed a pioneering role in developing technologies and services.

The aim of this book is to provide a comprehensive account of the evolutionary process of a modern communications technology sector in Israel through a highly innovative historical-genealogical approach. This approach enables us to trace the initial conditions under which a genealogy's founding parent firm was established. Those, in turn, affect the way firms spawn new ventures and have been shaping both the genealogy's evolutionary trajectory and its structure. This approach also provides a new lens for looking at intergenerational dynamics and sheds further light on the evolutionary dynamics of emerging industries and firms. Furthermore, by focusing on genealogical evolution, we are able to empirically trace the specific features associated with the founding processes of new ventures in terms of their birth origin along multiple generations, which influence the potency of the entire genealogy. Our genealogical approach focuses on ancestral origin and the intergenerational evolution of diverse Israeli ITC firms, and on the way that evolution unleashed forces that shaped the emergence and growth of industries and the firms' competitive advantage.

The historical evolution of the ITC sector is intertwined with those of individual entrepreneurs, the pioneers who were able to mobilize the country's unique resources, human capital, and cultural diversity. These capabilities have led many students of the Israeli high-tech industry to attribute its success to the nature of its social networks. In this book, we take a step further in understanding the growth dynamics of the industry. We hope to provide new insights by linking the past and the present and hinting at the future. We analyze the conditions under which the industry's pioneer founders operated, and we trace their genealogical trajectory. We decipher the process of firm founding and establish that it stems from parent-progeny relations, and we provide the reader with a complete account of the dynamics of evolution. We shed light on the question that has been asked by many researchers: How does entrepreneurial legacy and culture become so tenacious that the "DNA" of founding new and innovative start-ups leads to sustained growth over generations?

We also address questions of where new dynamic industries come from and what determines the early success of innovators in them. These questions are critical in light of the tremendous investments that such industries draw and the risk and uncertainty involved. The significance of the genealogical approach stems from its ability to facilitate the tracing of industrial evolution from early emergence to maturity. We hope that an understanding of the mechanisms and dynamics of genealogical emergence of the Israeli high-tech industry will help entrepreneurs, policy makers, and managers in the pursuit of starting and growing new technological industries.

This research was supported by the Israel Science Foundation (grant no. 1545/08). We acknowledge the financial support received from the following organizations: the Henry Crown Institute of Business Research at Tel Aviv University, the School of Business and Research Authority of the College of Management Academic Studies, and the William R. Berkley Center for Entrepreneurial Studies at the Stern School of Business. We are grateful for the insightful comments of Diane Burton and Brent Goldfarb. We also benefited from the comments of Joel Baum, Uri Bialer, John Carroll, Gino Cattani, Christina Fang, Moshe Farjoun, Avi Fiegenbaum, Steven Klepper, Joe Lampel, Robert Salomon, Rosemarie Ziedonis, and Ezra Zuckerman, who read various versions of a paper we had written as a part of this research project. We also thank our dedicated students who helped collect the data and construct the genealogies: Alon Gazit, Neta Kamin, Oren Ne'eman, Ayelet Noff, Snait Raz, Tali Stierler, Gidon Zundelevich, and Shir Zur. Without them, it would have been very difficult to complete this project. We extend our profound gratitude to the founders of the Israeli high-tech industry and the generations of women and men who are following their vision. Writing this book would not be possible without the generosity and guidance of many entrepreneurs and mangers that are building and sustaining the Israel high-tech industry. During our numerous encounters with them we were exposed to their knowledge and their willingness to share it. We highly appreciate their help in providing us a window into their fascinating world. Finally, we thank Rena Henderson for copy-editing the manuscript; Julia Kim for her dedicated and superb technical assistance; and our editor, Margo Beth Fleming, without whose encouragement and support this project would not have come to fruition.

The Evolution of a New Industry

Introduction

1

... The secret, then, of Israel's success is the combination of classic elements of technology clusters with some unique Israeli elements that enhance the skills and experience of individuals, make them together more effective as teams, and provide tight and readily available connections within an established and growing community. For outside observers, this raises a question: If the Israeli "secret sauce" is so unique to Israel, what can other countries learn from it?

Dan Senor and Saul Singer, *Start-Up Nation: The Story of Israel's Economic Miracle*

Since the late 1980s, the Israeli high-tech industry has witnessed unprecedented growth. The information technology and communication (ITC) sector in particular has exhibited innovative qualities and gained a leadership position worldwide—in spite of its small size, Israel is considered a global leader in this industry. Various studies have attempted to analyze the story of the Israeli high-tech industry and its trajectory to success. Most of them have focused on the processes and conditions that led to an agglomeration of resources and infrastructure and the formation of a unique high-tech sector (see, e.g., Avnimelech 2008; Breznitz 2007; de Fontenay and Carmel 2001; Saxenian 2002). However, the history and dynamics leading to the emergence of this sector have received little attention.

This book aims to reveal the environmental and organizational processes, as well as the critical paths, that underlie the evolution, structure, and comparative advantage of Israel's high-tech industry. We do not analyze its growth as a unified process stemming from the creation of a cluster. Instead, we present a complementary view in which we argue that Israel's ITC sector evolved out of diverse organizational models of founding that were embedded in two different institutional environments: an institutional-cooperative period that was followed by a competitive economic period.

We develop an evolutionary perspective on the development of the Israeli high-tech industry in general and on the ITC sector in particular. We do so by examining the context of inheritance and transmission of the sector's organizational characteristics while analyzing the prevailing institutional environments that represent the bedrock of its emergence and founding. Our theoretical conceptualization attends to both initial conditions and change, and uses a process-oriented mechanism to account for each. Furthermore, we predicate the evolution of the high-tech industry on its historical foundation.

As Stinchcombe (1965) asserts, initial conditions, including "the groups, institutions, laws, population characteristics and set of social relations that form the environment, have an enduring impact on industry evolution" (p. 142). This assertion implies a major challenge in explaining how the genesis of the institutional environment and the initial conditions under which key organizations were founded intertwined to create a particular momentum of growth for an entire industry.

We assert that initial conditions, socioeconomic processes, and geopolitical considerations, and the policy environment in particular, together influence the evolution of an industrial sector. They do so through the multilevel processes of inheritance and the intergenerational transmission of organizational forms, practices, routines, skills, and blueprints (see Phillips 2002, 2005). Furthermore, the evolutionary path of any industrial sector is shaped in response to the forces of competition, which affect an organization's mix and rate of change (Carroll 1984) and its corresponding entrepreneurial norms and opportunities.

The evolutionary mechanisms of competition and institutionalization dovetail with the persistent structures of organizational inheritance composed of certain practices and activities. In this perspective, both organizational and external forces are drivers of the Israeli high-tech industry's evolution. Such a comprehensive view allows us to assert the continuity between those who laid the foundation of the industry and their progenies who followed in their evolutionary path through direct inheritance structures. In the same vein, we can trace the changes in inheritance structures and processes that fostered a variety of organizational forms (Baum and Rao 2004; Stinchcombe 1968).

We first identify the origin of the founding firms in Israel's high-tech industry and their respective institutional environments; then we propose a genealogical framework for describing and analyzing the evolution of this industry.

In organizational terms, *a genealogy is a system of affiliation among organizations that originate from the same founding parents.* Because we focus on the founding process, we claim that the influence of founding parents is enduring and shapes the evolutionary trajectory of the entire genealogy. Thus, understanding the historical conditions at the founding of each genealogy is critical to our story. According to Stinchcombe (1965), the external environment at the time of founding is highly influential in shaping organizational characteristics that are imprinted with the "social resources available" (p. 168). Stinchcombe, a proponent of the imprinting perspective, explicitly contended that "organizations which are founded at a particular time must construct their social systems with social resources available" (p. 168). Once such social systems are built (in terms of structure, processes, and culture), they are maintained and further imprinted because "traditionalized forces, the vesting of interests, and the working out of ideologies may tend to preserve the structure" (p. 169).

Furthermore, founding parents of genealogies may not only constitute the potential bearers of new organizations through the spawning process (Klepper 2001)[1] but also be carriers of knowledge, values, and characteristics that encourage the spawning of new organizations. The assertion that progenies who found organizations rely on and learn from their parents has been widely discussed in recent literature (Klepper 2009; Baron and Hannan 2005; Burton 2001; Phillips 2002, 2005).

Our analysis of the evolutionary processes in the Israeli high-tech industry and our exploration of the industry's historical origins provide an understanding of how specific organizational genealogies are established and evolve. The genealogies presented in this book reflect the diverse structural characteristics, values, and routines associated with founding processes. We examine the different evolutionary patterns of the genealogies and their subsequent interrelationships, which characterized the maturity of this industry. These interrelationships stem from affinities between different genealogies and increase along generations with a genealogy's expansion. However, the different initial conditions that mark the founding of a genealogy's ancestors reflect different patterns of inheritance—namely, the spawning process and the transfer of capabilities and knowledge from generation to generation. For successful founding and survival, a new organization can rely on a number of sources for acquiring necessary resources: its management blueprints, norms, or values (Baron and Hannan 2005; Burton, Sorensen, and Beckman 2002; Hannan and Freeman 1989, 21; Baum and Singh 1994). However, the genealogical affiliation is its primary foundation. As we argued earlier, the relevance of genealogical evolution is twofold: in the founding of new firms and in the evolution of Israel's new high-tech communication and IT sector.

Founding parents and their incumbents carry entrepreneurial knowledge while spawning new firms through varied selection processes that tend to expand and diversify (Aldrich and Ruef 2006). A case in point is the small group of technology companies in the Silicon Valley, most notably Fairchild Semiconductor, which not only spun off numerous firms but also attracted other businesses in related technological fields and businesses (e.g., Castilla et al. 2000; Kenney 2000). The process of founding new firms is not only an issue of resource acquisition or agglomeration and clustering; it is also a genealogical progression, which relates to how founders develop entrepreneurial tendencies and acquire certain capabilities and skills that enable them to successfully launch new ventures. Consequently, our genealogical approach stresses the importance of both prenatal affiliation and heredity, both of which shape genealogical evolution through processes of selection. However, as we will demonstrate, parental affiliation does not necessarily imply that progenies are conditioned by their organizational "DNA" and indiscriminately mirror their parents. Environmental changes or selective adoption of managerial blueprints may introduce different models of founding, including different values and norms, that greatly influence the pattern of genealogical reproduction (e.g., Baum and Singh 1994; Hannan and Freeman 1989). Similar to the story of Silicon Valley, where, as mentioned, a number of genealogies descended from Fairchild Semiconductor (Rogers and Larsen 1984; Saxenian 1994), our case demonstrates that each ancestor of a genealogy spins off a "family tree" that exhibits its distinct characteristics in term of structure and reproduction pattern. The varied lines of heredity formed the entire ITC sector in Israel, which during the 1990s became a well-developed cluster with all the necessary complementary services.

This book explores a fundamental organizational process—the evolution of a new industry—that is due, to a large extent, to spawning. Spawning is the process by which employees of an incumbent firm found their own new venture, usually in the same industry. The value of this process is not unlike the influence of parents on their progeny because the experience, values, knowledge, and capabilities acquired during employment at an incumbent firm (parent) provide a basis for identifying and exploiting entrepreneurial opportunities. Furthermore, the strategic course—the managerial blueprints for routines and practices—and the culture and technology of newly minted firms in a genealogy are influenced by the characteristics of the parent company. This is the conceptual foundation of our work, which aims to provide a comprehensive account of the evolutionary process of a modern communication-technology sector.

In this book, we present the evolutionary process of a new industry by taking an innovative historical-genealogical approach based on the mechanism of spawning. This approach enables us to trace the initial conditions under which the founding parent firm is the first in what later becomes a genealogy. We show how those conditions affect the spawning of new ventures and shape the genealogy's evolutionary trajectory and structure. In this way, we offer a new lens for looking at intergenerational dynamics and shed further light on the evolutionary dynamics of the emergence of industries. Furthermore, by focusing on genealogical evolution, we can empirically trace the specific features associated with the founding processes of new ventures in terms of their birth origin and along multiple generations. These features, in turn, influence the potency, or the reproductive capacity, of the entire genealogy.

In his new book, *The Founder's Dilemmas: Anticipating and Avoiding the Pitfalls That Can Sink a Startup*, Noam Wasserman notes, "Stinchcombe (1965) argued that the liability of newness was due to three internal factors—the need for the team to develop working relationships, to find their newer roles, and to split financial rewards among themselves—and one external factor, the lack of relationships with potential suppliers, customers, and other external parties. The last factor has received vast amount of attention, the first three very little" (2012, p. 1). We agree with Wasserman, and the approach we pursue in this book emphasizes the effect of the external environment at the time of founding on several processes internal to a firm and to its genealogy. Thus, we hope to pursue a more comprehensive approach that follows Stinchcombe's framework in a more balanced manner. In this vein, the environment in which the Israeli high-tech industry has evolved features unique historical conditions marked by the government's active intervention in directing and regulating the industrial industry growth of the young nation. Objectives such as nation building, defense considerations, employment creation, and immigration absorption were the state's priorities, often irrespective of economic considerations. For example, from the state's early days, its defense policy emphasized resource mobilization and self-sufficiency. Consequently, the government established R&D facilities that focused on innovation in applied technology and that supported applied research in higher-education institutions (e.g., Drori and Landau 2011).

Theoretical Roots

The theoretical roots of our genealogical approach are grounded in institutional and ecological theories. These theories point, respectively, to the role of institutions in providing regulative, cognitive, and normative support to newly founded firms, and to the environmental determinants of organizational diversity, which influences their survival. Specifically, environmental conditions at the time of founding, as well as an organization's age, newness, and size, affect its structure and operations following the evolutionary processes of variation, selection, and retention. However, these theories do not explain how particular events generate a selection process that results in heterogeneous evolution patterns; nor do they illuminate the process by which organizational inheritance fosters a firm's persistence and transformation over time.

Other theories explore the origins of capabilities and core features of organizations. Imprinting approaches assume that an organization's core features imprint on its progenies and thus influence the entire evolution of an industry. Consequently, founders of new firms may introduce innovations that are based on knowledge gained while working at a parent firm. Such factors influence the number and size of firms in a genealogy. A new firm's strategies are influenced by pre-entry experience inherited from the parent company, such as human resource and employment blueprints and technological and market knowledge. Imprinting theories underscore exogenous forces and initial conditions, but they underplay the role of interactions among industry players and so offer limited insight into the forces that drive the emergence of industries and the competitive positions of firms. In contrast, our approach embodies a more comprehensive perspective that increases our understanding of the mechanisms and processes behind an industry's evolution.

Another approach to studying the evolution of industries emphasizes co-evolution processes. It identifies technological advancement as a driver of industry evolution and focuses on the interplay among innovation, industrial structure, and economic growth. Unlike aforementioned approaches, co-evolution takes into account the role of national institutions, among various other stakeholders, and emphasizes the interactions and causal linkages among organizations. Technological progress and industry evolution are considered both outcomes and drivers of change. However, aside from the general notion that evolving entities are interdependent, the co-evolution perspective prescribes no systematic patterns of evolution and pays no particular attention to the development stages of emerging industries.

Where new industries come from and what determines the early success of innovators in them are questions that have not been fully addressed in extant research. Some studies emphasize exogenous factors that drive corporate change; others consider endogenous processes and interdependencies across organizations. However, most ignore the founding stage of industry evolution and its influence on the prospects for industrial growth. These issues are critical in light of the largely risky investments that such industries make.

The significance of this book stems from pursuing a genealogical approach, which (1) advances research on industry evolution from its early founding to maturity; (2) uncovers the principles of genealogy construction and its potential for explaining the emergence and growth of a new industry; (3) analyzes the history of the Israeli ITC sector as an example of industrial development within an emerging economy; and (4) identifies key success factors in the telecommunications industry that can help policy makers and innovators in their investment decisions.

The Research Setting

We present the case of the Israeli high-tech industry and, in particular, its ITC sector, which has experienced tremendous progress in recent years. Renowned worldwide for its innovativeness and technological breakthroughs, Israel's ITC sector is considered a global success story and the growth engine of Israel's entire high-tech industry. In fact, the evolution of this sector is posited as an alternative model (Senor and Singer 2009) to Silicon Valley and is imitated by many advanced and emerging economies. Furthermore, Israel is a natural laboratory in the sense that it is a pioneer and innovator of modern communication technologies. Because it is a small country, we can effectively study most of the firms involved in the emergence of its telecommunications industry and combine field research with survey data as a means to establish a profound understanding of the industry from its embryonic through its mature stages.

Fiegenbaum (2007) presents a comprehensive paradigm of the Israeli high-tech industry that emphasizes its multilevel nature from a strategic management perspective. Focusing on the complementary activities at the global, state, individual, organizational, and industry levels, he shows how those factors, together, explain the takeoff phenomenon in the 1990s. Other studies have emphasized different perspectives, such as the role of venture capital (Avnimelech and Teubal 2003a, 2003b, 2004, 2006); the configuration and advantage of the Israeli high-tech cluster (de Fontenay and Carmel 2001); the role of national research and development policies and the "industrial-military complex" (including the defense industry at large) (Breznitz 2005a, 2006, 2007); and the institutional environment (Zilber 2006, 2007, 2011). Although these studies contribute significantly to our understanding of Israel's ITC evolution, their limitation is that they have focused on industry-related processes.

Our work explores the evolution of the Israeli high-tech industry over the last sixty years, focusing on two interrelated units of analysis: the industry and the firm. Again, our approach is genealogical, based on the theoretical foundation of parent-progeny relations, which have attracted recent attention in management research (Phillips 2002, 2005). By studying the full genealogical evolution of an entire industrial sector, we can trace the roots of founding and growth and predict and direct future sustainable growth at both the industry and the firm level. We focus on the founders of nine genealogies who have been involved both directly and indirectly in the creation of over nine hundred high-tech companies. Thus, in addition to contributing to theory, our findings can aid public and business policy makers in competing more effectively in global high-tech markets.

The Book's Structure

Chapter 2 presents the theories underlying the main approaches of the existing literature on the emergence of Israel's high-tech industry. These theories point to the role of environmental determinants of organizational diversity related to entry and survival of organizations, as well as to the ways in which institutions provide regulative and normative support. Specifically, environmental circumstances at the time of founding affect organizational structures and operations through the evolutionary processes of variation, selection, and retention. However, such theories fall short of explaining how particular events generate a selection process that results in heterogeneous evolution patterns. Consequently, we still know too little about the organizational inheritance that fosters firms' persistence and transformation over time.

As mentioned earlier, the co-evolution approach considers the role of national institutions (among various other stakeholders), emphasizing interactions and causal linkages among firms. However, it offers no systematic patterns of evolution and pays no particular attention to the development stages of emerging industries.

Chapter 2 also provides a detailed description of our genealogical approach, unfolding its origin and its intellectual and theoretical foundations and principles. The basic assumptions of our approach are as follows. First, new ventures' evolutionary paths are influenced both by their conditions at founding and by the imprinting effects of the organizational characteristics that shaped the founding processes. Second, those characteristics are transmitted through generations. Such a claim implies that "offspring" inherit certain "genetic" characteristics of "parents." We conjecture that the structure and characteristics of a genealogy and, ultimately, its size are affected by its particular line of heredity and affinity. The relations among founding firms and their progenies along different generations shape genealogical growth or potency, as measured by the number of newly spawned firms. We seek to understand the distinct influence of the founding parents on the evolutionary trajectory of the entire genealogy and, eventually, on its respective industrial sector. In so doing, we expand on the concept of heritage by analyzing the characteristics that are transmitted through intergenerational relations.

The chapter concludes by contending that tracing genealogies from founding parents to their next generations provides a new understanding of how industries grow.

Chapter 3 describes in detail the historical evolution of the founding parent organizations of the nine genealogies we examine and analyzes their particular characteristics. The chapter differentiates between the founding parents of two groups of genealogies—"old" and "new"—that were founded during two different historical periods. The old genealogies were created during a period we term the *cooperative economy*; the new genealogies, during the period we call the *competitive economy*. The former describes the institutional environment and policies during Israel's formative years—that is, from approximately 1948, the year of the country's independence, to 1977, the year of its political turnaround. This period is marked by centralized government intervention and substantial ownership of major economic enterprises by the country's labor federation. The latter period, the competitive economy, describes the institutional economy from 1977 through 2010, a time characterized by the country's transformation into a liberal, market-oriented economy and its integration into global markets. We describe the basic traits of each genealogy in terms of its historical development, its organizational characteristics, and its imprinting potential. We show how and why the new genealogies that evolved during the great communication revolution of the 1980s were more entrepreneurial and so have been more dominant in the sector's evolution.

Chapter 4 describes the structure and evolution of the nine genealogies we study, differentiating between those founded during the cooperative period and those during the competitive period. Through an analysis of founding models and processes, we demonstrate how the structure and characteristics of

the environment at the time of founding have an impact on the entrepreneurial tendencies of the founding parents. We also show that these tendencies are
transmitted along generational lines of the particular genealogy. These characteristics, which pass from one generation to the next, preserve the propensity of
the founding parents to spawn new ventures and influence the size and nature
of the entire industrial sector.

Chapter 5 presents an analysis of the processes that led to differences in
the genealogical evolution of Israel's high-tech industry. It also examines how
these processes affected the growth of the ITC sector and its ability to become
a technological and market leader. The chapter continues by considering the
implications of our theoretical approach and the ways in which it explains the
industry's growth.

Chapter 6 pulls together what this book has studied and accomplished—its
major findings and how they relate to genealogy theory. We conclude, first, by
considering the implications of our findings and, second, by speculating as to
why Israeli high-tech has been such a successful endeavor.

The Appendix presents the historical background of the Israeli high-tech
industry in general and the ITC sector in particular. It deals with the historical,
social, and political processes that led to the emergence of high technology in
Israel.

Summary

This book is about the mechanisms that brought about the evolution of Israel's
high-tech industry. Our genealogical approach rests on the idea that the entrepreneurial tendencies of a genealogy are the source of its diverse evolutionary
paths. Yet, among the genealogies we study, there is significant diversity in the
mechanisms that led to spawning. Such mechanisms influence a genealogy's
ability to spawn new firms. Different rates of spawning for each genealogy
determine its evolutionary trajectories and thus its influence and dominance.
We show how the historical path and specific characteristics of each genealogy
can help predict the evolutionary trajectory of the sector as a whole. Eventually, different genealogical characteristics stem from the *genetic variations* existing within and between offspring, families, or branches of lineages. These
are transmitted either directly, from parents to progeny in a successive line,
or indirectly, from the first to later generations. Ultimately, our analysis of the
growth process of Israeli high-tech may provide a conceptual framework for
explaining the evolution of an industrial sector, regardless of its type and/or
national origin.

A Framework for Genealogical Evolution

2

The idea of wireless solutions is rooted in my head since [my] first experience with the Internet. Then, I was working for RAD, and decided that if they [the Zisapel brothers, RAD founders] can do it, I can also. They taught me everything I know about the business. I [took] what I learn[ed], selectively and went on with my own start-up. We were working for big clients like Deutsche Telecom. Then I meet Hayim. He served in the same [military] unit, but in [a] different period. At [the] time he worked in Tadiran, but later with the crisis [in Tadiran, during the early 1980s] he moved to one of the Zisapels' companies and later founded one of his own companies. We decided to merge, not only because of technological complementarities—his company worked on wireless solution[s] for small and medium businesses in emerging markets—but because he was quite transparent for me. After all, we went to "kindergarten" together—[we] share the same history. From the beginning I knew that we are going to end-up with a half-a-billion-dollar company.

Interview with Yaakov, *a serial entrepreneur, 2006*

Studies of entrepreneurship beg the questions of how and why creation of a new venture ends in success or failure. To address this issue, we have developed a conceptual framework based on various theories regarding the founding of new firms and, consequently, the emergence and evolution of industrial sectors. In this chapter, we first present theories that explain how entrepreneurs—founders of new firms—shape the prospects of others in doing the same. We also examine the propensities and know-how needed for creating a new business venture from the ground up. Next we outline the various facets of our genealogical approach, which essentially claims that the initial conditions of founding lead to a spawning process of new ventures along generational lines. The genealogical affiliation, in turn, shapes the characteristics and the growth path of emerging individual firms and, in our case, the entire Israeli high-tech industry. These genealogical processes are instrumental to an understanding of the evolution of industrial sectors and to keeping or losing a competitive edge.

We have drawn on various theories of industry evolution to build our genealogical approach (e.g., Aldrich and Ruef 2006). We refer to "genealogy" as a group's record of descent or lineage (from its ancestors to the current generation) (Fox 1984). Genealogy reflects the degree of association and proximity within a network of relationships over time, characterized by path-dependent relationships (Arthur 1989, 1994; David 1994; Sydow, Schreyögg, and Koch 2009) among firms within a lineage system. We believe that the evolutionary trajectory of organizational genealogy is influenced by the genealogy members' affinity, mainly parent-progeny relations (Phillips 2002, 2005). Thus, investigating organizational genealogies may illuminate the processes leading to the transmission of organizational characteristics and the nature of the founding of new firms in certain industrial sectors.

A major theme of organizational genealogy is that conditions at the time of founding have an enduring effect on a firm's characteristics. These characteristics include prospective entrepreneurs' scope and degree of entrepreneurial or managerial know-how, which eventually lead to heterogeneity in the population of organizations (cf. Stinchcombe 1965). Moreover, our genealogical approach is related to imprinting perspectives in that inheritance dynamics influence the propensity to collaborate or compete. Thus, the study of the genealogical evolution of Israel's high-tech industry may demonstrate how a firm's behavior and performance are related to its lineage.

Genealogical analyses of organizations tend to focus on the nature of the environment and its effect on the initiation and growth of new firms. Because the pace of genealogical evolution cannot proceed without a certain influence of one generation on the next, any understanding of such influence implies that parents transmit relevant characteristics, values, practices, and blueprints to their progenies (Klepper 2001; Burton 2001; Baron and Hannan 2005; Phillips 2002). Accordingly, this chapter reviews the major perspectives that explain the various facets of a new venture's creation and the dynamic of inheritance and transmission of organizational traits, and it proposes a new direction in the study of industry evolution by introducing a genealogical perspective. This perspective can enhance our understanding of how industry emerges and matures in both depth and breadth. These objectives are compatible because, as we will demonstrate in this book, the success of the Israeli high-tech industry is closely related to the linkage between the ethos of new venture creation and the entire industry's evolution.

A Theoretical Framework of New Venture Evolution: External Determinants

In the next section, we review two major factors, the institutional environment on the one hand and initial conditions and imprinting on the other. These form the foundation of the genealogical evolution of a new industry.

The Institutional Environment

Studying the environmental and organizational processes—and critical paths—that drive the emergence of new industries is essential to understanding the evolution, structure, and comparative advantage of industries at both their embryonic and mature stages. In industries such as Israeli high-tech, the main challenges to emergence have stemmed from the environmental changes associated with availability of resources, technological feasibility, market needs, institutional legitimacy, and adoption of innovations (e.g., Aldrich and Fiol 1994). Challenges such as carving new markets, raising capital, and overcoming protective regulation pose hurdles to nascent industries, yet technological breakthroughs that are rapidly commercialized shape the socioeconomic environment and impact the prosperity of organizations.

Various theories view the environment as a primary factor in influencing industrial evolution. For example, institutional theory points to the role of institutions embedded in cultural worldviews and models that encourage isomorphism. Organizations operating in the same field exhibit tendencies toward uniformity of forms and structures as a way of gaining legitimacy regardless of efficiency considerations (Meyer and Rowan 1977, 1983). Furthermore, assumptions and assertions about organizational life are supported by regulative, cognitive, and normative frameworks that predetermine behavior or practices (DiMaggio and Powell 1983, 1991; Scott 2001). Thus, for example, viewing Israeli high-tech from an institutional perspective reveals certain cultural legacies that are common and shared. These cultural legacies may be reinforced by national ethos that feed into the industry and consequently shape its beliefs, values, norms, and vision as well as its practices and behavior (Zilber 2006, 2007, 2011).

Ecological theories focus on the nature of competition and its influence on various organizational forms and their chances of survival within certain environments (Carroll 1984; Carroll and Hannan 2000; Hannan and Freeman

1977, 1989). Accordingly, organizations strive to achieve a fit between themselves and their environment. Specifically, environmental circumstances at the time of founding and the organization's age, newness, and size determine its structure and operations via an evolutionary process of variation, selection, and retention (Aldrich and Ruef 2006; Campbell 1965). Thus, according to ecological theory, the Israeli high-tech industry consists of various specialized communities that compete (or cooperate) within certain ecological niches for the purpose of survival through reinforcing their relevance and status within their environment.

In our view, these theories fall short of explaining how particular events in the environment generate a selection process that results in heterogeneous evolution patterns. As Baum and Rao (2004) note, "We still know too little about processes leading to the emergence of new organizational forms, or the structure of organizational inheritance that fosters their persistence and transformation over time" (p. 213). The environment is thus considered an essential component in the emergence and growth of new organizations, in terms of both structure and forms. Evolutionary processes of variation, selection, and retention imply the idea that founding firms are associated with initial and boundary conditions that have an impact on the evolutionary trajectory.

Note that the two theories are not mutually exclusive[1] and that their integration facilitates the role of institutional ecology in the evolution of an industrial sector. For example, the interrelationship between various stakeholders in the Israel high-tech industry, such as venture capitalists, the Office of the Chief Scientist, and technological units of the army, shape the nature of the start-up culture in Israel as well as influence its co-evolutionary nature through flows of both information and resources (e.g., Avnimelech and Teubal 2008).

Initial Conditions and Imprinting

To understand the evolution of the Israeli high-tech, we resort to a theoretical framework that provides an explanatory "benchmark" for our genealogical approach. Stinchcombe's (1965) seminal work on the emergence of organizations provides us with a conceptual insight that situates the evolution of this industry within the framework of founding mechanisms. He asserts that new organizations are shaped by their ability to draw upon resources. This is particularly important in the nascent stages, when organizations are subject to what Stinchcombe calls the "liability of newness" (pp. 148–149). Stinchcombe outlines the social conditions that affect the degree of liability. These include new roles, which have to be learned; invention of new rules and standard routines and culture; social relations among strangers; trust—the need for social structure to reduce the differences in trustworthiness; and social network—stable ties to those who use organizational services. Stinchcombe points out that fledgling organizations that are vulnerable must align their rules and routines to facilitate relations with stakeholders who have the necessary resources. Further, the founding conditions imprint upon the new venture and have durable effects, both positive and negative, on its survival and development: "the groups, institutions, laws, population characteristics, and set of social relations that forms the environment," according to Stinchcombe (1965, 142), make up the context in which new organizations acquire the characteristics of the initial conditions that existed during their founding. Thus, we can assume that initial conditions may engender a certain similarity among organizations of the same sector, founded under the same conditions. This is because such organizations face similar environmental and survival challenges and, consequently, exhibit similar structural characteristics. Studies on the emergence of the Israeli high-tech cluster (Breznitz 2007; de Fontenay and Carmel 2001) have emphasized the unitary conditions under which the Israeli start-up culture flourishes. For example, entrepreneurs interviewed for this study claim that the nature of government incentive policies aimed at providing financial support at the nascent stage, and the support for complementary, not core, technologies, predisposed both investors and entrepreneurs to look for quick "exits" of new ventures.

Stinchcombe's (1965) imprinting hypothesis emphasizes the tenacity of a historical past. Stinchcombe claims that the environment and its characteristics, such as social relations, institutions, and legal systems, "are historically contingent and imprint an organization with the characteristics of the era when it was founded" (p. 142). In other words, the initial social and structural conditions at the time of founding, which include technological, social, political, economic, and cultural characteristics, exert enduring effects on future organizational development through inheritance dynamics. The assumption of the imprinting approach is that an organization's core features imprint on its progeny, which eventually influence the entire evolution of a specific industry. For instance, founders of new firms may introduce innovations that are based on knowledge gained during their employment with the parent organization. In the Israeli context, many start-ups—including Checkpoint, the flagship of the Israeli software industry—used the knowledge and technologies gained during the founders' army service in elite technological intelligence units.

Thus, imprinting theories suggest that chance events and exogenous factors influence the number and size of firms in an industry. Firms' strategies are influenced by pre-entry experience, such as human resource and employment blueprints (Baron and Hannan 2005) and technological and market knowledge (Agarwal et al. 2004), which are inherited from the parent entity. For example, an extensive study of blueprints that characterize entrepreneurial firms in the Silicon Valley (Baron and Hannan 2002, 2005; Baron, Burton, and Hannan 1996; Burton 2001; Hannan, Burton, and Baron 1996) developed three dimensions of employment blueprints that describe how high-tech start-ups drew on culturally appropriate templates to develop ideas about control, structure, work roles, and employee relations. These dimensions are (1) the basis of attachment and retention; (2) selection criteria; and (3) means of control and coordination. Within these dimensions, Baron and Hannan (2002, 2005) singled out five categories depicting employment blueprints that characterize most of the high-tech firms in their study. They labeled these autocracy, bureaucracy, commitment, engineering, and star. These blueprints correspond to the founding vision of the firm and, in turn, led to selection processes that instituted varied organizational forms. Furthermore, these human resource "blueprints" influence organizational outcomes such as turnover, costs, and performance, while changing "blueprints" may result in a decline in organizational effectiveness associated with performance and human resources practices.

In this vein, we note that Marquis (2003), in a study on how social technology available during the founding of inter-corporate networks continues to impact contemporary network structure, claims that "historically imprinted patterns have an influence on social forms beyond organizations" (p. 681). This means that societal and environmental conditions exert a wide range of influences on founding processes and, consequently, on the emergence of new industrial sectors.

Numerous studies following Stinchcombe's demonstrate that competitive founding conditions are critical in influencing organizational features that have lasting effects (Boeker 1988, 1989). Others have shown that initial conditions affect various organizational features, such as mortality rate (Swaminathan 1996) or pace of change (Tucker, Singh, and Meinhardt 1990). Implicit in the literature on the role of initial conditions and pre-entry experience at founding is the assumption that the characteristics of a new venture depend on the environmental context and the potential and activities of its founder(s). Accordingly, a founder may replicate the routines and related knowledge and know-how in the new founding organization (Klepper 2002). The initial social and structural conditions during a firm's founding thus imprint its capabilities and core features. As Dobrev and Gotsopoulos (2010) note, "Initial conditions exert a permanent, direct effect on subsequent developments regardless of the intermediary steps that have taken place since the start of the evolutionary process" (p. 2).

We assert that initial conditions influence the history-dependent evolutionary course of an industrial sector with the following implications. The initial conditions in different periods generate heterogeneous lines of firms, which may be affiliated with various genealogies. Here, Gompers, Lerner, and Scharfstein (2005) contend that the breeding grounds for entrepreneurial firms are more likely to be other entrepreneurial firms. It is in these environments that employees learn from their co-workers what it takes to start a new firm and are exposed to a network of suppliers and customers that are used to dealing with start-up companies. The spawning of entrepreneurial firms may also implicitly select less risk-averse individuals who are willing to bear the greater risk of starting a new firm. It is important to note that studies of Israeli high-tech claim that former affiliation, be it the army or the workplace, provide a strong impetus for founding new ventures (Senor and Singer 2009; Breznitz 2007). One of the most successful Israeli entrepreneurs confesses that he had waited for two years for two of his co-founders to be released from their army service before starting his firm.

The idea that economic, political, or social environments have enduring effects on the founding context has led to research on the influence of founders and top management teams on the future course of their organizations (Bhide 2000; Boeker 1989; Beckman and Burton 2008). Thus, the founding period and its initial conditions shape founding characteristics and how they are reproduced over time. As Stinchcombe (1965, 154) contends, the date of the (growth) spurt is highly correlated with the present social structure. More recent studies look mainly at two issues: first, the relationship between firms' entry characteristics and their performance, contingent on environmental turbulence and stage of industry life cycle (cf. Ganco and Agarwal 2009); and second, the process of behavioral imprinting and how founding characteristics imprint upon subsequent organizational features.[2]

By relating organizational behavior in Israeli high-tech to ancestors in incumbent firms, as well as to new start-ups that are composed of founders from different firms, these theories offer substantial insight into the forces that drove the emergence of the industry and its competitive position.[3] They stress that societal forms and characteristics of Israel's socioeconomic and political realities play a role in innovations that seem to be ahead of their time or that introduce a new technology or product—for example, the Internet security and communication technology based on fiber optics—which are prominent in the sector's success.

Theoretical Orientation: A Venture's Creation Mechanism

In this section, we elaborate on three models that characterize the creation mechanism of new ventures and their subsequent relationship with incumbent and new firms.

Spinoffs

Klepper (2009), in describing the nature of spinoffs, notes,

> Some are voluntary and are engineered by the parent firm. Some are motivated purely by an employee's desire to be his or her own boss, some to satisfy career aspirations, and yet others because of the failure or imminent failure of an individual's employer. (p. 160)

Accordingly, different industries and the nature of the parent firm—that is, its size or market position—influence the rate of spinoffs, their performance and survivability, and their role in the formation and development of clusters (Klepper 2001, 2009). Organizational scholars who study the theme outlined previously have investigated the spawning phenomenon—the process in which one or more employees of an incumbent firm create a new venture that harnesses the latter's potential contributions to the new venture. According to the spawning theory, experience gained during employment, including knowledge transferred to the spinoff, is extremely valuable to the prospective entrepreneurs of new ventures.

In a series of studies on the founding spinoffs in various industries, Klepper and associates (Klepper 1996, 2001, 2002; Klepper and Sleeper 2005; Klepper and Thompson 2010) identify three models to explain the patterns, motives, and characteristics of spinoffs. The first model, which is associated with agency theories (Klepper 2001), views the founding process as stemming from the ability of founders of new companies to introduce innovations related in some way to the activities of their parent companies (Anton and Yao 1995; Bankman and Gilson 1999). Thus, spinoffs emerge as the result of founders who exploit innovation and activities developed while working for their "parents." However, employees may be less inclined to take the risk of starting a new venture when in a secure management position in a large corporation.

The second model, which is based on organizational capability theories (Cooper 1985; Klepper 2001), focuses on the redundancy of discovery for incumbent firms and their difficulties in exploiting it for various business and organizational considerations—for example, diversion from core business (see also Tushman and Anderson 1986). Individual employees who are well positioned and armed with the necessary skills and abilities may seize the opportunity to start a new firm (Aldrich and Wiedenmayer 1993; Bhide 2000). Essential skills, knowledge, technological opportunities, and familiarity with market structure are embodied in the spinoff's former affiliation and history. Therefore, the nature of its relations with the parent firm, which is not necessarily a competitive threat, may be likely to influence both the type of its activities and its prospects for survival and success (Eckhardt and Shane 2003; Klepper 2001; Romanelli and Schoonhoven 2001; Shane 2000, 2001).

In the third model, learning theories claim that founders learn from their parents the knowledge and strategies needed to exploit similar products and services (Franco and Filson 2006; Agarwal et al. 2004). The learning model (Klepper and Sleeper 2005) suggests that employees with knowledge and initiative recognize that their employers might "cannibalize" their ideas for innovation or products. Thus, one option for such employees is to leave the incumbent firm and found a new one. However, the flip side of this claim is that employees with relevant ideas may prefer to remain in their organization and pursue them from within (Cabral and Wang 2008; Chatterjee and Rossi-Hansberg 2008; Klepper and Thompson 2010). Furthermore, Klepper and Sleeper (2005) suggest that firms continuously evaluate the merit of their employees' ideas. This practice has an impact on the employees' standing within the firm and thus affects the influence they have on the firm's policies and actions regarding ideas and innovation. Klepper (2009) contends,

> Firms are unable to recognize the best ideas and thus underweight them in their choice of what to do, leading to disagreements between the firm and its best employees about what it should do. If a disagreement is sufficiently large, then the employee leaves to found his own firm. At first, all employees have the same priors about what the firm should do, hence there are no disagreements. Then they receive different signals about what the firm should do, and disagreements materialize. (p. 167)

Others use theory grounded in evolution, contending that heredity relations between "children" (spinoffs) and "parents" (incumbents) involve the latter's providing resources, such as technical and market-related knowledge, models of organization, and entrepreneurial opportunities (e.g., Freeman 1986; Phillips 2002). Such support influences the prospects of founding and shapes the nature of spinoffs at birth. The genealogical approach we develop here contains mechanism of heredity relations through which resources and entrepreneurial culture are transmitted along generational lines. In addition, the rate of spinoffs is relatively high, particularly in "younger" industries such as semiconductor (Braun and MacDonald 1982; Freeman 1986), rigid disk drive (Christensen 1993; Agarwal et al. 2004), and lasers (Klepper and Sleeper 2005), as well as in service industries such as advertising (Garvin 1983) and law (Phillips 2002, 2005). The successful experiences of these industries, which innovate and globalize, encourage employees who are either self-motivated or discouraged by their employers' unwillingness to support their innovative ideas to leave the incumbent firm and pursue their own start-up (Christensen 1993; Klepper and Sleeper 2005; Romanelli and Schoonhoven 2001).

Furthermore, in these knowledge-based industries, prior acquired skills, knowledge, affiliation, and management models have a direct bearing on the prospects of entrepreneurial spawning (Franco 2005; Gompers et al. 2006). The nature of the parent firms also has a direct impact on the potency of their spinoffs. For example, better-performing firms in terms of "longevity, peak market share, early entry, product quality, and /or product scope, have higher spinoff rates" (Klepper 2009, 162). In the same vein, firms in less diversified environments that benefited from the support of venture capital (VC) spawn more VC-backed start-ups, as well as publicly traded companies in both Silicon Valley and on Route 128 (Gompers et al. 2006).

The importance of spinoffs is particularly relevant to the emergence of new industries. First, spinoffs promote the ideas that incumbent firms are reluctant to pursue (Klepper 2009). Second, they are models of newly founded firms that not only tap the experience of incumbent firm but also disseminate knowledge and managerial practices and innovations. Third, they are an integral part of the growth of innovative industrial clusters such as the Silicon Valley, U.S. biotech (Powell, Packalen, and Whittington, forthcoming), and Israeli high-tech sectors. Various aspects of the spinoffs' mode of founding firms are highly represented in the genealogy of the Israeli high-tech industry, as we demonstrate later in this book. Spinoffs in Israel emerge through various modes. Both those founded by employees of incumbent firms and new entrants seem to be associated with tightly connected networks. In addition, smallness and cultural tendency, which were described by many of the founders whom we interviewed in our research, emphasize "feeling comfortable and trust when we stick together with our own" (Interview with a serial entrepreneur, May 2006).

Nascent Stage and Inheritance

In the early days of their existence, nascent organizations operate in an unknown institutional environment in an attempt to ensure necessary resources, such as finance, skilled labor, and legitimacy. This implies that a venture's survival depends on external stakeholders favorably interpreting its prospects and potential (Lounsbury and Glynn 2001). Nascent organizations' relative lack of legitimacy exposes them to risks of premature death due to the liability of newness (Stinchcombe 1965; Freeman, Carroll, and Hannan 1983). In addition, new firms must gain cognitive and sociopolitical legitimacy for crucial activities, such as mobilizing resources, initiating products and markets, and establishing or linking with social networks and shared beliefs regarding their understanding of the business world (Aldrich and Fiol 1994). They also work to enhance their ability to cope with industry challenges such as technology and market (Aldrich and Ruef 2006).

An emerging field of research examines the founding of new firms that have inherited cultural beliefs, technological knowledge, or managerial blueprints from industry incumbents (e.g., Phillips 2002; Franco 2005). As Hannan and Freeman (1989) contend, "Although we have learned a good great deal about selection processes, we still know very little about the other side of the evolutionary process, the structures of inheritance and transmission" (p. 20). In predominantly evolutionary terms, this transfer of traits and blueprints from the incumbent firm to its spinoffs can be seen as the reproduction of the former's "genetic code."

Consider new industrial sectors such as those involving semiconductors (Freeman 1986), disk drives (Agarwal et al. 2004), or lasers (Klepper and Sleeper 2005). The success of these sectors has encouraged employees to leave incumbent firms and pursue their own start-ups (Klepper and Sleeper 2005; Romanelli and Schoonhoven 2001). Some studies have shown that human resource and employment blueprints (Baron and Hannan 2002, 2005), technological and market knowledge (Bhide 2000; Agarwal et al. 2004), nontechnical knowledge (Chatterji 2009), and access to venture capital (Gompers et al. 2006) are a few examples of what progeny (spinoffs) inherit from parents (incumbents) and what subsequently influence the former's behavior. It should be noted that while studies have focused mainly on parent-progeny relations or on spinoffs' abilities to survive, important questions regarding the imprinting effect of parents on *multiple-generation* progeny remain unanswered (Jaffee and McKendrick 2006). Studying the effect of multiple-generation spinoffs may provide important insights into the effect of potent progenitors on the survival of their progeny.

Of interest is the question of what is inherited. Recent studies have focused on the idea that founders of spawned start-ups carry with them experience, skills, and practices and apply them to the new organizations, thus shaping "the new firm behavior" (e.g., Beckman 2006; Boeker 1997; Kraatz and Moore 2002). So, for example, human resource blueprints created at founding may be relevant to the prospects of start-ups' effectiveness and survival (e.g., Baron and Hannan 2002), Research stemming from the Stanford Project on Emerging Companies (SPEC) (Baron, Burton, and Hannan 1996) shows how human resource blueprints associated with commitment and sustained patterns of reliability and accountability may become dominant templates to be relied on during change (Baron and Hannan 2002, 2005). Furthermore, Burton, Sorensen, and Beckman (2002) argue for reputation imprinting. That is, being a spinoff of a prominent parent—in terms of its position and status in the industry or its spawning reputation—may influence investment decisions in the new firm as well as access to opportunities and resources (Burton, Sorensen, and Beckman. 2002; Higgins and Gulati 2003). In this way, a well-positioned and prestigious firm may imprint its spinoffs with a legitimacy (Stuart, Hoang, and Hybels 1999) that signals to potential investors that a spinoff's founders and employees are trustworthy (Eisenhardt and Schoonhoven 1996) or that its technological innovations are important (Podolny and Stuart 1995). In the same vein, Phillips (2002, 2005) argues that position imprint determines the persistent of gender hierarchies in newly funded law firms.

Parent-Progeny Relations

As previously stated, if we consider the process of transferring traits and blueprints from a predominantly evolutionary perspective, we can say that the incumbent firm's "genetic code" is reproduced in its progeny. "Parents" influence their "progeny" through the "genes" (or "DNA") of experiences, skills, practices, and knowledge that offspring carry with them and apply them to the newly created organization. By doing so, they help shape the new firm's behavior (Beckman 2006; Boeker 1997; Kraatz and Moore 2002). Transmitting organizational "genes" may have practical advantages for progeny. Offspring may introduce innovations and practices related in some way to the activities of their parent company (Bankman and Gilson 1999) because they have inherited the knowledge and strategies needed to exploit similar products and services (Franco and Filson 2006; Agarwal et al. 2004). Research thus calls our attention to the varied situations, conditions, and requirements that bring about effective transmission of the "genetic code" from parent companies to their spinoffs.

Several studies outline the instrumental utility of parent-progeny relations. For example, employees learn and apply technological knowledge (Chatterji 2009; Klepper 2001), managerial routines, capabilities, and blueprints (Baron and Hannan 2005; Burton, Sorensen, and Beckman 2002; Phillips 2002, 2005; Klepper 2001, 2002). A new venture's chances to succeed go up if it has prominent "parents" that can provide supportive "assets" and tangible "tool kits" to help ensure its survival (and performance) over other industry entrants (Agarwal et al. 2004; Chatterji 2009; Ganco and Agarwal 2009; Helfat and Lieberman 2002).

By and large, in studying the nature of parent-progeny relations, including the characteristics of parent firms and their spinoffs (Helfat and Lieberman 2002; Jaffee and McKendrick 2006), scholars have focused mainly on what is being inherited (e.g., technological or marketing know-how) and its implications for the spinoffs' prospects of survival (Klepper 2001; Agarwal et al. 2004).

Studies of parent-progeny relations have focused on analyzing the characteristics of spawned firms in terms of taxonomical categorization—that is, *de novo* vis-à-vis *de alio* entrants (Agarwal et al. 2004) or pre-entry experience (Carroll et al. 1996; Klepper 2001)—or according to the parent firm's technological or market stance (Agarwal et al. 2004). Studying sources of the founding of VC-backed start-ups, Gompers, Lerner, and Scharfstein (2005) find that diverse initial conditions influence the prospects of entrepreneurial spawning. These include entrepreneurs who spun off from public companies and entrepreneurs who spun off from younger firms that were, themselves, backed by venture capital and are located in the main "hub" of venture capital (e.g., Silicon Valley or Route 128). Such firms also serve as fertile ground for spinoffs, as we demonstrate in our genealogical analysis (see Chapter 5).

Missing from current research on parent-progeny relations is the temporal aspect. Our study expands on the genealogical perspective in arguing that the influence of initial conditions extends beyond first-generation parent-progeny relations. We propose that organizational blueprints for entrepreneurship are transmitted not only between parent and progeny but also from the first generation along the entire organizational lineage. Moreover, a certain genealogy may exhibit traits and structural characteristics that enhance its potency and, consequently, its collective growth. When the founding parents possess entrepreneurial values that their progeny consider worth emulating, the progeny are more likely to benefit from their parents' experience and achievements, which may act as "templates" for the spinoff's members.

Principles of Genealogical Evolution

The framework developed in this book argues that genesis events serve as a mechanism for introducing variation, which, in turn, leads to selection processes that institute yet another set of variations (e.g., Aldrich and Ruef 2006). Thus, variation reflects an evolutionary process that stems from the historical circumstances of genesis and founding events. The source of variation resides within the individual organizations, starting with the founding events and following an evolutionary trajectory that is influenced by a genealogical chain of founders who are related to one another by parent-progeny relations and other, related founding affinities such as intergenerational or cross-generational founding.

A *genealogy* is a record of a group's descent or lineage from its ancestors to the current generation. It reflects the degree of association and proximity in a network of relationships created by genealogical connections that are characterized by evolutionary relationships among firms forming a lineage system. By and large, genealogical ties are modeled according to the natural relations of genealogical parenthood. However, inclusion in the genealogy may also be through affinity, as in the case of mergers and acquisitions or a founding event with an exogamous partner. Behind every genealogical evolution lies a basic founding event that triggers intergenerational progression—organizations that carry their parents' genetic codes in the forms of strategy, routines, technology, knowledge, market, and so forth (Klepper 2001; Phillips 2002, 2005).

Our genealogy approach is based on Thorstein Veblen's notion of affinity (Stahl-Rolf 2000). That is, the evolution of organizational genealogies is studied through tracing their common origin and multigenerational lines while following the relations between the founding events over time. It should be noted that an explanation of the genealogical process based on genealogical affiliation must include the influence and dependence of one organization in the line of the genealogy on another. As Stahl-Rolf (2000) states,

> Just as in evolutionary biological theories, a concept is necessary to explain why one organism is a member of an evolving species or, put in terms reflecting the historic context, why one problem arises as a phenomenon on a specific historic development path. Biology needs to explain stability, novelty, and the spread of novelty, and so do the social sciences. (p. 896)

There are two basic arguments in our genealogical approach. First is the liability of origin of genealogy: the new ventures' evolutionary paths are influenced by an imprinting effect and by the strategic managerial actions of the founding parent—the *founder* of the first firm in the genealogy. This implies that certain "genetic" characteristics of the founding firm of an entire genealogy affect the evolutionary processes of the whole genealogy. Furthermore, certain characteristics of the founding firm are inherited by offspring, or certain strategic decisions of the founding firm might determine, for example, whether new firms will join the genealogy by birth or by marriage. Thus, the nature of the *origin of genealogy* may determine how the new venture's capabilities are shaped or how they evolve or vary. The research, then, investigates the diverse interrelationship between the *founder effect* and the evolutionary path of the various genealogies of the Israeli ITC sector in order to predict the causal circumstances under which parenting events shape the nature of parent-progeny and cousin (exogamous) relations. This may, in some cases, be a blessing, as parents provide the relevant necessities and resources for early consolidation and future growth; or the progeny's replicating of successful organizational forms of a previous generation may sometimes come at the expense of the parent (Phillips 2002). For example, the higher the rank of the child in his or her parents' organization, the greater the parent-progeny transfer—and thus the more hazardous the parenting event to the parent and the more beneficial the parenting event to the offspring (reallocation of human and social capital).

Our second argument is associated with the evolutionary path of the genealogy and its implications. The main process affecting the evolutionary path of a genealogy stems from the characteristics of founders (parents) that result in the various ways that new entrants emerge and evolve. This, in turn, has a direct bearing on the genealogy structure, its characteristics, and its strategic direction. However, spinoffs may trace their difficulties in the market or R&D directly to their parents, which provide them with distinctive but rather limited knowledge (Klepper and Sleeper 2005).

Building on existing diverse research that has studied how incumbent firms influence their progenies (e.g., Klepper 2001; Phillips 2002, 2005; Baron and Hannan 2005), we explore the notion of genealogical potency—that is, the extent to which parents influence their offspring through imprinting and transfer of resources, values, and practices (Nelson and Winter 1982). Consequently, the progenies' qualities, which stem from their "history" or path dependence (David 1994) may reflect on the genealogies' potency and predict their likelihood of survival and growth. It should be noted that research also suggests that the interaction between internal structures and external environment (Thompson 1967), or the interaction between structure and internal and external environment, may be the dominant factor influencing organizational outcome.

In applying a genealogical approach to the organizational evolution of the Israeli high-tech industry, we give special attention to the notion of network dynamics, and we acknowledge the environmental context in which new firms evolve (Burt 2000; Hoang and Antoncic 2003). Advocating the study of networks of macro-dynamic evolution, Powell et al. (2005), state, "the linkage between network dynamics and the evolving structure of fields needs to be made in order to make progress in explaining how the behavior of actors or organizations of one kind influence the actions of organizations of another kind" (p. 1134). In the same vein, network dynamics is also helpful to the study of entire industries (Granovetter and McGuire 1998; Castilla et al. 2000). Thus, our theoretical approach is based on a dynamic mapping of the Israeli high-tech industry's networks and their evolution over time. By doing so, we attempt to reveal the meanings of the evolutionary paths that stem from various founding origins, which eventually shaped the Israeli high-tech industry's distinctive organization. In this regard, we can glean from the industry's genealogical patterns, which consist of founders, spinoffs, spinoffs of spinoffs, mergers and acquisitions, and so on, a valuable insight regarding the evolution of this industrial sector and its outcome.

In genealogical evolution, an organization's initial standing in terms of the ability to draw on the parent's resources and capabilities leads to isomorphism regarding the progeny's strategy (Klepper 2001). Inferring from such an "imprinting" process of parent-progeny relations, Phillips (2002, 2005) also claims that intergenerational closeness and homogeneity within a population of organizations may predict the progenies' chance of survival through a predetermined evolutionary course. As Phillips (2005) points out,

> Populations producing a high proportion of progenies increase population homogeneity by reproducing social structure and organizational forms across generations. Not only do progeny receive routines and resources from the previous generation, but they are also rewarded with improved life chances that make them candidates to produce the next generation of organizations. (p. 503)

A few recent studies have investigated the role of a genealogy's structure and in particular the relationship between parents and spinoffs in conditioning the performance of its members' (Ito and Rose 1994; Ito 1995; Rose and Ito 2005). Looking at spinoff strategy in Japan, Rose and Ito (2005) contend that "creating offspring appears to be an approach to enhancing familial survival" (p. 10). Moreover, they show (Ito and Rose 1994) that Japanese parent companies tend to behave somewhat "altruistically" by distributing core competencies or allowing operational freedom to spinoffs. By doing so, they risk being outperformed for the sake of the survival of the whole family.

In fact, prominent parents with an ability to directly imprint their progenies with effective skills, practices, knowledge, or blueprints may well end up creating genealogies that are more potent; namely, they are "virulent" in spawning spinoffs. Potency is understood in terms of both the degree of transmission of practices, routines, or values from parent to progeny and the parents' reproduction potential. Furthermore, the genealogical approach suggests that strength and consistency in the transfer of resources and routines between parents and progeny directly influence the progenies' viability. The potency of each genealogy can play a key role in its own evolution and in the growth of the entire industry sector. Because potency represents the potential for cooperation and resource and information sharing among a certain genealogy's members, new firms coalesce around a dominant business model or technology that may serve as a "security net" against competitors. To the extent that the potency of a genealogy enhances the interaction among its members, it also promotes interdependencies and a transfer of practices, routines and values among them. This, in turn, may produce a "bandwagon" effect, which benefits each member as a bearer of its predecessors' inheritance.

Thus, the behavior of the genealogy's members across generations depends on (1) the continued existence of the parent company as a model and a source of cultural values that legitimate its descendant firms, and (2) the parent's ability to transfer these values to its descendants. On the face of it, the parent company needs to have a set of values, shared beliefs, norms, and capabilities that are stable over time so that new firms "born" to the genealogy can engage in imprinting, emulating its founder; also, the genealogy must have a structure that facilitates the imprinting process. For example, in genealogies with more "insect relations" and more serial entrepreneurs, traits may be transferred directly from early to later generations. In other words, the structure of a genealogy in terms of composition of affiliation may influence the efficiency of the imprinting.

Dyck (1997) studied 60 self-governing religious congregations, applying a conceptual framework based on the human-family metaphor and classifying new ventures according to their intergenerational organizational lineage. His analysis suggests that the ancestry origin of an organization predicts the nature of future organizational procreation activities, as well as their "fertility rate," but not necessarily their performance. For example, unwanted children beget unwanted children; siblinglessness increases the number of offspring, and firstborns are more likely to be unwanted (Dyck 1997). However, Dyck's study concludes that the effect of type of birth on future offspring performance is unclear. Other studies on the founding process have claimed that shared parents are more likely to enhance successful outcomes. Neck et al.'s (2004) study on new venture creation in Boulder County, Colorado, presented the genealogy of local high-tech firms that had spun off from "trunks" of seven primary incubator organizations. These incubators served as the genesis bedrock for new organizations, which followed a well-defined path. Although this path was marked by the establishment of supporting systems and institutions (universities, VCs), the creation of new ventures was also dependent on "events experienced by existing organizations in the population" (p. 206). Thus, a genealogy emerged from a distinct founding father, its evolutionary path embedded in relational and structural contexts that can be defined by the nature of its heredity line.

Organizational Genealogy: Operational Definition, Domains, and Outcome

A *genealogy*, in our study, refers to a multigenerational lineage of firms that originated from a common ancestor and can be traced to this ancestor by either direct or indirect affiliation. Affiliation of a single firm to the genealogy's founder reflects the degree of association and proximity along generational lines. By and large, the genealogical ties are modeled according to the natural relations of genealogical parenthood. However, inclusion in the genealogy may also be through affinity such as mergers and acquisitions or a founding event with an exogamous partner. Our main assertion is that the structure and characteristics of each genealogy represent a corollary of its genesis and founding events and the nature of its particular line of heredity and affinity. Thus, in this study of the genealogical evolution of the Israeli high-tech industry, we primarily focus on how parents imprint the nature of multigenerational evolution within an industrial sector and how the potency of parents' inheritance (or "genes") fosters the persistence and transformation of genealogical structures (e.g., Baum and Rao 2004). Adapting a genealogical perspective (Phillips 2002, 2005), our study also points to an elaboration of Klepper's (2001) notion of heritage relations. In doing so, it expands on both Klepper's (2001) and Phillips' (2005) conceptions that refer to the nature of heritage, in terms of traits transmitted through intergenerational relations, and the imprinting conceptions that reflect the utility of the transmitted models and blueprints (Burton,

Sorensen, and Beckman 2002; Burton and Beckman 2007). The focus on multi-generational evolution offers a theoretical framework that is mainly concerned with the ability to detect the tenacity of founding along historical periods. We claim that disparate founding models affect the evolution and eventually the performance of firms who belong to a certain genealogy in spite of cluster factors that may converge on the evolution of an industrial sector. Our genealogical approach is thus set to understand the distinct role played by founding events in the evolutionary trajectory of an industrial sector.

In addition, variations within the genealogy determine its selective transformation, its composition, and the nature and source of affiliation. For example, unlike familial (human) genealogy, which is normally made out of linear affinity in terms of generational path, our genealogies are varied in terms of affinity and linearity. Familial genealogies are usually constraints by cultural or social norms and rules that usually define who is entitled to perform a reproductive role, the degree of affinity, and the social and other roles attached to it (Fox 1984). Thus, a genealogy is founded by ancestors (real or mythological), grows by its children and then its grandchildren, and so on. Our definition of genealogy transcends familial societal norms of affiliation. For example, in our research "insect relations" are common; spinouts are founded out of "marriage" between parent and grandchild or out of marriage between founder, grandchild, and progeny from the fifth generation.

Within a broader environmental context, organizations of a certain genealogy make intentional and unintentional choices about the path they wish to pursue in terms of their survival strategy. These choices eventually draw the boundaries of each genealogy in terms of its structure, its potency, and its reaction to its business environment. In turn, they become the building blocks of intergenerational evolution of various genealogies. In genealogical terms, this is a matter of understanding the evolutionary course of organizations, which revolves around two dimensions. First is the evolution of strategic orientation and the extent to which this strategy bears uncanny characteristics that increase the genealogy's entrepreneurial tendencies. Second is the genealogy's imprinting potential, the degree to which the organizational blueprints, shared beliefs, and values set up by the founders can be transferred through the genealogy's successive generations.

Affiliation and Its Formation

The main thrust underlying our genealogical approach relates to the fact that the birth event of an organization is performed by social actors that affiliate in a certain point of time to both parents and progeny. These birth events take place in each generation and originate from direct descent and/or exogamous affinity. The genealogical lines might predict what types of new organizations will be born, their structural-institutional and organizational characteristics (e.g., organizational models, technology, knowledge, markets, alliances, access to human, social, and financial capital, legitimacy), and, consequently, their likelihood of survival and growth.

In principle, organizational genealogies have two basic dimensions: origin and affiliation. The former refers to the ways in which a firm belongs to an organizational genealogy, either by "birth" or by "marriage." An organization may belong to two nuclear families: one in which it is a child (new enterprise, new acquisition, or merger) and one in which it is a parent (original founder or acquirer or ex-employees from this organization who are the founders or acquirers). The former is called the *family of child or orientation*; the latter is called the *family of spouse or procreation* (de Nooy, Mrvar, and Batagelj 2005).

The second dimension is the nature of affiliation: endogenous or exogenous. In *endogenous affiliation*, a firm is defined as a member of a particular genealogy if it is related to it by "birth." Accordingly, we identify six types of membership in genealogies of firms: (1) the *founding parent*, the origin of the genealogy; (2) *independent start-ups* (de-novos), firms founded by independent entrepreneurs who have left an incumbent firm; (3) *spinoffs*, firms that used to be a division of an incumbent firm or of one of its offspring and have become new independent entities, in which—the incumbent firm has an ownership stake (Ito and Rose 1994); (4) *firms* founded by members, new ventures directly established by incumbent firms; (5) *acquired firms*, companies that were acquired by a company belonging to the same genealogy, that is, by an incumbent firm or one of its offspring; and (6) *mergers*, new firms created by merging two or more firms, at least one of which is already a member of the genealogy.

In *exogenous affiliation*, a firm is defined as an exogenous member of a particular genealogy if its origin is from another genealogy and related to the former by "marriage"; thus, the new joiner is a co-founder, co-acquirer, or co-merger. All of the firms of exogenous origin are affiliated with at least two genealogies. They are the nodes that link different ones. Each genealogical line presents a different reproductive process and path, leading to the various characteristics of, and relations among, different genealogies.

Each of the ways in which a firm belong to a genealogy may vary according to the following characteristics: number of incumbents (one or more founders or acquirers), incumbent's source (the founding firms or ex-employees are from the same genealogy, from an external genealogy within the same industry, or from an external genealogy and different industry), kind of industry (the new firm remains or does not remain in the same industry).

Genealogies may vary in different ways depending on characteristics such as the number of incumbents (one or more founders or acquirers), the incumbent's origin (he or she may come from the founding firm or may be an ex-employee of a company in the same genealogy, or may come from an external genealogy in the same or a different industry), and the type of industry. Genealogies can also vary according to particular types of relations among members. Unlike a familial (human) genealogy, which is normally linear in terms of generational path, organizational genealogies vary in terms of their affinity and linearity. Moreover, familial genealogies are usually constrained by cultural and social norms and rules that define who is entitled to perform, for example, reproductive and social roles, and by the degree of affinity. Thus, a genealogy is founded by ancestors (real or mythological) and grows by their children, their grandchildren, and so on (Fox 1984). Note that a genealogy is affected by origin of founding, that is, whether the new venture was founded by one or more ex-employees from a firm in the same genealogy or a different genealogy in the same industry, or by mix of founders from two separate genealogies within the same or a different industry.

Our perspective on genealogical evolution transcends familial societal norms of affiliation. For example, cross-affinity relations (which can be described as a kind of "incest") are relatively common in our study. They exist when a spinout is founded by a parent teaming up with a grandchild or great-grandchildren along the generational line. They can also be created by a spinout founded by a parent and a progeny with kinship affinity (e.g., a kinship relationship that resembles those of "blood": siblings, brothers, uncles, etc.). Finally, multigenerational genealogies give us the opportunity not only to identify unusual intergenerational relations such as incest but also to identify extremely potent members such as serial entrepreneurs who found new ventures in a few successive generations.

We conjecture that the structure and characteristics of a genealogy and, ultimately, its size are affected by the nature of the particular line of heredity and affinity. The relations among founding firms and their progenies along different generations shape genealogical growth or potency as measured by the number of newly spawned firms. We attempt to understand the distinct influence of the founding parents on the evolutionary trajectory of the entire genealogy and eventually on its respective industrial sector. In doing so, we expand on concepts of heritage by analyzing the characteristics that are transmitted through intergenerational relations (e.g., Jaffee and McKendrick 2006; Klepper 2001; Phillips 2005; Beckman and Burton 2008).

Conclusion

The basic assumptions of our genealogical approach are, first, that new ventures' evolutionary paths are influenced both by their founding conditions and by the imprinting effects of the organizational characteristics that shaped them during founding; second, that those characteristics are transmitted along generations. Thus, pre-entry ecologies of incumbent firms may affect how progenies' capabilities are shaped and how they evolve (cf. Helfat and Lieberman 2002; Carroll et al. 1996; Ganco and Agarwal 2009; Klepper and Sleeper 2005).

Such a claim implies that certain "genetic" characteristics of parents are inherited by offspring (Agarwal et al. 2004; Chatterji 2009; Gompers et al. 2006; Klepper 2001; Phillips 2002, 2005). Furthermore, we focus on the idea that founders of spawned start-ups carry with them "genes" of experiences, skills, practices, and knowledge, and apply them to the new organization; consequently, they shape "the new firm behavior" (e.g., Beckman 2006; Boeker 1997; Kraatz and Moore 2002). Thus, for example, human resource blueprints created at founding may be relevant to the prospects of start-ups' effectiveness and survival (e.g., Baron and Hannan 2005).

It should be noted that the relevancy of the inheritance model is related to contextual factors. For example, Chatterji (2009) found that in the medical device industry successful spinouts inherit not technical knowledge from their incumbent firm but rather nontechnical knowledge. Carrying parents' "genes" may have practical advantage for progenies that may introduce, say, innovations and practices related in some way to the activities of their parent company (Bankman and Gilson 1999), because they learned from their parent company the knowledge and strategy of exploiting similar products and services (Franco and Filson 2006; Agarwal et al. 2004). The notion of carrying, then, reflects the affinity nature of the spinoff's relations with its parent organization, which can influence both the type of its activities and the prospects of its survival and success (Eckhardt and Shane 2003; Klepper 2001; Romanelli and Schoonhoven 2001; Shane 2000, 2001).

Furthermore, the genetic composition of a genealogy may determine its resilience in terms of potency, or its prospects for spawning new firms. In organizational terms, we may postulate that certain genealogical characteristics can predict the types of new organizations that will be born as well as their organizational characteristics (such as organizational models, technology, knowledge, markets, alliances, and access to human, social, and financial capital). Eventually, different genealogical characteristics stem from the *genetic variations* existing within and between offspring, families, or branches of lineages, which are transmitted directly from parents to progeny in a successive line or indirectly from first to subsequent generations.

The idea is that a genealogy develops from a parent company, which has certain values as described previously. However, the existence of a genealogy over time depends on the continued existence of its parent company as a model its descendant firms. Thus, the parent company needs to have a set of values that is stable over time so that new firms that are born in new generations in the genealogy can look up to the founding parent, emulate its values, and engage in imprinting.

If the set of values is changing and unstable, new companies that are born into the genealogy at different points in time may identify with different values and may not feel that they are members of the same genealogy. Note that we talk about "constitutional" values, those that withstand changing conditions in the environment and provide stable guidelines for future generations. Values that should be stable for the development of a genealogy include, among others, the commitment to innovation and the commitment to maintain and develop core professional personnel. Along with values, there are routines that exist in the parent company that must be stable to facilitate their transfer to new generations.

The genealogical approach in this study aims to capture how new ventures are created through the recombination or interaction of their progenitors—in particular, what types of network structures produce which forms of genealogical progeny: multigenerational, flat, dispersed, or concentrated (see also Saxenian 1994). Also, we ascertain that genealogical evolution portrays diverse features because of the *variations* in offspring positioned in different locations within the structure of the genealogy. In this sense, firms within the generational line of the genealogy create offspring, which may be similar or different or more or less potent than the parents are.

The genealogy's evolutionary process, its structure, and its composition of firms are nested in its environment. In our case, we can assume that the Israeli high-tech industry's position in terms of niche, products, technology, and market is shaped by its genesis and founding events, which, in turn, configure a certain variation. The variation mechanism serves as the bedrock of a continual selection process. The criteria for this selection are already shaped by the exiting variation. The genealogical structures, which stem from the varied founding events, represent ongoing variation configurations. These configurations are the repertoire for selection of those genealogies and the firms that affiliate with them, which fit a certain environment.

Within the genealogical approach, we attempt to take a step forward in understanding the evolution of an industrial sector by adopting a two-stage perspective. The first stage pertains to how initial conditions at founding shape both the entrepreneurial propensity and the know-how of the founding parents. The second stage relates to how these entrepreneurial characteristics are ultimately transmitted to their descendants along time. By entrepreneurial propensity, we refer to the set of intelligence, skills, and motivational attributes of people who engage in an entrepreneurial process (Shane, Locke, and Collins 2003). The skill component in this definition refers to "entrepreneurship know-how" and consists of capabilities, skills, routines, and managerial blueprints. Such know-how can be explicit and implicit (cf. Nonaka, Von Krogh, and Voelpel 2006), and both types are crucial to the knowledge accumulation that leads to the founding of new firms and the evolution of an industrial sector. The ability to identify and materialize founding opportunities gained from founding parents is passed on from one generation to the next and preserves the propensity of the founding parents to spawn new ventures over time. The transfer of know-how from various parents to their descendants is the source of diversity of genealogical evolution.

Chapter 3 relies on the idea of genealogical transmission, particularly the notion of imprinting. We describe how different historical periods breed different genealogical founding parents and whether and how the genesis events of founding parents that led to the formation of the Israeli high-tech genealogies shaped the evolutionary trajectory of the entire sector.

Economic Conditions at the Time of Founding and the Founding Parents of the Genealogies

3

I had a single motive, to create something from nothing. Then, one day the motive changed. I wanted to create something for others. I remember when, a couple of years after founding, the company organized a fun day for the workers and their families, many of them new immigrants from the Soviet Union. We took them for sightseeing in the Galilee. I remember looking at the fully loaded buses with families and I thought, "I'm responsible to these people and I'm their provider." Suddenly, a thought strikes. "I have a responsibility for this country." It brought memories of the tiring stories of my grandfather about "drying out the swamps and conquering the desert." Of course, you know, each of us has grown up on these stories of our elders and building up this country, and we all sang in singing class—"we will dress you with cement and concrete. . . ." I remember, smiling to myself, and a thought came to mind. I'm building this country with innovative technology and through the global market—what would my grandfather say had he still been alive?

Interview with Yitzhak, *a serial founder of communication companies, RAD genealogy, May 2006*

Imprinting theory emphasizes the importance of initial conditions and supports the basic logic of our genealogical approach, which proclaims that history matters. This chapter starts by analyzing the socioeconomic and political conditions that existed during the founding events of the firms that we have identified as founders of genealogies (see the Appendix). By capturing the history of foundation, we provide the context for the evolutionary path undertaken by the Israeli high-tech industry. It is important to point out that documenting such historical conditions and events poses a challenge because a company's founding events are not usually recorded.

The lion's share of this chapter is devoted to the meticulous description of an individual founding event for each genealogy. We describe and analyze the historical legacy of the founding companies in the communication sector of the Israeli high-tech industry. We trace the founding stories as recorded by various sources, including, when available, evidence from founders and relevant managers. By uncovering the individual history of each founding firm, we can identify its genesis events and the initial conditions that had, according to our theory, differential influences on the various genealogies.

We review the founding process of the pioneering firms against the backdrop of both the formative and the recent socioeconomic and political history of Israel, distinguishing between two major periods: before and after 1977. In 1977, Israel experienced political change when the Labor Party lost the elections to the right-wing and liberal parties. The "institutional-cooperative" period (before 1977) was characterized by the emergence of an economy that was highly dependent upon government intervention and support. The "competitive" period (after 1977) was characterized by relatively high environmental uncertainty and a competitive economy (Ben-Bassat 2002). Whereas social movements and the labor parties in Israel drove the first economic period, the liberal parties led the second one . As this chapter illustrates, the challenge in understanding how history has shaped the evolutionary path of the Israeli high-tech industry is highly contingent upon this insight.

Historical Legacy

In what follows, we describe the two historical periods that differentially shaped the evolutionary path of the Israeli high-tech industry. The first period, the institutional-cooperative economy, marked the formative years of the State of Israel and its centralized industrial development policies. The second period, the competitive economy, marked the transformation to a market economy and reflected the state's aggressive privatization policies.

Formative Years: The Institutional-Cooperative Economy

The formative years of the Israeli state were marked by a distinct ideology, one that elevated the collective above individual interests while harnessing the resources of all for the task of nation building (Aharoni 1993; Daniel 1976; Greenberg 1987). During these years, Israeli society formulated its demographic, territorial, and socioeconomic foundations and consolidated its ideology as a combination of three central elements: (1) *national values*: establishing a *politically* independent homeland for the Jewish people; (2) *economic values*:

ensuring economic independence; and (3) *social values*: creating a community based on equality, social solidarity, responsibility, and mutual help (Greenberg 1987). These three ideological elements shaped not only the evolution of the new Israeli nation and its institutions but also the character of the organizations founded in this period.[1]

Three institutional pillars played a pivotal role in shaping the society and cooperative economy of the State of Israel: the government, the ruling Labor Party, and the labor unions. The first pillar, the government, designed and implemented centralist and protective policies, which provided incentives to those sectors that were considered in line with the task of nation building. The second pillar, the ruling Labor Party (Mapai), served as the government's political power base. Mapai supplied the government with both politicians and technocrats who, as the "party emissaries," implemented and monitored the execution of government policies that it endorsed. During the years of the cooperative economy, the state and the ruling party were seen as interdependent, and this blurred the boundaries between them (Horowitz and Lissak 1989). This was in spite the fact that Israel's multiparty system had always dictated rule by majority coalition, which gives voice and power to small parties (Eisenstadt 1969). However, during Israel's formative years the overreaching goal of nation building—through the creation of cooperative sectors and the government's high involvement in directing the economy—was dominant in every facet of Israeli life (Aharoni 1976, 1993; Daniel 1976).

The third pillar was the labor unions, led by the national union, the Histadrut,[2] and its economic arm, Hevrat Ha'Ovdim.[3] The immediate objective of these institutions was to improve members' working and living conditions by increasing their share in the national income. This led the Histadrut to take an active part in founding, owning, and managing industries and companies (Daniel 1976). The involvement of the union in ownership and management thus accelerated the formation of an "administrative economy" in which criteria for founding and managing businesses were closely linked to the societal objective of creating employment opportunities (Daniel 1976).

Israel's industrial development evolved in tandem with three major needs that affected virtually every facet of society and the economy: the need for nation building and security; the integration of mass migration influxes; and economic development. During the early 1950s, the Israeli population increased by more than 100 percent, when about 600,000 immigrants arrived from post-war Europe and from Arab countries in Asia and North Africa. This mass migration, which was heterogeneous in ethnic and cultural backgrounds, education levels, and skills and occupations, placed an enormous burden on the nascent economy, forcing it to restructure swiftly. The restructuring was marked by intensive state intervention and planning in both capital and labor markets, including political and union intervention in every economic sector (Levi-Faur 2001).[4] With the pressing task of providing employment for new immigrants, priority was assigned to labor-intensive industries, most prominently agriculture. Only with the exhaustion of agricultural assets was the first industrial policy adopted, designed to substitute local production for imports to ease foreign-currency shortages. Barkai (1990) observed three different periods during the formative years of the Israeli state, characterized by different social, political, and economic realities. The first, immediately following the Second World War (1945–1947), was termed the *economy in transition*. This pre-state period, although politically hectic, was nevertheless considered one of growth in which the economy consolidated a modern economic structure based on developed agriculture and rapid growth of the industrial sector. By and large, the pre-state economy was highly integrated with the British war effort. The second period, the *economy at war* (1948–1951), was characterized by the need to mobilize the economy in part because of the hostilities during that period and in part because of the need to care for the many new immigrants. The government was faced with insurmountable expenses while building its embryonic economic and financial institutions. The third period, the *economy in growth* (1952–1956), saw the emergence of a new economic policy that consolidated the state's industrial, socioeconomic, and political structure. This period was marked by increased economic activity due to the flows of foreign aid and increased private sector involvement, mainly in industry. Events during this period also helped shape the Israeli welfare society and precipitated significant government involvement in the growing economy—including financial markets—and the increasing economic power of the Histadrut. In the 1960s, new efforts were undertaken to enhance exports. This was achieved by subsidizing exporting companies and by selectively encouraging certain industries, such as textiles, that were expected to perform well in the international market (Shafir and Peled 2002, 58).

The prevailing ideology of nation building implies that the state expands its influence and implements comprehensive economic policies. In Israel's case, these not only provided direct incentives for industrial development but also shaped ownership structures (Aharoni 1993). Numerous studies have documented the prominence of the state and its bureaucratic apparatus in planning, directing, and organizing industrial development through specific policies that channeled resources and incentives directly to industries that were aligned with state ideology. Levi-Faur (2001) claims that Israel's political choices shaped the path of industrial development but not the economic priorities of market mechanisms or the political clout of individual industrialists (p. 269). He further contends that the state shaped industrial development through mediation with other social and economic factors, based on a pattern defined by four conditions: high state autonomy, weak social actors, explicit central policy, and social mobilization for the execution of policy. Accordingly, in its quest to develop industry the state was able to employ various strategies that promoted, blocked, or even replaced certain social actors. For example, the encouragement and emergence of the private sector and private entrepreneurs as industrial champions were direct corollaries of the state's strategy, not to mention its assessment that the private sector, and not the state, represented the best mechanism for industrial development. During its formative years, then, Israel's objective of nation building—the first pillar of its ideology—generated incentives and policies that favored the private sector as the prime engine of industry.

Israel's socialist legacy has had far-reaching effects on the country's economic development. This diverse and complex society, with its long-term volatile geopolitical standing, has shaped the formation of the country's economy—particularly the coupling of the economic burden of national security with the social policies that characterized the state's formative years. Furthermore, in its early years Israel's deep government involvement in every facet of economic activity, including its substantial control over economic assets, caused a severe misallocation of resources. The polarization of the Israeli economy and excessive government involvement brought about a paternalistic system, which resulted in the dependence of most businesses on the government. As Aharoni (1993) remarked, "Government intervention shifted from rationing, ad hoc decisions and administrative controls to the control of virtually all sources of capital and their administrative allocation at varying rates of subsidy" (p. 14).

The organizational structure and ideology of many of the main enterprises founded during this early period were shaped by the increasing economic and political challenges of the new state. The governing ideologies triggered the establishment of new organizational forms, such as the *Kibbutz* and the *Moshav*. Various industrial cooperatives aimed, on the one hand, to "bloom the desert" and, on the other, "to unify, on cooperative foundations, laborers engaged in any manner of work upon the land or undergoing agricultural training" (Histadrut Constitution, 1952, 12). The inability to differentiate between national and social values or national and labor institutions led to a blurring of the boundaries between ownership and control. The Histadrut, for example, was both the employer of the workers and their sole representative.[5]

A case in point is Koor, an industrial conglomerate owned by Hevrat Ha'Ovdim, the economic arm of the Histadrut. Koor mirrored the business culture in Israel during the first decades of the newborn country, having been derived from the unique connections among the Zionist movement's vision, the government, the political parties, and the labor unions. It was a spinoff of Solel Boneh Construction, which the Histadrut had founded in 1924 in British Palestine to pursue the Zionist vision of constructing roads and buildings. Through Solel Boneh, the Histadrut provided a livelihood for settlers in an attempt to found a new state in Palestine. The company began planning for independence as early as 1944, when it created an industrial arm called Koor Industries. As noted, Koor not only pursued economic targets through its diverse economic activities but also undertook other social and national endeavors. For example, after World War II, it employed many concentration camp survivors and refugees from Arab nations, and provided much needed job training and employment for these immigrants, in cities as well as in remote villages. Later, because it was so closely tied to the Histadrut, Koor often made business decisions according to workers' welfare rather than to profit potential. Naftali Blumenthal, Koor's CEO from 1977 to 1982, proudly recalls,

> Once a year, I used to produce not only a financial balance sheet, but also a social balance sheet, reflecting Koor's social accomplishments and values. (Interview, August 2010)

Moreover, during the first decades of statehood, until the recession of the mid-1960s, the Israeli economy underwent rapid growth. One important result was the accumulation of capital by large corporations, many of which were owned by the Histadrut. During this period, only a few of Israel's leading companies were privately owned. Hevrat Ha'Ovdim became the economic arm of the labor government and was used to accomplish the political and economic goals of the young country: bringing in Jewish people from all over the world to settle the country, providing employment, and enhancing the country's ability to defend itself.

With respect to entrepreneurship, one may argue that this threefold ideology of the Jewish community in Israel in the first half of the twentieth century not only shaped the new Israeli nation and its institutions but also directed its entrepreneurial inclination. All creative and entrepreneurial resources were harnessed to fulfill the Zionist dream: to revive the "dead" Hebrew language;

to bring in and settle hundreds of thousands of Jewish refugees from all over Europe, Asia and Africa; to establish an economic system to absorb them; to create an excellent academic system; and to establish effective military forces and sophisticated defense industries. This extensive effort required not only creativity, improvisation, and daring, but also the ability to delay gratification. These important capabilities played a key role during the years to come—that is, during the competitive economy period.

With respect to private entrepreneurship, in retrospect the cooperative environment limited the development of an entrepreneurial private sector's ability to fully exploit its own initiatives and resources. If there were any major private ventures, most of them were encouraged, supported, or directed by the state or the Histadrut. In particular, the government allocated handsome incentives to entrepreneurs who founded new industries, mainly by subsidizing employment opportunities for new immigrants arriving in Israel in the aftermath of its independence. A case in point is the establishment during the 1950s of the textile industry in developing towns in the southern region (Drori 2000).

Furthermore, all entrepreneurial activities had to be carried out within existing institutions. Bonne (1958) argues that Israel lacked the entrepreneurial incentives that usually originate or prosper in a middle-class milieu, similar to those that played such a prominent part in the development of Western countries. In particular, the values of individuality, status, property, and personal profits, which are typically associated with business success, were missing. History tells us that the Jewish pioneers who immigrated to Israel after World War I did not represent groups with this middle-class ideology. Nor were they part of entrepreneurial groups that could advance the development of new fields of economic activities or unorthodox methods of economic expansion. Furthermore, the combination of a socialist ideology with the Zionist movement, which embodied both and advanced the national revival, provided an excellent breeding ground for the increasing strength of the collective enterprises backed by strong labor organizations. In this national and social environment, any entrepreneurial activity was interpreted not in terms of personal benefits or ambitions but in terms of the public interest or the Zionist mission.

Transformative Years: The Competitive Economy

During the 1980s, the political and business environments in Israel changed, turning more global and competitive. East and West drew nearer to one another, and the Western capitalist system became much more influential around the world. The State of Israel also experienced political changes and challenges and had to struggle not only for its physical existence but for its socioeconomic survival. The year 1977, in particular, marked a major turning point in Israel's political status, which had significant socioeconomic implications. In that year, Israel underwent a political change, with the Labor Party losing the elections to the right-wing and liberal parties, Gahal (Gush Herut liberalism in Hebrew), an alliance between the nationalistic Herut Party and the Liberal Party. This was followed by the abolition of foreign currency regulations and travel taxes, as well as reductions in prices of imported goods. It quickly became evident that the Israeli economy was not prepared for such drastic changes, as could be seen by the deterioration of the balance of payments (net external debt amounted to 80 percent of GDP in the subsequent years after the 1977 elections), the mass increase of imported goods, and the sharp rise in the inflation rate (of more than 400 percent per year).

Furthermore, the new regime changed or threatened to change the position of many "sacred" institutions of the labor government, such as the *Kibbutz*, which underwent a deep crisis that nearly wiped out the entire *Kibbutz* movement.

In 1985, the Israeli economy was on the verge of a severe crisis, necessitating dramatic changes in economic policy (Ben-Bassat 2002). The Economic Stabilization Program, implemented in July 1985, not only halted the economic deterioration of Israel but also signified the first step in the transition of its economy from a socialist-oriented regime, in which the government was deeply involved, to a modern, capitalist regime based on market forces.

The main objective of economic policy makers after 1985 was to stimulate growth by providing substantial incentives to the private business sector. To attain this objective, the government gradually downscaled its expenditures and freed up resources for use by the business sector. In a bold move, the government seriously trimmed the defense budget. This was enabled by a worldwide trend in defense-expenditure reduction coupled with a decrease in the level of Israeli-Arab conflict and greater economic discipline in the defense sector. The government took measures to create a comfortable economic environment for investment and growth in order to ensure the absorption of labor and capital by business. Furthermore, it initiated structural reforms in the country's main markets to reduce its involvement in directing resources to failing state- or union-controlled enterprises. All of this was aimed at making the markets more competitive. Finally, the new stabilization program shaped monetary policy to support the growth process by making financial and capital markets more flexible, maintaining relative stability, and significantly lowering real interest rates.

By the 1990s, ideological transformations and globalization trends opened the Israeli economy to foreign influences and facilitated the reduction of government intervention in business affairs. Over time, these trends contributed to the liberation of capital markets and the massive privatization of large state banks and corporations. Some salient results of the liberalization process included an increase in foreign investments, public stock issues by Israeli firms on foreign stock exchanges, and a growing trade balance surplus. Also, neoliberal ideology and policies were based on reduced state intervention in the economy, large-scale diversification, and substantial cuts in welfare and social services. Consequently, the Israeli economy exhibited contradictory trends. On the one hand, high economic growth: 4.9 percent in 2006 (Bank of Israel 2007); on the other, increasing economic and social inequality, deterioration of welfare services, economic degradation of the weakest part of the population, and high poverty rates. For example, in 2004, 20.3 percent of households were living below the poverty line (Bank of Israel 2005). At the same time, the changes in Israel's economic structure helped in creating a dynamic competitive advantage in world markets through a high level of investment in human capital.

In addition, the shift toward a market economy, which coincided with the shift in political power and ideology, brought about income and social inequalities and gave rise to the coexistence of two parallel economic systems: modern and traditional. The first system was based on the country's advanced technological and knowledge-based industries, including advanced service and financial sectors that exhibit substantial growth and skillful integration into the global economy. The second was a manufacturing and a less advanced service sector, which suffers from low productivity and growth and is barely able to compete locally and globally. Furthermore, the rapid modernization of the economy, particularly through aggressive privatization processes, resulted in the re-formation of a powerful few business groups, which accelerated the skewed distribution of the country's wealth and power.

Indeed, the global and local events that triggered the Israeli economy were (1) the information technology (IT) revolution, along with the rise of knowledge-intensive industries and the decline of labor-intensive industries in the 1990s; (2) the collapse of the Histadrut in the mid-1980s, including the divestiture of its assets; (3) the privatization of many of the country's biggest corporations, especially the major banks; and (4) the large inflow of human capital to the private sector due to mass immigration from the former Soviet Union and the dismissal of workers from the defense industry in the late 1980s and early 1990s. These events led to the dominance of the private sector, changes in the

composition of Israel's business elites (Aharoni 2007), and the precipitous rise
of the high-tech sector.

One may say that Israel entered the 1990s equipped not only with a different economic strategy but also with a set of transformed socioeconomic values.
The ideological combination of *nation, economy,* and *society* that was nurtured
during the cooperative period and embodied in the cooperative movement no
longer dominated. The national labor union and the Labor Party were now
transformed, giving way to a new ideology and a new set of policies and values (Yaar-Yuchtman and Shavit 2001). Israel's economic difficulties in the early
1980s and the subsequent stabilization program required changes—changes in
the economic system as well as in the national value system and culture. Insti-
tutionally led entrepreneurship was not appropriate to either the new competitive environment or the dynamic character of the emerging high-tech industry.
Many products, inventions, or ideas from the defense industry that were previously confidential were set free for use in the civilian sector. Even the so-called
"deserters"—derided by Prime Minister Izhak Rabin in 1976 as having dared to
leave the *Kibbutz* or the State of Israel in order to make money, study, or work
abroad—gained legitimacy. They later became the new generation of pioneers
who were willing to give up their successful careers abroad to return and help
the local high-tech industry develop and prosper. The qualities of friendship,
creativity, improvisation, and daring were now channeled toward the national
high-tech sector. The individual and national ability to shun personal gratification for the sake of the collective was now replaced by sophisticated calcula-
tions of how much to invest and when to exit—in other words, developing
business strategies and organizational systems that balanced exploration and
exploitation (March 1991; Lavie, Stettner, and Tushman 2010).

The Synthesis Approach to Historical Legacy

The two periods just described both influenced the evolutionary path of the Israeli high-tech industry. The cooperative past of the Israeli state presented early
opportunities, as government involvement provided resources and incentives
for those industries considered essential for nation building. The competitive
environment, marked by a series of industrial policies, has proven conducive
to the emergence of the Israeli ITC sector and its global linkages. Although
these periods differ in fundamental ways, it is important to acknowledge that
both have shaped the emergence of Israeli high-tech. Thus, an understanding
of the interrelationship between them calls for synthesis—a particular synthesis based on two elements. The first is the representation of key features that

stem either directly or indirectly from the cooperative period or the competitive period. The second is the new features, which represent an adaptation to the competitive period; however, they are embedded in historical processes.

To illustrate our point, we turn to the Israeli defense industry because it is directly linked to the emergence of the civilian high-tech industry. The defense industry was established in the early days of the state, but its foundations were laid even earlier, during the struggle for independence (http://www.imi-israel.com). Following the French arms embargo in 1968 after the Six-Day War, the government decided to adopt self-reliance measures that aimed to free the country from dependence on foreign suppliers. Consequently, it made a concerted effort to develop a sophisticated and state-of-the-art weapons system by channeling resources to the military-industrial complex and national laboratories (Dvir and Tishler 1999; Sadeh 1995). In this way, the Israeli defense industry gained its unique status and centrality while benefiting from generous government incentives. It is important to note that the government, because of national interests, also owned a large part of this industry (Bonen 1995; Galai and Schachar 1993; Klieman 1992). As Drori and Landau (2011) state,

> The linkage between the government and the defense industry has been further reinforced due to the nature of the products and services developed by the industry. These were regarded as exclusive, secretive, and as one of the keys to achieving the country's innovative and qualitative edge, a view that served to further enhance the interdependency between the government and the defense industry. Such interdependency brought national objectives and priorities to the forefront, sometimes to the point of overshadowing economic and market considerations. (p. 4)

The 1980s, however, saw a more relaxed geopolitical atmosphere, both globally and locally. In particular, the end of the Cold War and the peace process between Israel and Jordan and Egypt brought about a considerable shift in government priorities. Primarily, the Israeli government's allocation of resources to the defense industry was reduced, as was the demand for its products and services (Sadeh 1995). The defense industry, which had always been highly dependent on the government, faced a severe existential crisis. By the beginning of the 1990s, it was apparent that it would need to change or risk default (Dvir and Tishler 1999).

While the crisis negatively affected the defense industry, it also posed a unique opportunity. It forced the industry to "convert" and revitalize itself by looking at the prospect of civilian commercialization. Thus, during the 1980s and 1990s reduced global and local demand and, consequently, reduced government support led to divestment and conversion to civilian use of military innovations and technology (Blum and Tishler 2000; Dvir and Tishler 1999). This transformation brought about changes in the industry that reflected its shifting priorities—it began to invest in innovation and technology to exploit the opportunities presented by the civilian market. Furthermore, it became more open to new business models, including joint ventures, partnerships, and the outsourcing of its expertise in R&D. The necessity of such transformations led the industry to reevaluate its main objectives and reexamine its primary mission and goals (Ringer and Strong 1998).

The Historical Background of the Genealogies' Founding Parent Firms

In what follows, we outline the evolution of high-tech genealogies that emerged during the two periods—institutional-cooperative and competitive. These genealogies represent, to a certain extent, a mirror of their past, which significantly influenced their evolutionary trajectory. We describe in detail the events that led to the emergence of the founding parents of these genealogies and refer to the socioeconomic conditions that prevailed during the time of their founding.

We collected the data for identifying the genealogies of the founding parents of the Israeli ITC sector from two sources: Israel Venture Capital (IVC; www.ivc-online.com), which lists all technological firms established in Israel since 1948; and interviews with 65 CEOs and founders of high-tech and venture capital (VC) firms. We used the IVC to compile all the companies listed in communication-related categories. We first searched for those founded prior to 1985 (the early 1980s are considered the start of the modern ITC sector in Israel, according to Breznitz [2007]). We found 18 that had been founded before 1985: BA Microwaves, Comverse, ECI Telecom, Elisra, Fibronics, Gal-Op, Galtronics, Leadcom, Microkim, Micronet, Motorola Israel, Orbit Technologies, RAD Data Communications, Source of Sound, Telco, Teldor, Telrad Networks, and Tadiran. For each of these, we identified its spawned, merged, or acquired ventures. We used the interviews to verify whether all founding parents of the ITC sector were included in this group of firms and which of them could be titled "founding parent of ITC in Israel." Five firms were selected by most of our interviewees: Telrad Networks (Telrad), Tadiran, ECI Telecom (ECI), Comverse Technology, and RAD Data Communications (RAD). However, our genealogical analyses revealed three additional relatively important genealogies, Elisra, Orbit Technologies (Orbit), and Motorola Israel (MIL), that evolved during the institutional-cooperative period and one important and unique genealogy, Fibronics, that evolved during the competitive period. Interestingly, although Fibronics was not mentioned by many interviewees, it had a tremendous effect on the evolution of the Israeli ITC sector. The other nine firms (four that were established in the institutional-cooperative period and five that were founded in the competitive period) did not have the minimal record of spinouts and were not included in our study. Finally, it should be noted that only ITC companies were included in the list of founding parents. Therefore, holding companies such as Koor or construction companies such as Solel Boneh were omitted.

Table 3.1 shows that the founding parent firms can be divided into two groups: those that were established during the institutional-cooperative period and those that were founded during the competitive period. The first group consists of six companies: Telrad, Tadiran, Elisra, Orbit, ECI, and MIL. As we will see, only Tadiran and Telrad were associated with Koor and the labor unions. ECI, Elisra, and Orbit were private ventures, and MIL was a subsidiary of an American corporation. The first four companies, Telrad, Tadiran, Elisra, and Orbit, were oriented toward the local institutional market, at least in their first ten to twenty years of existence. Although ECI was started as a private venture in 1965, with its efforts targeting the institutional market, its leadership in 1977 transformed the organization into a private entrepreneurial venture and changed its goals and culture. All the other founding firms were born after the political change to the right-wing and liberal parties' regime but before the stabilization program—that is, before the transformation of the economy from institutional/centralized into competitive/privatized. Furthermore, all the parent companies in this group were founded as personal private ventures, motivated by different goals and values and in different business environments. One may say that ECI, RAD, Fibronics, and Comverse (and a few others in other sectors) were the spearhead of the IT revolution that started during the early 1980s.

The Institutional-Cooperative Economy (1951–1977)

As noted above, six companies were established during the institutional-cooperative period: Telrad Networks, Tadiran, Elisra, Orbit, Motorola Israel, and ECI Telecom. This section outlines their founding processes and the environmental conditions prevailing during their respective founding era.

Telrad Networks (Telrad)   Telrad Networks (Telrad) was founded in 1951 as a joint venture of Koor and CNEC (Consolidated Near East Company). At the time of founding, however, Koor was still an integral part of Solel Boneh, which

Table 3.1

Major genesis events and initial conditions of the founding firms of the nine genealogies

	Institutional-cooperative period						Competitive economic period		
	Telrad	Tadiran	Elisra	Orbit	MIL	ECI[a]	Fibronics	Comverse	RAD
Year of founding	1951	1962	1967	1951	1964	1965	1977	1982	1983
Company type at birth	Joint venture of American company and holding corporation controlled by unions	Merger of two private companies owned by Ministry of Defense and holding corporation controlled by unions	Subsidiary of a U.S. company; acquired in 1980 by holding corporation controlled by unions	Start-up: private company	Subsidiary of American corporation	Start-up: private company; acquired by a holding corporation in 1980	Joint venture of two private companies	Start-up: private company	Start-up: private company
Founders	Assigned managers from owners, Koor and CNEC	Professional manager (director general of Ministry of Defense)	Engineer, owner of American company	Five engineers	Engineer (manager of electronics and engineering factory)	Engineer (former U.S. colonel, new immigrant)	Engineer (serial entrepreneur and owner of American company	Two engineers and finance expert	Two engineers (former chief scientist of military intelligence unit and owner of electronic equipment agency)
First IPO	—	—		1991	1965	1990	1983	1992	—
First market	Institutional-cooperative	Institutional-cooperative	Institutional-cooperative	Institutional-cooperative	Competitive	Institutional-cooperative	Competitive	Competitive	Competitive
	First stages: knowledge acquisition—2 knowledge-sharing contracts; later stages: knowledge creation—investment in R&D	First stages: knowledge acquisition—4 knowledge-sharing contracts; later stages: knowledge creation—investment in R&D	First stages: knowledge acquisition—2 knowledge-sharing contracts; later stages: knowledge creation—investment in R&D	Knowledge creation—investment in R&D	Knowledge creation—investment in R&D	Knowledge creation—investment in R&D	Knowledge creation—investment in R&D	Knowledge creation—investment in R&D	Knowledge creation—investment in R&D

[a]ECI was founded as a private venture in 1965, targeting it efforts toward the institutional market. In 1977, its new leadership transformed the organization into a private entrepreneurial venture and changed its goals and culture.

was predominantly a construction company; it was legally separated from its parent just a few years later. Koor's CEO was Hillel Dan, and the co-founder on its behalf was Moshe Zitron, who was not an entrepreneur but a project manager assigned to this mission. The strategic thinking behind this move was, according to Solel Boneh's diversification strategy, to strengthen its industrial arm—that is, Koor. The co-founder, on behalf of CNEC (owned by M. E. Moss), was Lee Ruthenberg.

Dan, who had worked at Telrad during its formative years in the beginning of the 1950s, analyzes, in retrospect, Telrad's vision in those days:

> The business policy of Telrad was first and foremost to provide work for the residents of Lod [a developing city near Tel-Aviv], who were mostly new immigrants. A factory was set up to provide jobs for them. Later, in 1965, another factory was built at Ma'alot in the Galilee for the same purpose. As you may understand, the first item on . . . the business policy agenda was the welfare of its employees. Only the second or third items spoke about earning money. . . . (Interview, October 2005)

Telrad's first product was a telephone. The company signed knowledge contracts with two European companies—General Electronic Company (GEC; United Kingdom) and Albis Wire Telephone (AWITEL; Switzerland)—that provided it with all the relevant know-how. Telrad was the first manufacturer of telephones in Israel, and the Post Office was the first government ministry to purchase them. In fact, the Post Office Ministry was obliged to use German reparations money to buy whatever Telrad manufactured.

In 1962, Telrad began to produce public switching equipment in Israel. Again, it was the first to manufacture this product and, again, the Post Office Ministry was its main customer. The 1960s were very good years for Telrad, and the company grew considerably. It had exclusive manufacturing rights and sold products at very good prices to the Post Office Ministry, which later became the Ministry of Communications and, subsequently, Bezeq Ltd. Hillel Dan, who was at this time a senior manager at Telrad, recounts,

> We had close to 800 people. Telrad was considered a large enterprise. New plants were built and others purchased. I remember the ceremonies when a new factory was opened. All the important people in the country came. I even remember Shimon Peres [the current Israeli president] coming. . . . The organizational climate was also special. There was no clear hierarchy at Telrad, with a technician being lower than an engineer and so on. Everyone was respected on the basis of what he proved he was capable of doing. I remember technicians without academic creden-

tials managing whole departments of engineers and it working very well. (Interview, October 2005)

During the 1970s, Telrad imported knowledge from various European and North American companies, such as STR, Penta Conta, and Northern Electric (later Nortel). Business agreements with the latter proved very significant to Telrad during the 1980s and 1990s, as they denoted a change from European to North American technologies and standards. In the 1980s, Nortel developed a small digital telephone exchange, which Telrad adopted and distributed in Israel, eventually supplying 60 to 70 percent of the market.

Dan describes the rationale of the transformation:

> When we brought the digital exchange to Israel, it swept the market. No one in the private market bought private exchanges anymore. They all started buying digital exchanges and there was no end to the demand. In fact, that was the beginning of the digital era in the telecommunications of private exchanges. In our wildest dreams, we had not expected such success. We thought it would last for a few years, but it continued for 20 years and it is still being sold today. (Interview, 2005)

Interestingly, in spite of being a part of Koor and the risk involved with technological change, Telrad preserved its original social values. Naftali Blumenthal, Koor's CFO, explains:

> For years, Telrad employed a group of destitute, hard-working women who [wove] the wire braids for the exchanges. This is what they did and this is the only thing they knew. The decision to produce only digital exchanges left them with no work at Telrad. Guri Meltzer, the CEO who was responsible for this strategic change, did not want to fire these women. He approached the Post Office Ministry with an unusual request: "Please make each year a five-unit order of the old exchanges." They responded positively and he did not have to fire this group of women. (Interview, September 2005)

At the beginning of the 1990s, Israel was 100 percent digital, one of only a few such countries in the world at the time. The Nortel-Telrad partnership was further strengthened when Telrad developed specific telephone-related hardware for Nortel. Eventually, Nortel bought up to 20 percent of Telrad without interfering with its management and operations. This involvement facilitated the transformation of Telrad from a company that was basically dependent upon acquiring technology into a company that acquired technological capabilities and knowledge of its own.

By the end of the decade, the market in Israel began to be saturated, and orders from Bezeq (Israel's phone company) dropped dramatically. In addition, the government enforced restrictive trade laws, and Telrad faced serious difficulties in coping with this development. It not only had to lower prices but also found itself with no major product of its own to replace the digital exchanges. Furthermore, at the end of the 1990s Koor, which owned Telrad, underwent a severe crisis that, for all intents and purposes, dismantled the company—it was sold to the Claridge Group.

The privatization of Koor brought about changes in its structure and culture. With the new values that the acquiring owner brought to the firm, workers' welfare and loyalty to the organization became secondary to competitiveness and profitability. Hillel Dan comments on this transformation:

> Jonathan Kolber, who had joined Koor and was a finance man and only concerned about money, decided to sell the sausage in slices. They cut up the company and sold it slice by slice. They destroyed Telrad for money. Reuven Avital, the CEO at the time, fired good people—the software veterans who knew the product well—because they received high salaries and he wanted to save on costs. It isn't clear why. He destroyed the team spirit and the atmosphere of appreciating innovation and people coming up with good ideas. This is what Reuven Avital destroyed. Until then, Telrad had a grading scale for professionals in order to promote geniuses that were not good at management. There was no other way for the company to promote these people and express its appreciation of the work they were doing. It was a special group engaged in important work, and Reuven Avital destroyed it. (Interview, October 2005)

From a firm boasting 3,200 employees and a market value of $800 million, Telrad had become an employer of 530 workers. In 2005, it sold 21 percent of its shares to Fortissimo Capital for just $21 million. Under its new leadership, Telrad has slowly regained a leading position in the communication sector. Today, the company focuses on integrated network solutions and develops products in the areas of IP NGN, gateways, optical, metro, enterprise, wireless, and switching.

Tadiran Tadiran was established as a merger between two firms—Tadir and RAN—in 1951 by an American named Segnof, who dreamed of founding a modern factory for radio crystals in the young State of Israel. Segnof brought from the United States all required equipment, as well as technical experts who trained the new employees. The factory implemented advanced technologies and processes that were not common in Israel at that time. Segnof was very mindful of employee well-being and introduced a human resources (HR) practice that emphasized fair employment conditions and employee rights. Since the demand for crystals was relatively weak, Tadir opened an electronics department and started to develop car radios. In 1956, the military demand for crystals for radio systems increased sharply because of the war with Egypt, resulting in a major boost to Tadir's financial performance. That same year, Koor, which specialized, in part, in military communication equipment, acquired Tadir.

RAN Battery Industries was founded as a battery factory in the southern part of Tel Aviv in 1932 by three engineers who had emigrated from Poland: Rautenshtein, Aisenshtat (Ardon), and Neuman. They purchased machinery in Germany and manufactured additional equipment in their factory.

RAN ultimately became a very successful establishment, selling batteries not only in Israel but in Jordan, Syria, Turkey, and Iraq. According to Aisenshtat (Haspel 1990), the company was unique because the founders had brought traditional practices from European industries and combined them with the scientific standards they applied in their processes. RAN's managerial strategy, as shaped by its founder, emphasized technological innovation, market orientation, and employee satisfaction and well-being. The company experienced rapid growth during World War II, when it became the sole supplier of batteries to the British army. In these years, it broadened its product portfolio, moving from just batteries to electric transformers, ventilators, and other electronic equipment.

RAN's involvement with the defense sector intensified after Israel's independence. The military's rising demand for batteries forced RAN to devote the lion's share of its production and R&D activities to military use. Consequently, in 1957 the Ministry of Defense acquired a part of it.

At the beginning of the 1960s, the director of Israel's Defense Ministry, Moshe Kashti, estimated that the need for electronics in the Israel Defense Forces (IDF) would grow and become critical to the young country's survival. A charismatic leader, Kashti convinced his colleagues of the need to create an electronics industry, both in the defense establishment and in the private sector, with the intent of decreasing Israel's dependence on external procurement. Because the Ministry of Defense held a significant percentage of RAN's shares and was Tadir's biggest customer, he was in a position to approach Koor, the owner of Tadir, with an invitation to unite RAN Battery Industries and Tadir in one enterprise that would develop and produce communication equipment for the IDF. Kashti succeeded in convincing the management of both companies that such a merger would benefit each and, of course, contribute to strengthening the security of the State of Israel. Koor Industries, Ltd., purchased the shares of the other partners in RAN, and the merger was carried out in 1962. A few years later, Koor gained full ownership of the new firm, Tadiran, which soon became the leader in Israeli electronics and communications. Kashti invited RAN's CEO, Elkana Kaspi, to be the first CEO of the merged company, and Kashti himself served as the first chairman of the board (Barak 1987).

This business process exemplifies the deep involvement and influence of social-Zionist values in the evolution of the high-tech (including communication) industry during the first decades of the newborn country. Kashti did not think in terms of today's strategic language, such as competition or survival. He truly believed in the following four factors that shaped his role as the Director General of the Ministry of Defense and later as the first chairman of Tadiran's board of directors: (1) The existence of the State of Israel depends on its ability to defend itself (". . . a people under blockade must develop a military industry"); (2) Israel's security depends on healthy and sound economics; (3) Israel should have independent capabilities when it comes to national security; and (4) based on its economic capabilities and the talents of the Jewish people, Israel can do all this (Naor 1977). Indeed, Kashti's energy, vision, and determination were the motivational forces behind the development of the electronics and communication industries and their applications in weapon systems, aeronautics, rockets, and the like (Yona 2006).

The new firm, Tadiran, became a one-stop shop for military communication equipment. As a holding company, Koor used it as a hub for its strategy of diversification through new technologies, knowledge acquisition, and mergers. The Israeli Defense Ministry sold its 50 percent interest in Tadiran to the U.S. firm General Telephone and Electronics Corporation (GTE) in 1969. This new ownership gave Koor access to GTE's superior technologies and helped Tadiran become Israel's largest electronics and communication manufacturer as well as one of its largest employers.

Tadiran expanded its interests in the communication domain in two directions: telephone and military communication equipment. In 1968, it entered the telephone business by signing a knowledge agreement with GTE and by obtaining a contract with the Post Office Ministry to be one of its exclusive supplier of telephone switchboards. In 1969, Koor acquired Telco and merged it with Tadiran to enhance its existing efforts to develop its capabilities and markets in the telephone domain.

At the beginning of the 1970s, the Ministry of Communication decided to move toward a new generation of public switchboards. To be able to join this venture, Tadiran signed a new knowledge contract with the Swiss company ITT and started manufacturing the Crossbar switchboard in Israel. The next step was to develop and manufacture a relatively small multi-line switchboard (60 lines) for GTE—the Tadex. This allowed Tadiran to enter what they called "the big elephants' tracks" or, in other words, the game of the big competitors in international markets. In the 1970s, the Communications Division of Tadiran completed some very important projects, such as a computerized telephone book. In the late 1980s, after signing a long-term contract to manufacture the Coral switchboard for American giant Bell South, the division was considered a giant, too, in Israeli terms, employing 1,700 workers.

As noted earlier, telecommunications was not Tadiran's only division developing and manufacturing communication products. In 1976, it had created a different division that manufactured mainly military radio communication equipment. Although it based its products on American knowledge, Tadiran invested in further improvements of American shelf products by promptly responding to the needs of Israeli soldiers who had emerged from training and battlefields. Alex Milner, the CEO of the Communications Division since 1981, provides an interesting example:

> One day, in the summer of 1969, a young captain, a paratrooper, identified by the red beret on his head, knocked on my door.
>
> "I came from the Jordan Valley. Yesterday, my deputy was badly wounded while chasing a team of terrorists. I identified the terrorist who started firing at us. I tried to warn my deputy and called him to find a shelter. Unfortunately, he did not hold the earpiece close enough to his ear and he did not hear me. If the communication equipment had an external loudspeaker, he could have heard me in the midst of storming the target and we could have prevented his serious injury. Can you do something about it?"
>
> After three days, the Captain returned to his unit with external loudspeakers in his bag. After a short while, all the relevant communication equipment [was] similarly modified. This is a small example. It should be noted that the immediate feedback from the battlefield triggered many of our technological innovations. (Michalson 1985, 34)

The Radio Communication Division grew very rapidly and, in the beginning of the 1980s, was split in two: Radio Communication and Electronic Systems. Four plants belonged to the Radio Communication Division: tactic radio communication, radio communication equipment, numeric equipment, and electronic assemblage. Tadiran acquired the American company Nomex, which helped it improve its marketing deployment in the United States and to process orders from the U.S. Army.

Over the years, the Radio Communication Division increased its investment in R&D dramatically in order to develop products that could be exported to other countries and to decrease Tadiran's dependence on the local market. In 1985, it reached an impressive 30/70 balance between local and external markets. In the beginning of the 1980s, management had decided to unite the production of all Tadiran product components under one divisional roof. This decision facilitated the marketing of these components to industrial clients as well and accelerated the pace of production of the various products at the other divisions. The plants that were passed over to the new division included telephone cables, crystals, printed circuits, batteries and accumulators, and lithium batteries, among others.

During the 1970s and 1980s, Tadiran consolidated its structure into five major divisions, three of which were communication-related: Radio Communication, Telecommunication, and Components. The other two were Mechanics and Electrical Equipment, and Electronics. Tadiran made huge investments in the development of new products that might have been attractive not only to local institutional markets but also to international ones. It succeeded in demonstrating technological capabilities and a commitment to innovation by independently developing advanced military electronic systems, including a Mini Remote Piloted Vehicle (MRPV). At the end of 1987, the company had $750 million in revenues and about 12,000 employees, half of them engineers and technicians. Its market value was about 30 percent that of its parent company, Koor. As one of the largest organizations in the country, it was considered not only an innovative firm but also an attractive workplace for technicians and engineers and for many graduates of the security forces.

Starting in the late 1980s, Tadiran encountered serious financial difficulties for several reasons: massive cutbacks in the portion of the IDF budget allocated to orders from the local industry; major cutbacks in government R&D projects; and significant depreciation of the dollar on the international market. During the first half of the 1990s, Koor divided Tadiran into several smaller firms, and the original founding firm, Tadiran, Ltd., ceased to exist. In 1999, the Tadiran Communications Division, was sold to the Shamrock group, First Israel Mezzanine Investors, and a group of managers. Five years later, in 2004, Koor (which had sold Tadiran Communications in 1999) bought back a 33 percent stake in the company, with the intent of merging its business with Elisra, for $150 million. Ironically, the sum that Koor paid for reacquiring this stake was equal to the value of the entire company when it was sold off five years earlier.

Elisra   Dr. Leon Riebman, an electrical engineer and entrepreneur in his native United States, founded Elisra. In 1950, he was one of the founders of American Electronics Laboratories (AEL), which, under his leadership, became a premier electronic-defense-systems manufacturer. AEL designed and manufactured electronic countermeasures systems, simulation systems, radar receivers, microwave integrated circuits, and other electronic equipment, and contracted avionics installation as well as integration services. It also provided other services, such as aircraft modification and maintenance, calibration, product testing, and technical publication, to the commercial and public-sectors. In the mid-1980s, AEL Industries grew to employ close to 3,000 people in Israel in addition to those in its worldwide distribution network. It was among the first U.S. corporations to develop an Israeli subsidiary.

Riebman was immersed in various activities related to Israel's economic development and was chair of the science-based Industries Committee of the Prime Minister's Council for Israel's Economic Development. When he founded Elisra in 1967, his interests in Israel were not purely business-based or scientific. He was also driven by Zionist ideology and a desire to contribute to Israel's security. As an owner, Riebman was not involved in Elisra's daily operations. The first CEO of the company, Zalman Shalev, a retired artillery colonel, shaped Elisra's organizational structure and strategy, including its shift from telephone equipment to defense-related technologies, mainly electronic warfare. As Alex, one of the senior managers, testifies,

> The decision to change the business domain and to start developing and manufacturing electronic warfare products was at the national level and was derived from the needs of the military (IDF) and because of the expertise of its senior experts [such as the CEO]. (Interview, June 2009)

Shalev, the legendary CEO, also oversaw the change of ownership. In 1980, Riebman sold his shares in Elisra to Tadiran for 6 percent of Tadiran. It seems that Shalev was most influential in shaping Elisra's corporate culture, including its beliefs, values, and behavior, especially in light of its civil-defense conversion. Furthermore, the merger with Tadiran, which belonged to Koor, exposed Elisra to the influence of Tadiran's culture, which was inspired by the workers' unions. Yaron, a senior Elisra manager, explains:

At the time of the merger (1980), Tadiran was already the leading electronic company in Israel, working mainly for the defense industry. It had established best practices and know-how regarding the best way to work with IDF and to meet its specific requirements. First and foremost, it implies a keen understanding of how military people think and how to approach them. This is why Elisra's many managers are army and air force veterans. This is quite common in the Israeli military-industrial industry; you adopt the culture of the military through the colonels and generals who have their second career as civilians, but still build on their military past. (Interview, June 2009)

Elisra, which had started operating in the institutional market (producing switching terminals for the Israeli government), moved into a new domain— the defense industry. Shalev, at least in the eyes of the company's workers, played an important role in Elisra's stability and in protecting its employees' rights. With such a caring CEO, the Zionist commitment of the founder, the socioeconomic and national values of the acquirer, and an association with the Histadrut, it is no wonder that employees had no incentive to leave the organization in order to initiate new ventures, even when the high-tech market was prospering.

In the mid-1980s, Elisra became less dependent on government funds for R&D. Once the government allowed it to export its products, the company increased its activities in international markets. However, the local market and, in particular, the IDF continued to be a secure and important source of revenues. Elisra, one might say, was always poised with one foot in the institutional market and the other in the competitive market.

Elisra has become a world leader in the fields of electronic warfare, intelligence, and communications. Its 1,300 employees (as of 2010) design, develop, manufacture, integrate, and support advanced system solutions for electronic warfare in four divisions of expertise. Elisra's advanced solutions are deployed on a wide range of platforms for air, sea, and land applications in over 40 countries, Israel included. Particularly important are its laboratories for electromagnetic compatibility and environmental testing. Because of its superior capabilities, Elisra was awarded the precious and valuable Israel Defense Prize of Excellence, given by the Israel Ministry of Defense to only a select few deserving companies.

In November 2002, 30 percent of Elisra shares were sold for $100 million to Elta, an Israeli electronic defense company and Elisra's fierce competitor. The two companies developed a common strategy in order to improve their ability to compete in the international market. As of November 30, 2005, 70 percent of Elisra shares had been sold to Elbit. Since then, Elisra has operated as a subsidiary of Elbit Systems, Ltd. Ironically, a few years later, Elisra acquired two "Tadiran Companies"—Tadiran Systems and Spectralink—and changed its name to Elisra Group.

Orbit Alchut Technologies (Orbit)   In contrast to Tadiran, Telrad, or Elisra, Orbit started as a new venture. It was founded in 1950 as a modest technology shop serving Israeli industry, under the name Alchut, as a cooperative association, by five ambitious entrepreneurs: Teddy Beeri, Walter Cohen, Moshe Myk, Karol Kirshner, and Yiftah Stein. The company's initial goal was to supply radio services to agricultural settlements. It equipped a vehicle with instruments that enabled simple repairs to be carried out on-site and also opened a lab in the coastal town of Netanya. As Karol Kirshner, Alchut's first CEO, writes,

> While in the beginning we provided only services, our real dream was to establish a manufacturing facility that would have a smoking chimney of at least 20 meters. In time, the plant was indeed established, but as for the chimney, it still has not been put up. . . . (http://www.orbit-cs.com)

Shortly afterward, Alchut found its niche—radio receivers and reception devices became its main business, and it garnered a substantial part of the market, providing services to a few of the biggest Israeli firms of the 1960s, such as the National Bus Company, Egged, and Rafael, a leading designer and developer of sophisticated military technologies. The work with Rafael proved to be crucial, as it allowed Alchut to develop professional know-how and to meet Rafael's high-quality business standards.

Alchut developed a reputation for reliability and fast turnaround, and other leaders of Israel's military industries, such as Israel Aircraft Industries (IAI), joined its group of customers. The real leap forward, however, was in 1967, when Alchut was asked to manufacture an antenna pedestal for a special defense project. After that, the company began to specialize in pedestal antennas and became a key supplier of antennas and related equipment for the Israeli defense establishment, including the IDF. By 1980, Alchut was recognized as an expert in pedestal solutions, and in 1981, renamed Orbit Alchut, it was granted an export license by the Israeli government and won its first international contract with a leading European firm.

During the 1980s, Orbit Alchut started to establish business relationships with Flam & Russell (FR), which specialized in antenna measurement and had developed a distribution network with a presence in the United Kingdom, Italy, Germany, Korea, and Japan. In 1988, Orbit Alchut acquired FR and opened its first office in the United States. Three years later, the company went public on the Tel Aviv Stock Exchange. Later, in 1994, Orbit Alchut reorganized its core business lines into two companies, Orbit ACS and Orbit Communications. The new company, Orbit ACS, was selected by Rockwell Collins to supply audio management systems for the U.S. Air Force. In 1997, Orbit FR went public on the NASDAQ and ventured into the space industry by launching its first Satellite Communication Tracking System for Trains.

During the last ten years, Orbit Alchut has grown relatively fast. The company established two U.S. subsidiaries: Orbit CT&T, Inc., and ACS, Inc., which were selected as first-choice vendors to supply a SATRACK product to the Sky Bridge project as part of the ISIS consortium, and it established ties with Sharp of Japan. Orbit also won a contract to supply airborne satellite communication tracking systems for commercial aircraft in the United States. It launched the new and most advanced generation of the two-way marine VSAT as well as the Orsat antenna system Ku-Band Marine Stabilized Tx/Rx.

In sum, starting as a small technological service shop, Alchut became a world-leading public company, with hundreds of employees, that operates from its modern facilities and is active all over the world. Orbit is a company in which all the technological know-how and experience is developed in-house; among its customers are world leaders such as Boeing, Gulfstream, Lockheed Martin, Rockwell Collins, Israel Aircraft Industries, Embraer, and more. Additionally, many leading navies and air forces are using Orbit's equipment and solutions.

Orbit and its subsidiaries are today known as "Orbit Defense Group." Its line of products aimed at military use in Israel and abroad hints at the potential growth of Orbit as a genealogy.

Motorola Israel (MIL)   Motorola, the world's leading provider of integrated communications and information solutions, brought its business to Israel in 1948 through a company called Moshe Bassin Electronics & Engineering, Ltd. It began operations as a small factory for car radio installation and, over the years, broadened its spectrum of activities to managing complicated technological projects in Israel and abroad (e.g., Iran). In 1964, with active involvement by the Israeli government, Motorola opened its first non-U.S. plant in Israel—Motorola Israel, Ltd. (MIL).

MIL was established as a wholly owned subsidiary of Motorola, Inc., a U.S.-based multinational electronics corporation. Its primary business concerns include integrated communications and embedded electronic solutions. More than 80 percent of its products have been developed locally, and its R&D center in Israel works primarily on the development of chips for cellular phones, as well as other innovative products for the parent company. In fact, the Israeli center has been developing in the first few years of the twenty-first century the next generation of processors for Motorola's palm devices. In 1998, MIL and Page Call founded Pelephone, Israel's first cellular carrier. It was not long before Pelephone had garnered a substantial portion of Israel's cellular communications market. Overall, MIL has experienced steady fiscal growth and now employs more than 4,000 workers, placing it among Israel's leading telecommunication companies. Figures for 2004 indicate a sales turnover of $798 million and total exports of $349 million.

MIL is different from the other founding parent companies already discussed, such as Tadiran, Telrad, and Elisra. As the first U.S. technology conglomerate with a subsidiary in Israel, Motorola USA provided the resources to establish this venture and also brought its corporate culture to the Israeli subsidiary. Yehuda Porat, human resources manager, explains:

> Although we are an Israeli company for all matters regarding management and strategy, and Motorola USA allows us to do most of the things our way, still many facets of Motorola culture are forced on us. For example, we have to follow the headquarters' directives on issues of diversity of employees or online evaluations. We are a microcosm of Motorola worldwide in the sense of both the variety of business domains and the culture. The Motorola culture is dictated from the upper echelons in the United States and penetrates every sector at MIL. It doesn't mean that there are no cultural differences between MIL and other subsidiaries, or between different sectors, but the general managerial culture of Motorola worldwide is dominant. Our great challenge is how to "paste" the Israeli culture onto the Motorola worldwide culture. We try to link between the Israeli and the American (corporate) culture by having as many Israelis [as possible] all over Motorola, headquarters and subsidiaries. Every Israeli in Motorola is first and foremost an Israeli. (Interview, September 2009)

MIL has three operating divisions: Communication Systems Operation, Service, and Next to Core Solutions; four business units: Network Services Applications, Defense Center of Excellence, Radio Network Division, and Motorola Ventures; and three daughter companies: MIRS Communication, Beeper Communication Israel, and Taldor Communication.

Elisha Yanai, MIL's CEO, attributes the firm's success to the unique characteristics of the Israeli high-tech industry. The entrepreneurial inclination of the average Israeli engineer is stronger than in any other place in the world. As a result, Motorola has welcomed many of MIL's ideas and has been a key factor in its growth. Yanai dubs the entrepreneurial culture "the spider tactics" and explains its rationale as follows:

> Since MIL mirrors Motorola USA, it is easier for us to enter into their shoes and to analyze the business decisions that Motorola is supposed to take. In the next stage, we are using our network to gather evidence supporting or not supporting our prior analyses. We have an "ambassador" in Motorola. He [or she] organizes and monitors these activities. For this purpose, he or she uses the "spider"—the Israeli network in Motorola Worldwide. This tactic helps us to be the first to submit relevant proposals to Motorola USA and to generate ideas that will ultimately be accepted by them. (Interview, September 2009)

With its impressive achievements, MIL is considered one of the most successful subsidiary of Motorola USA. It develops, manufactures, and markets communication solutions for government and enterprise networks and the mobile solutions sector. MIL's Design Center carries out the design and development of a variety of products and solutions for all Motorola markets around the world and is a major contributor to many prestigious global Motorola projects.

ECI Telecom (ECI)   ECI (Electronic Communication of Israel) Telecom is a leading producer of global telecom networking infrastructure, specializing in the area of communication platforms and solutions. Cellular service providers, cable/multiple-system operators, and government and defense entities from all over the world make up its core of customers. ECI's arenas of expertise include multi-play services, business services, voice services, wireless, cellular backhaul, optical networking, Ethernet networks, TDM-to-Ethernet evolution, migration to all IP, network security, carrier of carriers, and wavelength services.

A group of 50 Israeli Air Force veterans, led by Sol Gudelman, established ECI in 1965. The group joined forces with French partners and started developing and manufacturing electronic products. "Schneider Radio" was its most famous. ECI soon established itself as a pioneer in the field of advanced electronic equipment.

During the same period, in another location, a different group was established. Uri Goren, a chief commander in the Intelligence Force of the IDF, and

David Rubner, a young engineer from Westinghouse, established Electra Electronics, which employed five people. After a short time, Clal Industries became its owner. Together with Clal, Electra Electronics acquired Gudelman's Electronic Communication of Israel and kept its name. However, the core of the business was changed as Uri Goren and David Rubner focused on the military market. Together, they formed a team of 55 employees producing televisions and control tables for the Israeli Air Force. Electronic Communication of Israel developed into a totally different company.

Throughout the 1970s and the first half of the 1980s, ECI's main clients, the Ministry of Defense and the IDF, represented the largest portion of the company's growth. For 1974, ECI reported about 90 employees, with a breakdown of 80 percent mechanics and 20 percent electronic engineers. At that time, ECI was focused on providing solutions for systems within the army, and, as time passed, it branched off into the design and construction of air traffic control towers. The fledgling company's products helped to coordinate the air command of the various divisions of the Israeli army with products such as the ultra-wide-band antenna comparator for airborne applications; internal communication equipment for sea-based vessels; and mobile communication equipment for police vehicles and airplanes. Employees perceived the company as flexible and innovative, as CEO Uri Goren proclaimed, "We can invent anything as long as there is a purchase order!" (ECI archive, 1974).

The story of how ECI changed its strategic path in 1976 is quite amazing. The IDF asked for an analogical conceal mixer for conversation over the telephone. ECI and Tadiran competed to win this project and "unfortunately" Tadiran won. ECI's R&D group had worked hard on its proposal and succeeded in developing new technology that was not related to the army's project. This was the major turning point in the evolution of ECI. Its engineers focused on long-distance multiplexing, that is, simultaneous transmission of multiple telephone messages over one physical line. One device took advantage of the fact that phone lines were strung in pairs—one line sent signals one way while the other conducted the return signal—and each was actually only in use about half the time during the course of a typical conversation. ECI recognized the system's potential and decided to market it for commercial applications such as the "Telephone Line Doubler" for conducting two conversations over one line. With this, ECI, a modest Israeli factory, astounded the world! Recognizing the potential of this innovation for the communication market, it decided to shift back to the civilian market and develop the doubler, its major application, for the global market.

A second turning point was the appointment of Mair Laiser as ECI's CEO. In 1970, Laiser was the company's production manager and, at age 36, was appointed CEO in 1977. He had a strict work ethic that he expected everyone to follow. He was highly influential in molding an organizational culture based on the values of familiarity, solidarity, and a total commitment to the company and its customers. This is demonstrated in an anecdote involving a senior Deutsche Telecom (DT) executive and Laiser's predecessor, David Rubner. The DT executive claimed that DT worked with ECI because, as he said, "You are 'suckers; we just have to put some pressure on, and you deliver." To which Rubner answered, "You are right. For us, the customer is number one" (ECI archive).

It can be argued that Mair Laiser re-established ECI and turned it into a true high-tech company. Under his leadership, management started to steer the company away from the defense industry and toward civilian constituencies. Laiser deepened ECI's hold on the civilian communication market, at the expense of its defense involvement.

ECI developed Time Assignment Speech Interpolation (TASI) technology, which tracked the beginning and end of each segment of a telephone conversation and wedged the elements of a different conversation into the spaces in between. Launched in 1979, this device increased the potential use of long-distance analog lines by a factor of two. ECI's product beat even Bell Laboratory's (now Lucent Technologies) entry into the market. TASI was used especially on international undersea cables, where efficiency was a paramount concern. The digitization of telephone switching that began in the 1970s foreshadowed a decline in demand for TASI, but it challenged telephone equipment manufacturers to develop complementary devices. Digital telephone switches convert sounds into binary code for more efficient, computer-managed transmission, and then translate the code back into sounds at the receiving end. Digital Circuit Multiplexing Equipment (DCME), developed by ECI and others, bundle these digitized signals for maximum efficiency during transmission, thereby allowing standard long-distance phone lines to carry more information than was originally intended.

In 1977, ECI began building what was to become a long-term, strategic, and very successful relationship with Deutsche Bundespost (today known as Deutsche Telecom or DT). The German company became ECI's primary client, enabling ECI to go public in 1982, with its shares issued for the first time on the NASDAQ. At the same time, ECI grew into a global force with regard to the doubler telephone technology. By the mid-1980s, ECI was providing support for major carriers and private-line users in 18 countries on five continents.

In 1984, ECI embarked upon a global expansion plan, which included expansion of its U.S. office and the establishment of two representative offices in France and Australia. The company also opened two new subsidiaries—in

West Germany and Panama. A name change was enacted, and a new logo was unveiled that emphasized the company's new persona as a multinational corporation: ECI was now ECI Telecom, Ltd., with the word *Telecom* highlighting what had became the company's core business.

The years 1985 to 1986 brought a number of precarious developments that threatened to throw the company into crisis. Not only was inflation high but the profitability of going public was never really manifested. Overall sales declined by about 12 percent (approximately $19 million); as a result, ECI dismissed nearly one-third of its employees. Moreover, the company took a blow from lower sales of Telephone Circuit Multiplication (TCM) systems, which had not met expectations. Finally, ECI experienced increasing operating costs because of changes in various Israeli economic policies that cut earnings substantially.

The danger of a deeper crisis dissipated when ECI received the opportunity to furnish its communication equipment (DCME) for the connection of both ends of an international underwater cable (TAT-7, TAT-8). This was the main communication channel between Europe and the United States (as well as additional locations). The order for the DCME was worth $4.5 million, and the initial phase of the TAT-8 deployment brought an additional $13 million-plus in orders from 20 countries. As DCME grew to be used on satellites as well, there was virtually no country in the world that did not use ECI's products. The now very profitable company experienced 44 successful quarters, operating in 23 offices around the world servicing 144 countries. The late 1980s saw excellent gains in sales and earnings, with most of the growth driven by the DCME product line.

The 1990s reflected the leadership of David Rubner as CEO and Mair Laiser as chairman of the board. These were extremely fruitful years, and revenues grew steadily. The company now had a presence in several key developing regions in the world—Asia Pacific and Central and Eastern Europe—as well as in North America. It forged ahead into two new areas: data communications and video. In 1998, ECI agreed to merge with Tadiran Telecommunications, keeping the name ECI Telecom. The main strategy behind the deal was to secure and maintain ECI Telecom's position as a leading supplier of advanced telecommunications solutions to the world's telecom service operators and business users. Innowave, Business Systems, and the Transport Division (Bandwidth Management), including a plant in Kiryat Shmona and Innowave's plant in Omer, were incorporated as part of the merger.

As the turn of the twentieth-first century approached, the DCME market declined sharply. Again, ECI went into crisis mode just a few short months before the high-tech sector crashed, as revenues from their new technologies,

Synchronous Digital Hierarchy (SDH) and DCME, simply could not hedge the losses. The company was faced with reconstructing the core of its operations and downsizing. Before the bottom of the market for DCME fell out, ECI decided to spin off its divisions into five independent companies: Innowave, Inovia, Enavis, Lightscape, and NGTS. A few years later, NGTS merged with an American company, NexVerse, to form Veraz Networks, a leading global provider of soft switch–based, toll-quality packet telephony solutions. As of 2002, ECI had a 43 percent interest in the new company. Another division was spun off under the name ECTel, which became a leading developer and worldwide supplier of monitoring solutions and revenue assurance applications. It is now traded on the NASDAQ.

Following the bubble burst and the crisis in the telecom industry, ECI's management decided to reincorporate all of the independent companies into one strong ECI. Innovia became the Broadband Access Division, and Lightscape and Enavis were merged into the Optical Division. ECI kept its share of Veraz Networks and sold Innowave to Alvarion.

In 2005, ECI acquired full control of the outstanding common shares of Laurel Networks, Inc., a provider of Next-Generation IP/MPLS Multi-Service Routers, which became the company's Data Networking Division. Notwithstanding its ups and downs, ECI has remained a world leader in its field since it established operations in 1961. Today, it employs more than 3,000 people around the globe, with a network of sales operations conducted from regional divisions.

According to an ECI senior technology manager,

> You look at ECI and notice that many of ECI's veterans founded new firms. This is a company that gives a unique education to its worker—"Take responsibility, be creative and dare to do things out of the box." This is in spite of the fact that we are big. But look at the company; we are always at the state-of-the-art technology. ECI was a kind of a core for many Israeli entrepreneurs. You can see such places, like Stanford for the Silicon Valley. To my mind, ECI was very instrumental in inventing the most crucial aspect of the growth of the Israeli high-tech, the networking. People sought people there, and ECI was a great place where people with ideas and drive could be found. (Interview, September 2009)

The Competitive Economic Environment (1977–2005)

Three major companies were established in the "competitive" period (after 1977). As noted above, this period was characterized by relatively high environmental uncertainty and a competitive economy. During this period, the State of Israel was led by the liberal parties, and the country went through transformational change that was reflected in its goals, values, and economic system. This section outlines the founding processes and the environmental conditions prevailing during the founding of Fibronics, RAD Data Communications, and Comverse.

Fibronics   The idea for establishing Fibronics originated in 1977 in a meeting in Boston between Dr. Morris Weinberg and Uziah Galil, who was already a high-tech icon in Israel and was among the founders of Elron, Elscint, and a long list of technological ventures. Galil was considered one of the contributors to the transformation of the industry in Israel from institutional and agricultural into high-tech entrepreneurial. A graduate of the Technion–Israel Institute of Technology and Purdue University, he was the founder of Elron Electronic Industries, Ltd., the first high-technology multinational holding company based in Israel and operating worldwide. Galil used Elron to initiate various technological ventures. Elron, indeed, developed about 25 high-tech companies in medical imaging, defense electronics, communications, machine vision, and semiconductors. Galil served as CEO of Elron for 38 years (1962–1999) and as chairman or director of most of the companies founded by it. Prior to founding Elron, he worked in R&D for Motorola in Chicago (1953–1954), as head of Electronic Research in for the Israeli Navy (1954–1957), and as head of the Electronic Department of the Faculty of Physics at the Technion (1957–1962). Galil's partner in founding Fibronics was Morris Weinber, an American who was working at Waltech at the time. Morris had great trust in the future of Israeli electronics and dreamed of bringing to Israel the know-how for manufacturing fibers as well as the equipment that would connect them to the system (Levav 1998). Galil testifies that "of the two of us, Morris Weinberg was the real entrepreneur" (Interview, 2008).

In their first meeting, Weinberg and Galil raised the idea of setting up a partnership to develop connection parts for local communication networks based on fiber optics. Later, they decided to establish Fibronics International in the United States, to serve as the focal base, and a second company, a subsidiary of Fibronics, in Israel. They further decided that product development would be carried out in Israel while marketing and sales would be based in the United States. This model is still the preferred business arrangement for Israeli high-tech companies that see the United States as their prime market and source of knowledge and finance (Saxenian 2006).

Fred Adler, a venture capitalist who was active in Israel at the time, joined the Fibronics initiative right at the start. Elron, of which Uziah Galil was president, made the first investment in the new company. At the time, fiber optics was a new field and the hope was that it would replace cable for transferring data in fast files. However, the plan to manufacture fibers in Israel turned out to be insufficiently viable economically; there were better options elsewhere in the world. Thus, the focus shifted to the development of equipment that would transfer information on optical fibers. The company was built on the know-how that Weinberg brought to Israel and the work of the development staff of Elbit, a company that was part of Galil's group (Elron).

In its first two years, Fibronics moved rather aimlessly from one idea to another and, in fact, came close to the point of closing down. Most of the development and manufacturing was for the military, the main client being Rafael (the Armaments Development Authority). Elbit transferred a development team to Fibronics, headed by Moti Gura, that developed multiplexers for data communication on the basis of optical fibers (Timor 1997a). The products that Moti Gura developed raised great interest around the world, and Fibronics was marked as a possible success story.

Shortly after he joined the company in 1980, Gura was appointed CEO of Fibronics Israel, a position he held until 1984; during this time he played a key role in the Fibronics story. Gura had served in one of the best intelligence-technology units in the IDF, a unit that had a reputation for being very entrepreneurial. Gura himself was known in this unit as very creative and innovative and as one who would do everything to reach his goals. The founders of Fibronics, Morris Weinberg and Uziah Galil, were not sufficiently involved in its daily operations, so Gura had a lot of freedom. His bold and fearless style, together with the founders' financial backing, led to the opening of several divisions and to a significant boost in the volume of sales. Gura says,

> There was an atmosphere of innovation and pioneering in the area. Fibronics was perceived as a serious and innovative high-tech leader. Everyone wanted to leave a mark and make a change. (Interview, 2008)

In its first years, the company developed communications-compatible systems for IBM. The main device in these systems was the multiplexer, a passive product that gave the cable the power to convey the traffic of two terminals. From this, an entire line of IBM-compatible products was developed, based on the 32/70 communications protocol. The line sold extremely well.

It was Gura who led Fibronics (when it was still a start-up) as it went public on the NASDAQ in 1983, when the world was beginning to understand the potential inherent in fiber optics. Fibronics managed to raise $6.7 million on Wall Street by issuing 26 percent of its shares at a company value of about $26 million. The income of the company in the first half of the year was $1.84 million, but it was four times that for the same period in 1982. Many investors made a lot of money, and Fibronics changed the face of the venture capital (VC) industry in Israel.

But everything changed at Fibronics in 1984 when Gura suddenly decided to leave after not being appointed Morris Weinberg's successor as CEO of Fibronics International (Levav 1998). He was not interested in staying on as a salaried employee and believed that he had the capability to succeed independently.

In 1985, Fibronics closed 5 product lines and decided to dedicate its efforts to FDDI (Fiber Distributed-Data Interface). Moti Gura had left the company and been replaced by Joseph Maayan. Gura set up a competing company called Adacom, taking with him most of Fibronics' senior management and highly knowledgeable employees. This was a serious blow to Fibronics regarding its profitability, image, and morale. Avinoam Rubinstein, one of the founders of Nicecom and Atrica, came to Fibronics as a third-year student at the Technion, just before Gura left. He comments on the atmosphere at the company at the time:

> There was complete hysteria about the fear of knowledge theft and industrial espionage. A very high level of compartmentalization and secrecy emerged, alongside very low morale. (Interview, 2008)

Moshe Levin, who joined Fibronics in 1986 as Vice CEO for Marketing and Sales, describes a great sense of uncertainty: "It was a company that had lost its raison d'être after the establishment of Gura's Adacom" (Interview, 2008).

After Gura's departure, Fibronics changed its strategic course. The new CEO, Dono van-Mierop, who had joined Fibronics in 1984 as Vice CEO for Development, shifted the company's focus to FDDI, a technology that enables construction of the fastest high-speed data communication networks on optical fibers. The company developed the product line and, at the same time, strove to establish the protocol that it developed with the IEEE standards committee. "A new spirit of innovation and entrepreneurship returned to Fibronics. Many new employees joined the organization and there was a feeling of being capable to conquer the world" (Avinoam Rubinstein, 2008)

The years from 1987 to 1990 were a time of important breakthroughs and great morale. Fibronics carried out a number of large projects: the networking of many of the main highways in Italy; the networking of the racetracks in Hong Kong with optical fibers; and the networking of Euro Disney in Paris. These were projects for which all the major companies, such as Digital and IBM, had competed, and Fibronics won the right to carry them out.

With these successes, Fibronics ended 1989 with sales of $48 million and 469 employees. In 1990, sales increased still further, to $62.5 million. CEO John Hail declared at the time, "Our products lead the market and we foresee a bright future for Fibronics" (Timor 1997a).

From 1990 onward, however, there was a distinct slowdown in the company's development. Fibronics placed all its hopes on FDDI in the belief that in the distant future fiber optics would dominate the market, but it failed to correctly evaluate the power of the cable infrastructure with which its products competed (Levav 1998). Fibronics continued to lose valuable time by betting on FDDI (Timor 1997b). The mistiming, combined with the outbreak of the Gulf War in 1991, led to a drastic decline in sales.

Fibronics' failure was attributable not only to its unfortunate choice of an industry standard but also to many other factors. For example, Harry Yuklea, the founder of Optosortage who joined Fibronics in 1988 and eventually became the head of business development, points to the company's main weakness: operations-oriented rather than R&D-oriented management. Amir Eldad, head of the European marketing desk at Fibronics from 1986 to 1994 and founder of Atternity, describes a situation of alienation among managers in the lower echelons:

> The organizational culture that prevailed in the lower echelons was very much that of a start-up: Work around the clock, an aggressive schedule, doing the impossible. Against this, the management style of the senior echelons was very cautious, conservative, and even regressive. The senior management was not a party to the creative spirit and did not succeed in channeling the positive energies that abounded in the company. (Interview, 2008)

Dr. Orna Berry, founder of Ornet, who had been brought to Fibronics as a senior project manager in 1989, adds to this by describing an aggressive regime of shouting, threats, and arrogance:

> The success of the company attracted talented, motivated young engineers who wanted to be a part of that success and be exposed to cutting-edge technology. The

company hired personnel capable of independent, high-quality work and turned them into nothing. By clipping their wings, they chased away much brainpower and talent. (Interview, 2008)

Fibronics operated in a market with enormous growth potential. Having had its stock traded on the international market was a rare situation on the Israeli high-tech scene, which in the 1980s was still in its infancy. It exposed the best engineers to innovation, to cutting-edge technology, and to acquaintance with the main clients and players in the industry.

In sum, during Gura's tenure Fibronics' employees were exposed to an entrepreneurial spirit and a willingness to take risks, which had not been the case before. They also experienced the process of going public and saw that it was possible. In contrast, an unfocused management style and the appointment of unsuitable CEOs made it difficult for Fibronics to retain talented employees and led to a brain drain. Endowed with the knowledge, the tools, and the right spirit, some of those driven away from the company chose to establish their own enterprises.

At the end, in 1994, Fibronics was sold to Elbit Systems of the Elron Group in a circular transaction (since Elbit and Fibronics were both owned by the Elron Group). Later, in 1996, it was sold to MRV Communications.

Uziah Galil, a co-founder of Fibronics and its chairman, sums up:

> Fibronics, in my view, is a painful story and a failure in the chain of successful companies that I established through Elron. It may be that mistakes were made in the appointing of CEOs and that we did not correctly understand the need to place emphasis on marketing. We chose to appoint CEOs who came to us from big companies (like Gil Weiser from Digital), people with rich operational experience (Zvi Axelrold from Elbit, Joseph Mayan, past Director General of the Defense Ministry). Had I been aware of the entrepreneurial forces buried under the surface at Fibronics, I would have appointed a CEO who would have known how to harness these forces and channel them in positive directions—a strong CEO respected by the workers, someone who understood their aspirations. (Interview, 2009)

At the same time, Galil did not blame the failure of Fibronics just on the choice of its CEO. He attributed its decline to other factors, too, such as being ahead of its time in terms of technological vision and the inability of Elron (Fibronics' mother company) to provide the required managerial backing. It should be noted that within the high-tech community in Israel, Fibronics was considered the greatest missed opportunity of the decade.

Comverse Technology (Comverse)   The primary business activities of Comverse Technology, Inc., include the design, development, manufacturing, and marketing of computer and telecommunications systems for specialty multimedia communications and information-processing applications. By 1995, an international sales force had helped place Comverse's products in more than 30 countries around the world. Indeed, the mid-1990s represented a period of rapid growth, not only through the expansion of international markets but also through the introduction of new technology to the global marketplace.

Three individuals came together to establish Comverse in 1982: Boaz Misholi, Kobi Alexander, and Yechiam Yemini. Alexander had studied economics in Tel Aviv before moving to New York in the early 1980s. In New York, he worked full-time as an investment banker at Shearson Lehman while attending New York University at night to earn his M.B.A. degree. Although Alexander had always had an entrepreneurial spirit, he didn't expect to be able to actualize it so early in life. In 1982, he met Boaz Misholi, an Israeli engineer who had an idea for a business venture. "The week after I met him, I resigned from Shearson. I always knew I wanted to have my own company" (Bernstein 1990).

Misholi, who already owned a software development company in New York, remarks,

> In those years, there were not too many possibilities in Israel for young people to get rich. . . to make big money. The high-tech was the best venue for young talented entrepreneurial people to make their way to it. (Interview, 2010)

Misholi's idea was to develop a voice and fax messaging system that would allow customers to store, process, access, and transmit information from any telephone or fax machine. The system would offer a far more comprehensive alternative to answering machines and other rudimentary gear available at the time. Misholi and Alexander recruited engineers to help them develop the system. They also decided to move back to Israel and take advantage of the government's incentive package for technology entrepreneurs.

In Israel, Alexander and Misholi operated their fledgling business as Efrat Future Technology, Ltd. With Misholi taking the lead from a technological standpoint, the two began work on a digital listening system that would be used for intelligence purposes by the Israeli army. This development was crucial to providing the young venture with financial stability. According to Misholi, the army was the only entity that could afford such intensive and costly R&D efforts. Along with Alexander, he spent two years with the army's development team in Israel. At that time, Yechiam Yemini was the company's chief scientist and was not completely vested in running the new venture. In 1984, however, he joined Alexander and Misholi in their move back to New York to establish the foundations of an infrastructure through which they could market the new digital listening system once it was ready.

Comverse (a fusion of "communication" and "versatility"), incorporated in New York in 1984, is the result of that move by the three founders. Formally, it was the parent company of Israeli-based Efrat Future Technology, Ltd. For the first three years of operations, Comverse generated a few million dollars annually. In 1986, it went public on the New York Stock Exchange to generate additional capital.

During the next two years, Misholi served as president and chief executive of the newly public company, but he left the post in 1988 after he and Alexander failed to come to terms regarding Comverse's strategy. Alexander took over Misholi's position, counting on Yemini's help. He was well aware that he would need a unique and compelling marketing strategy if his small venture was to compete successfully among telecommunications technology giants such as AT&T. He consequently decided to target the international market early on, particularly in Europe, which was scheduled for economic unification in 1992. Alexander believed that Comverse could benefit tremendously from developing an early lead in a newly unified Europe with its particular products.

Alexander implemented his plan successfully during the late 1980s by securing exclusive relationships for Comverse with several top European equipment distributors. Specifically, between 1987 and 1990 the company signed marketing agreements with six large distributors that had managed to launch comfortable and inviting relationships not only with national governments but also with major equipment buyers. Among the companies that agreed to distribute Comverse systems were Ascom (Switzerland), GPT (United Kingdom and Australia), Voice Data Systems (Netherlands), and Oki (Japan). These first agreements gave Comverse a definitive advantage over its larger competitors because the distributors often knew what was happening with deals on the market well before Comverse or its rivals found out. Comverse could step in and push its product to clients early in their decision-making process.

Comverse's foray into the European market included the former Eastern Bloc, ready and poised to drive long-term industry growth. It also expanded its U.S. sales by working primarily with domestic telephone companies, such as the wireless divisions of the Regional Bell Operating Companies, and independent cellular companies, such as PacTel and McCaw.

There were several fortuitous factors that came together in the early 1990s, propelling Comverse's income and profit. In 1991, for example, the company agreed to purchase the assets of the Irvine, California–based Startel Corp., a leading supplier of transaction-processing systems used mostly by the telephone answering service industry, hospitals, and corporate message centers. In 1992, Startel became a subsidiary of Comverse, bringing with it important new technology to Comverse's R&D lab, as well as access to a new segment of the market.

In late 1992, the company experienced another major achievement: an agreement with global communications giant AT&T, which offered Comverse's multilingual voice-processing system to corporate customers and telecommunications providers outside of the United States. In essence, AT&T was giving an endorsement to Comverse's technology, an invaluable vote of confidence by the industry leader.

Beyond these accomplishments on the global market, Comverse continued to reap the benefits of its work in the development and introduction of cutting-edge technology. Its Trilogue and Audio Disk systems, surveillance technologies for the intelligence and policy markets, exploded onto the scene in the mid-1990s. In fact, as a result of that major growth, in February 1994 Comverse spun off its entire surveillance business into a new subsidiary—Interactive Information Systems Corporation, which changed its name to Comverse Information Systems Corporation two years later. By 1999, Comverse Technology, as it was now called, had reorganized its operations into two divisions: Comverse Infosys (a merger of Comverse Information Systems with Comverse Info Media Systems) and Comverse Network Systems.

The rapid increase in the popularity of cell phones in the late 1990s brought yet more changes. While Comverse Information Systems quietly sold its Audio Disk systems through the Comverse Infosys Division, Comverse Network Systems was thriving with its wireless voice messaging systems. Soon, a majority of its revenue—nearly three-quarters of $1.2 billion—came from the sale of mobile mailboxes. At this point, Comverse Technology was in danger of over-concentration in one particular arena: voicemail. In the face of the cell phone market reaching a plateau, management began an aggressive plan for diversification, acquiring promising technologies that would help the company develop new products, and at the same time adding assets to Comverse Infosys. In July 2000, Comverse acquired Loronix Information Systems, Inc., a company that developed software-based digital video recording, networking, and live Internet video-streaming technology. This deal yielded a digital video-monitoring system used by government agencies, such as the U.S. Department of the Treasury, as well as by commercial customers, including the Mohegan Sun Casino and Federal Express.

In 2001, Comverse management reorganized and split the company into five divisions after having acquired several other concerns. Comverse Infosys was one of the five, but it became increasingly apparent that it did not really fit in with the rest of the company, not least because it sold its products to entities that were entirely different from the telecommunications companies that bought Comverse's voice and data messaging services. Not surprisingly, management started to consider a means by which it could split off the security and intelligence division.

It was not long before the opportunity to do so emerged. After the terrorist attacks of 9/11, the need for all forms of security-related products rose exponentially. A struggling economy and a depressed stock market, however, left the demand for initial public offerings rather soft. Nevertheless, Alexander arranged for the sale of shares of Comverse Infosys in a "carve-out" agreement that would leave Comverse Technology with a majority stake in the company while unlocking shareholder value. Comverse Infosys was renamed Verint Systems, Inc., in February 2002, and the company was now ready to go public. Alexander became the chairman of Verint, while Dan Bodner served as president and CEO, positions he had held since Comverse Technology established Interactive Information Systems in 1994. Media assets under Comverse Media Holding, Inc., were sold back to the parent company. Concurrently, Verint, through Lorinix, beefed up its video surveillance business with the acquisition of the digital video-recording business of Lanex, LLC. By 2005, Comverse Technology consisted of four divisions: Comverse, Verint Systems (formerly Comverse Infosys), Startel, and Starhomes.

RAD Data Communications   RAD Data Communications is the cornerstone of the RAD Group, a family of independent companies that develops, manufactures, and markets solutions for diverse segments of the networking and telecommunications industry. Unlike ECI, Telrad and Tadiran, the founding parents of RAD Data Communications are still its active owners and are involved in both its operational and its strategic decisions. Consequently, Yehuda and Zohar Zisapel, the two brothers who founded RAD in 1982, still have a meaningful impact on the evolution of their group and, respectively, on the entire genealogy. Both brothers had studied electronics engineering at the Technion–Israel Institute of Technology. In 1973, they founded (with a partner) a company importing and distributing computer networking equipment as a cooperative association called Bitcom. Later, Yehuda parted company with his initial business partner and started a new firm, Bynet. This company imported various electronic components, but its main business was distributing the Codex Corporation's products. Bynet's contract with Codex made it a market leader in Israel. In 1977, Motorola USA acquired Codex and insisted on taking over Yehuda Zisapel's distributorship. Because of its successful performance, Bynet maintained the distribution rights for its products for another three years. In 1981, Motorola decided not to renew the distribution agreement with Bynet and to sell the former Codex Corporation's products in Israel directly.[6]

In 1981, Bynet experienced a serious crisis, which led Yehuda Zisapel to change his business path. He asked his younger brother Zohar to join forces to establish RAD Data Communications. For Zohar Zisapel, the cost of accepting this offer was high. It meant leaving a highly interesting and prestigious position in the military system (head of the Electronic Research Department of the Ministry of Defense). "We will produce and export," promised Yehuda. "You have the technological knowledge and I know the market. We will succeed." Zohar agreed immediately, in spite of the fact that he did not know much about his brother's business. He believed in Yehuda and wanted to help (Levav 1998). In an interview, he described his decision to leave the army and join Yehuda in founding RAD as a one originating from a deep familial connection:

> If there is a single turning point in my whole professional career, then that was my decision to leave my position in the military in 1981 and to accept my brother's offer to try our luck at establishing RAD Data Communications. You can say that RAD Data Communications was founded because of my mother's cholent. It is a tradition on Saturday, the Jewish Sabbath, to gather around the family table for lunch and be served a dish commonly called cholent, which is a heavy stew filled with meat, potatoes and beans that has been cooked all night. And it was there, seated around the table, that we originally developed what was then the unheard-of idea of a company that would manufacture data communication products in Israel for export abroad. (Goel 2007, 94)

After graduating from the Technion, Zohar Zisapel enlisted in the IDF and served in one of the most prestigious military technical intelligence units, one that raised and nurtured many successful inventors and future entrepreneurs. Thus, because his last position in this unit was as chief scientist, he was the ideal partner for establishing the new venture. He brought with him not only technological knowledge and a creative mind but also the entrepreneurial culture that he and his colleagues had developed in their special military unit. This was an atypical unit—informal and relatively undisciplined—which Zohar used to call a "positive mess." He believed that tough discipline inhibits creativity and decreases innovation. In regular army units, soldiers' behavior is shaped by tough routines and top-down-dictated procedures. This culture cannot promote entrepreneurship and innovativeness. Technological industry, in contrast, needs a climate of free and independent thinking—a climate like that of the special units of the Israeli army (Levav 1998).

The brothers established the new venture—simply named RAD, for Research and Development (Levav 1998)—in 1981 with the goal of developing their own products. Zohar and Yehuda Zisapel were among the first pioneers of the Israeli high-tech industry. They did not have any corporate or wealthy investors behind them. Zohar worked for a low salary, with Bynet covering all expenses. He was not used to working under these conditions. From a leading unit in the army, supported by almost unlimited budgets and brilliant personnel, he found himself in a small start-up with a low budget and a relatively mediocre team.

The Zisapels started by developing the "short-range modem" and the "remote-line monitor." Whereas the modem was not innovative enough, the monitor preceded its time, and both failed (Levav 1998). The company's breakthrough was marked by its creation of the miniature computer modem, which quickly became a commercial success, and by 1985 RAD's annual revenues had reached $5.5 million. Since then, RAD has sold hundreds of thousands miniature modems. "Small is good" became the company's new slogan. "It is not ingenuity," explains Zohar Zisapel. "Without my experience in the army, it wouldn't have happened."

Today, RAD earns about $1 billion in revenues per year and maintains 26 offices on six continents, supporting 300 sales offices in 165 countries. Approximately 30 percent of RAD's 1,000 employees are engaged in R&D. Such heavy emphasis has contributed to the company's unprecedented achievements. RAD was the originator of Single IP, which enables multiple users to share a common IP address for Internet access, as well as of numerous pioneering developments in communication technologies and the miniaturization of communication hardware such as modems.

The slogan "Small is good" manifested itself again when the Zisapel brothers teamed with Benny Hanigal, a young engineer who had worked on the Lavi, the Israel Aircraft Industries' fighter aircraft project. Together they developed a miniature intranet product that was extremely successful. The next start-up, Armon, was followed by many others. After RAD, up to 2005, the Zisapel brothers founded 26 ventures. During those years, they developed a rather un-usual and singular business philosophy that employs a decentralized approach. Working individually and autonomously under a common strategic umbrella, the companies in the RAD Group experience the advantages inherent in small businesses, such as flexibility, entrepreneurial spirit, and management focus. When the parent company locates a new market niche that cannot be filled under the existing umbrella, the brothers create a new company in response to the identified need. In a 2007 interview (Mohney 2007), Zohar Zisapel sum-marized the RAD Group's achievements:

> My brother and I have started 27 companies, five of which we closed and one of which left the group; six companies trade on the NASDAQ; seven were acquired and eight are still private. We have done that repeatedly during the last 25 years, so, on the average we have started one company every year, except of 1991 when we started three companies. (p. 22)

Few of RAD Group's companies are traded on the NASDAQ; they remain in the hands of the Zisapel brothers along with several VC firms. The found-ing company, RAD Data Communications, has never attempted to go public; instead, it acts as a key strategic resource for the innovative moves of its found-ing parents. The strategy for firms founded under its guidance usually follows a similar pattern: First, RAD matches an innovative idea with a prospective founder, either from within or outside the group. It then provides the main portion of the initial funding and directs strategic development based on its vast experience. Even though the group is known for its successful exits, it tends to focus on the deliberate and calculated founding of new firms, rarely resort-ing to mergers, acquisitions, or strategic spinoffs. The ventures established by RAD Data Communications regularly share technology, market channels, and valuable market information—cooperation is central to its organizational cul-ture. Start-up companies initially receive administrative and marketing assis-tance from the group, which lowers operating costs at the crucial early stages of operation. Furthermore, RAD fosters the motivation for success among the employees of these start-ups, who often share in the profits and the decision making at this critical juncture.

According to Amnon Yaakobi, one of the founders of an Armon-sponsored company,

RAD provides me with the infrastructure, mainly administrative services, and seed money. They didn't create dependency, but let me do many things on my own—take responsibility. I will give you an analogy. Teaching a baby to walk is good, but at a certain point you would like him to walk on his own. This is their model, to help you, but at the same time to encourage you to develop your own capabilities and abilities to survive. This sharpens your entrepreneurial instincts. (Interview, 2004)

Summary

Table 3.1 summarizes the environmental context and the major genesis events of the nine founding parents' firms discussed in this chapter. As can be seen, the founding parents used different strategies with regard to resources—knowledge creation versus acquisition—and with regard to target markets—local and institutional versus competitive and international. Tadiran and Telrad differ from Elisra, Orbit, and Motorola, as well as from ECI, RAD, Fibronics, and Comverse. They represent organizations that operated in the centralized and protected Israeli market until the 1980s. Through their holding company, Koor, which was horizontally integrated and politically well connected, the two firms were both practically free from external competition that would have threatened their survival. Thus, they did not have to invest in R&D beyond the direct needs of their institutional clients. They had to cope only with the uncertainties of competitive markets during the 1980s, when the Israeli economy underwent a process of liberalization and privatization that forced Tadiran and Telrad, which were heavily involved in government projects for either the Ministry of Defense or the Ministry of Communication, to turn around and invest resources in innovation and knowledge creation. Finally, the managerial culture and vision of both organizations were anchored in labor, national, and Zionist values. As noted earlier, these values were intertwined with their business considerations and had a great impact upon their evolution.

All of the other founding companies were private enterprises, four of which (Elisra, Orbit, ECI, and MIL) were established either by Israeli entrepreneurs or by foreign investors during the institutional-cooperative economy period. Although ECI was founded in 1965, it experienced a major transformation in the 1970s that allows it to be considered an entity founded in the competitive-economy period. The common denominator of Elisra and Orbit is their orientation toward defense products. From their employees' perspective, being a part of an industry that contributed to Israel's defense meant much more than their actual roles. As one of Elisra's senior employees stated, "You will not abandon an organization where you feel as if you are an integral part of the tremendous effort to defend your country" (Interview, June 2010). Furthermore, the projects created for the military were, generally speaking, bigger and much more technologically challenging than those created for the civilian market. Such factors contributed to the motivation of the organizations' members and increased their organizational identification.

The remaining three firms, RAD, Fibronics, and Comverse, were founded during the competitive-economy period. In contrast to the other firms, they were start-ups and from the very beginning based their strategy on knowledge creation for a globalized competitive environment. Furthermore, their founding teams had been nurtured in the most creative and innovative scientific units of the IDF.

RAD was founded by two brothers, both of whom were involved in technology and business development through the founding of 26 sister firms, each of which adopted a similar business model, albeit engaging in different technologies. This model was based on RAD's founders' serving as mentors and coaches of the CEOs of the initiated companies. RAD also provided resources, knowhow, and market linkages. In this vein, it served as a repository for the companies' entrepreneurial blueprints as well as for their practices and resources. In contrast, Comverse's model involved channeling its efforts toward development and business control of a particular interrelated technological niche—voicemail and surveillance. To this end, it invested in R&D and also acquired a large number of firms to gain competitive knowledge and reduce competition. RAD avoided going public because its founders preferred to retain absolute control over their first founded firm. In contrast, Fibronics and Comverse went public on the NASDAQ a few years after founding. They differed from RAD in their growth strategies. Whereas RAD expanded by founding new innovative technological firms, Comverse expanded mainly through mergers and acquisitions. RAD consistently exhibited an entrepreneurial strategy, while Comverse opted to control its niche by developing new technologies and reducing competition in its domain.

Unlike RAD and Comverse, Fibronics, which was a world leader in fiber optics technology, neither initiated nor acquired even a single firm during its 17 years of existence. The event that triggered the rapid growth of this genealogy was an internal conflict that led to the exit of the firm's creative and influential CEO, who left in 1984 to found Adacom, which later became Fibronics' main competitor. We have been able to trace 23 companies founded by Fibronics deserters (almost 10 percent of the highest number of Fibronics' employees at its peak) between 1984 and the end of 2005. It seems that the initial conditions and the genesis events of RAD, Fibronics, and Comverse had greater potential for triggering stronger entrepreneurial inclinations than those of Tadiran and Telrad.

ECI, although formally founded in the institutional-cooperative economy period, appears to belong to the RAD, Fibronics, and Comverse group in terms of the potential impact that its initial environmental conditions and genesis events might have had on its entrepreneurial inclinations. ECI was not founded as a start-up but as a merger between two small companies. Taking its first steps as a unified company, it focused mainly on the defense market. However, ten years later, in the late 1970s, following a change in its leadership, it modified its strategy and made extensive investments in innovative R&D, carving its way into international competitive markets.

This chapter reviewed the initial conditions and the historical legacy of the founding parents of nine of the genealogies that form the Israeli ITC sector. We observed that the companies founded during the cooperative and competitive environments, respectively, possessed certain underlying characteristics that shaped them for years to come. Companies founded in each period depict a coherent model that allows for different evolutionary paths. The characteristics of the different genealogies stem from the initial conditions that prevailed during the founding of their parents' firms. However, in both periods the companies reviewed in this chapter possessed a culture that regarded the mission of nation building as a prime mover for their own missions. Companies that were founded in different periods exhibited varied business models. However, the Israeli ethos of mobilization for the sake of the nation never waned. Zohar Zisapel, the founder of RAD, eloquently explains:

> We are pretty much attuned to the American culture because our high-tech work originated in America. We grew up there. The first generation of Effie Arazi [the founder of Scitex], the second generation of Dov Frohman [the founder of Intel Israel], returned to Israel and brought with them an American corporate culture and business models. We use the same terminology as the Americans. But there is a difference because we are a small society, which leads you to improvise to find a way, by all means. This is why I don't accept "no" for an answer. "No" is not an answer when we have to develop the best product. When I try to explain our entrepreneurial culture to Americans, I tell them the story about my car engine, which fell off in the middle of the desert while I was in the military. We improvised, using the branches of shrubs and then we drove on. An American would have waited for a tow truck. We are like that because we are living in a country which is under constant threat, and everything we do—at least in my generation—is first for our survival as a nation. This gives you extra motivation and resilience. (Interview, 2006)

Genealogies in the Making
The Process and Structure of Their Evolution

4

The only power that can serve to moderate individual egotism is the power of the group; the only power that can serve to moderate the egotism of the group is that of some other group, which embraces them.

Emile Durkheim, *The Division of Labor in Society*

Genealogy implies a line of descent. Human genealogy is governed by a series of rules that are embedded in cultural, social, and ethical norms handed down from one generation to the next. With regard to organizations, one can say that industries evolve from founding parent companies that spawn progenies. Organizational genealogies assume change processes that guide an industry's evolution through a predetermined sequence of heredity. A genealogy is, in fact, the reproduction sequence of organizations that expands the population of organizations responding to emerging opportunities. This leaves the question of where capabilities and core features of organizations come from. As we stated in Chapter 2, according to imprinting theories, initial social and structural conditions at the time of an organization's founding exert enduring effects on future organizational development through inheritance dynamics (Klepper 2002; Stinchcombe 1965). The underlying assumption is that an organization's core features imprint on its progenies through heredity processes, which eventually influence the entire evolution of a specific industry. Thus, the "inheritance" dynamics (Franco and Filson 2006; Klepper 2002) may have influenced the genealogical evolution of the Israeli high-tech industry.

Genealogical evolution is influenced by the initial conditions of founding. Those conditions affect various characteristics of a genealogy's members, including the variation in firms' forms and strategies (Boeker 1988); the pace of growth and change (Eisenhardt and Schoonhoven 1996); managerial models and blueprints (Baron and Hannan 2005; Burton and Beckman 2007; Beckman

and Burton 2008); and the mortality rate (Carroll and Hannan 2000; Swaminathan 1996).

In this chapter, we explore the formation of organizational genealogies of
the information technology and communication (ITC) sector in Israel and its
characteristics. In particular, we trace the evolutionary trajectory of each genealogy and its growth strategy. We show how genealogies and their respective
environments evolve and influence their growth. We also demonstrate how the
conditions at founding influence the entrepreneurial tendencies of a genealogy's affiliates, and how the different institutional environments at founding
shape entrepreneurial capabilities and the inclination to spawn progenies. The
data show that certain genealogies prosper when pursuing innovation in line
with the trajectory of change in their industry (McGahan 2004). Hence, our
genealogical perspective presents the evolutionary dynamics that ultimately
shaped the Israeli ITC sector—in both its embryonic and mature stages. We
also show how the prospects of genealogical evolution are ascribed to the ex
ante capabilities embedded in their founding environment.

Studies on the evolution of the Israeli high-tech industry claim that it has
evolved from start-ups to a mature stage as a result of specific event sequences
and generative mechanisms (Avnimelech and Teubal 2006). In this vein, the Israeli case exhibits a unique model of start-up clusters that co-evolved in phases
(Avnimelech 2008; Avnimelech and Teubal 2006, 2008). Avnimelech and Teubal
relate industry evolution to time-dependent changes rather than to contextual
events that shape industries at their embryonic stage. Industry characteristics
are assumed to be constant during each stage, with no accounting for industry
heterogeneity. Our genealogical approach, however, does consider context and
enhances understanding of the conditions and processes that have led to the industry's prosperous growth by claiming that founding rates and their patterns
depend upon the policy and socioeconomic conditions at the time of founding.
Furthermore, at the embryonic stage of industry evolution, innovators compete for market acceptance and funding sources, knowledge, and other essential resources needed to support their entrepreneurial activities. Therefore, the
genealogical tradition proposes that parents shape their progenies' prospects
for success (Phillips 2002, 2005).

Genealogies create opportunities and constraints for their members and
evolve through reproduction processes that reflect lineage affinity and serve
as the basis for formation of new ventures along generational lines. The selection of reproduction patterns that bring together entrepreneurs and shape the
potency of an entire heredity line plays an important role. Genealogies may

oscillate between high potency and low potency—that is, producing more or fewer offspring over time. Some genealogies may spawn a substantial number of new ventures much later in their life cycle. This occurs because certain types of contextual triggers, such as the existence of well-developed high-tech clusters (Breznitz 2007; Kenney 2000; Saxenian 1994), may affect why and when a genealogy gravitates toward greater potency. In this chapter, we show the evolutionary path of nine genealogies that developed at different times from different founding parents. In the first part of the chapter, we explain how the genealogies were constructed; in the second, we describe their evolutionary paths and structure. Finally, in the third part, we show how the nine genealogies differ from each other in terms of potency.

Mapping the Genealogies

The data for mapping the genealogies of the founding parent firms in the Israeli ITC sector came from the following sources: (1) the Israel Venture Capital (IVC) Research Center's historical and current archives; (2) Israel's Central Bureau of Statistics (CBS) databases; (3) the Israel Association of Electronics & Information Industries (IAEI) databases; (4) firms' websites; (5) LinkedIn; (6) newspaper archives; and (7) interviews with 65 CEOs and founders of high-tech ventures and venture capital firms. Constructing the ITC genealogies involved the following steps.

Compiling the Data

We used the IVC (www.ivc-online.com) historical and current records to identify all the companies listed in communication-related categories. The IVC database is divided according to industrial sectors, and the ITC firms are aggregated in separate domains. The database includes over 6,500 high-tech companies and venture-capital funds. It is considered a major, reliable source for the Israeli high-tech and venture capital industries and is widely used in academic research (cf. Avnimelech and Teubal 2004; Fiegenbaum 2007), as well as by government and private sector analysts. We constructed the genealogies by tracing the origin of each company in our sample.

To construct the genealogies, we searched for founders who had been employed by one of the nine parent firms before founding their own.[1] This allowed us to add the de-novo firms—spawned start-ups founded by independent entrepreneurs who left their incumbent firms—to the basic configuration (incumbents and their different progenies). Then we searched for firms that were spawned from, acquired by, or merged into each of the nine founding firms. We identified the founding team of each firm and the companies they founded or worked for before founding what became the genealogy's parent company. The same process was applied for each offspring to identify all subsequent generations. In other words, we repeated the same procedure by moving along generational lines. In this way, we were able to build a succession line of firms and to identify the origin of their founding characteristics. In cases in which there was more than one founder, we traced their employment histories and marked the genealogical affiliation as endogenous (or exogenous) if they were employed by a firm that was (or was not) part of the genealogy. We traced firms not only through top-down procedures (as described previously) but also from the bottom up. We selected the firms of the last generation and identified their founding teams and employment histories. The most recent employers were identified as the parent companies of these teams. In this way, we continued to trace each genealogy's origin until we reached the founding parents of the entire genealogy. This procedure was carried out to ensure that we did not miss any firm or founder in the top-down method.

Drawing the Genealogy Maps

We drew network maps of each genealogy using the Pajek software (see Figures 4.1 through 4.9). These maps illustrate the interrelationships among the members of each genealogy and between genealogies, enabling us to understand the nature of each genealogy's intergenerational relations.

The nine genealogies consist of 769 firms. Because some firms may be affiliated with more than one genealogy, the total number of firms in our nine genealogies was 998. The firms included in each genealogy were divided into two major groups: endogenous and exogenous. A firm is exogenously affiliated with a particular genealogy if it originated in a different one and then became a part of a new genealogy by incorporation. A firm has an endogenous affiliation with a genealogy if it is related to it by "birth" or by "legal adoption." According to this principle, we identified seven types of membership in genealogies of firms (see also Chapter 2). These types are (1) founding parents' firms; (2) de-novo firms founded by employees who left their organizations to pursue their entrepreneurial ambitions; (3) firms founded by member firms founded by existing endogenous members of a genealogy; (4) mergers and acquisitions (M&As)—those that were either merged into or were acquired by a member of a genealogy; (5) mergers—firms that were established following a merger of two or more firms; (6) spinoffs—those that used to be a division of an incumbent firm or of one of its offspring and became new independent entities; and (7)

Exhibit 1

Ventures' frequency: Genealogy by type of affiliation

Type of affiliation	Telrad	Tadiran	Elisra	Orbit	MIL	ECI	Fibronics	Comverse	RAD	Total
					Genealogy					
Founded by member	3	4	1	0	3	4	0	2	34	51
Spinoff	2	11	2	2	5	7	1	8	5	43
M&A	4	6	0	1	0	6	5	8	3	33
Merger	2	0	0	0	0	1	0	2	2	7
De-novo	15	85	23	4	22	69	86	67	110	481
Founding parent	1	1	1	1	1	1	1	2	2	11
Exogenous	22	28	27	4	15	68	42	69	97	372
Total	49	135	54	12	46	156	135	158	253	998

exogenous firms—co-founder, co-acquirer, or co-merger, whose origin is from another genealogy. The distribution of firms according to the type of affiliation in each genealogy is presented in Exhibit 1.

In the following sections, we describe the evolutionary path of each of the nine genealogies. Since de-novo firms best reflect the entrepreneurial spirit of a genealogy or, in other words, its potency, and because they are the majority of the genealogies' members, our analyses focused mainly on them. A figure and a table accompany each description. The figure is a pictorial description (map) of each geneaology's evolutionary path; the table provides information on the genealogy's potency by presenting the number of de-novos that were founded in it across generations and years. The maps comprise two main objects: vertices (nodes) and edges. The vertices denote the firms in the genealogy, whereas the edges reflect the links between them. Most of the vertices are associated with two kinds of edges: inbound and outbound. The inbound edges connect a firm with its acquirers or founders (the higher the number of inbound edges, the higher the number of acquiring organization or founders), whereas the outbound edges connect the firm with its de-novos, acquired or merged firms (the higher the number of outbound edges, the higher the number of the firm's de-novos, spinoffs, and M&As). Note that members of a genealogy that have outbound edges are exogenous members only—they did not have any kind of association with other members before co-founding or co-acquiring firms in the genealogy. In addition, there was some missing data on the former employment of some entrepreneurs who came out of a genealogy to co-found a firm (i.e., exogenous). In such cases, we marked the name of the firm as "company."

The Genealogy Maps

The following sections discuss the maps of the genealogies in our study.

Telrad Networks (Telrad)

As shown in Table 4.1 and Figure 4.1, Telrad, founded in 1951, is historically the second communication company (after Orbit) in Israel's ITC sector. Telrad's genealogy consists of only 49 companies along five generations, including the exogenous members. The entrepreneurial activity of Telrad, the founding company, was relatively dull and did not begin until the 1990s—more than 40 years after its founding. In fact, except for founding a single company at the beginning of the 1980s (PV-Etc), members of this genealogy did not exhibit significant entrepreneurial activity until Be Connected was founded in the 1980s (see Figure 4.1). Toward the end of the 1990s, Telrad acquired and founded a few firms, such as Media Gate NV and Telrad Connegy, but these did not contribute to the genealogy's future expansion. Allegedly, the genealogical branch of Be Connected has been extremely fruitful. However, one may see significant traces of founding parents from other genealogies in this branch—RAD and ECI in particular. An entrepreneur from Radwiz Systems was involved in founding Be Connected, and others from RAD and ECI were involved in founding Broadlight. The structural difference between this branch and other branches that originated from the parent firm, Telrad, is quite salient. Whereas the Be Connected branch sprawls over three generations and consists of six companies (excluding the exogenous ones), all the other branches have one to three generations and two ventures at most. Interestingly, the branch of Be Connected, comprising of de-novos as well as acquisitions (ComGates, Telco Systems, and Analog Optics), reflects an interesting combination of the entrepreneurial tendencies of both—Telrad and RAD.

Table 4.1

Telrad's genealogy: Distribution of de-novos as a function of generation and founding year

Generation	Founding year					Total
	1981–1985	*1986–1990*	*1991–1995*	*1996–2000*	*2001–2005*	
2	1	0	0	3	2	6
3	0	0	0	1	5	6
4	0	0	1	0	2	3
Total	1	0	1	4	9	15

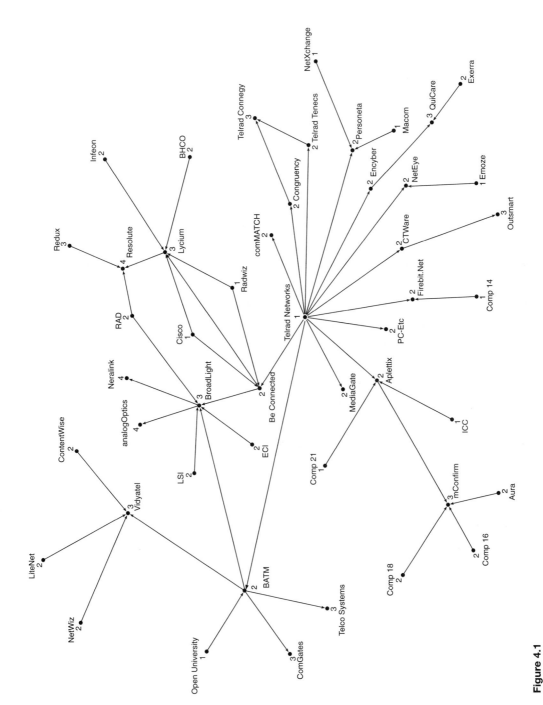

Figure 4.1

Telrad's genealogy: Founded firms by generation

In sum, the three or four decades of its evolution as part of Koor provided Telrad with a stable institutional environment and a secure market. Furthermore, Telrad hardly invested in R&D beyond the direct needs of its institutional clients and faced a competitive market only during the 1980s, when the Israeli economy underwent a process of liberalization and privatization. Note that, although Telrad went through continuous crises in the 1990s and many engineers left the company, very few among them directed their energy and knowledge toward entrepreneurial activities.

Tadiran

The distribution of firms within the Tadiran genealogy according to affiliation type is presented in Exhibit 1. Table 4.2 displays the frequency of de-novos as a function of founding year and generation. The interrelations structure of the whole genealogy is presented in Figure 4.2.

The prominent growth of Tadiran during the 1970s and early 1980s (see Chapter 3) was not reflected in the growth of its genealogy. Before 1988, the firm did not establish new ventures and acquired only three firms, Mavletan, Simtech, and Telco. Telco was slated to be given by Koor to Telrad, but accidentally found its way to Tadiran and, ultimately, facilitated Tadiran's entrance into the communication sector. Note that only one start-up (de-novo) was founded by a former Tadiran employee before 1990. The genealogy expanded mainly through new divisions (that were later spun off and sold) or by M&As for knowledge acquisition and market penetration (such as Media Gate and Elisra). Furthermore, the majority of the spinoffs were outside Tadiran's core business, and during the early 1990s, when Tadiran experienced financial and

Table 4.2

Tadiran's genealogy: Distribution of de-novos as a function of generation and founding year

Generation	Founding year						Total
	1976–1980	1981–1985	1986–1990	1991–1995	1996–2000	2001–2005	
2	1	0	0	5	9	2	17
3	0	0	2	5	14	8	29
4	0	0	2	1	10	7	19
5	0	0	0	0	2	8	10
6	0	0	0	0	1	3	4
7	0	0	0	0	1	4	5
8	0	0	0	0	0	1	1
Total	1	0	3	11	37	33	85

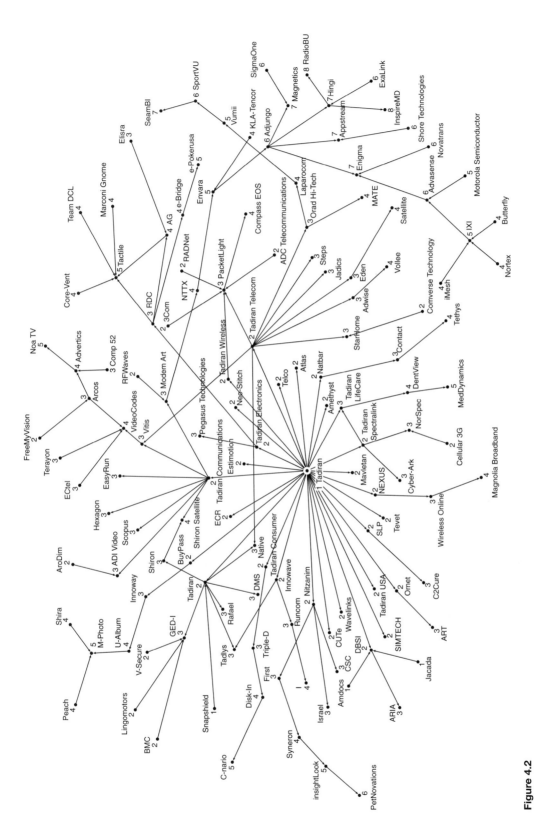

Figure 4.2

Tadiran's genealogy: Founded firms by generation

business crises, those spinoffs were first sold as part of restructuring and cost cutting. In fact, the basic skeleton of the Tadiran genealogy comprises the founding parent and its spinoffs that had been established earlier as divisions or initiated in preparation for being sold to external acquirers.

From 1993 to 1999, four major spinoffs were established: Tadiran Communications, Tadiran Telecom, Tadiran Telecommunications, and Tadiran Wireless Communication Industries. These companies, along with other parts of Tadiran, were sold. Tadiran Telecom, which manufactures business telecommunications equipment, is now owned by Africa Israel Investments, Ltd. Tadiran Batteries, one of the world's largest suppliers of lithium batteries, was sold in 2000 to Alcatel, which was later (2004) acquired by Saft Groupe (France). Tadiran Air Conditioners (Tadiran Appliances) is now owned by the Carrier Corporation, the world's largest manufacturer and distributor of heating, ventilating, and air-conditioning systems. In 1988, Tadiran Telecommunications, a manufacturer of networking infrastructure solutions for carrier and service providers, was merged into ECI Telecom, Ltd. Tadiran Electronic Systems, a manufacturer of military electronic equipment, and Tadiran Spectralink, a leading supplier of advanced wireless communications products for manned and unmanned aircraft, are both now part of the Elisra Group. Tadiran Communications, one of the world's largest suppliers of Military HF and VHF tactical radios and communication systems, was acquired in 2008 by Elbit Systems, which brought all three of these companies under one umbrella (the Elisra Group is a subsidiary of Elbit Systems). Finally, in 2007, Aerotel Medical Systems acquired Tadiran LifeCare, a division of Tadiran Spectralink established to design and develop innovative wireless monitoring solutions for healthcare applications.

The first two generations of Tadiran lasted about 20 years, and the pace of generational exchange and of founding new ventures accelerated only in the mid-1990s, several years after the beginning of the firm's financial crisis. Former Tadiran employees established only four new ventures before the Internet bubble burst (2000–2001). By the end of 1995, former employees had founded only ten start-ups, and established only 38 start-ups during 1996–2000. Thirty-three start-ups were added to the list of Tadiran's de-novos in the next five years. This number is below the surge of new firms among all the other genealogies in the post-bubble period (2001–2006). Interestingly, it seems that the actual entrepreneurial potency of Tadiran's genealogy does not reflect the *potential* potency of a firm with 12,000 employees (during the end of the 1990s) or the broad technological knowledge and expertise that the company had accumulated since its formation.

The relatively high potency of the Tadiran genealogy during generations three through six can be attributed to the fact that the companies in these generations were established by founders who had not been employed by Tadiran before initiating their new ventures. Thus, these entrepreneurs had not been directly influenced by the strategy and values of Koor (Tadiran's parent company). Rather (mainly in generations three and four; see Table 4.2), they had spent several years in other start-ups and had absorbed the appropriate values, entrepreneurial spirit, and knowledge for establishing successful new ventures.

In sum, Tadiran did not portray strong entrepreneurial tendencies and did not inspire its employees to leave the company to exploit their valuable knowledge to create new companies. Tadiran's ex-employees who moved to other start-ups and absorbed real entrepreneurial values, skills, and knowledge have established new ventures and have even brought them to successful exits.

Elisra

Exhibit 1, Table 4.3, and Figure 4.3 demonstrate that Elisra is a relatively small genealogy that resembles the genealogical structure of Telrad. From its beginning until 2005, Elisra neither founded nor acquired any new company. In fact, only one branch of its genealogy looks very potent—Radcom. The majority of the de-novos in Elisra's genealogy belong to this branch. As with Telrad's genealogy, this branch belongs partially to the genealogy of RAD. The structure and potency of the Radcom branch are very different from those of Elisra's other genealogical branches. Whereas the Radcom branch evolved to five generations and about 15 start-ups, the others reached only the second or third generation and entailed just one or two ventures.

Interestingly, Tadiran, which was one of Elisra's shareholders in the 1980s, sold two of its spinoffs, Tadiran Spectralink and Tadiran Electronic Systems, to Elisra in 2005.

Table 4.3

Elisra's genealogy: Distribution of de-novos as a function of generation and founding year

Generation	Founding year			Total
	1991–1995	1996–2000	2001–2005	
2	2	2	1	5
3	2	1	5	8
4	1	1	3	5
5	0	0	1	1
6	0	1	3	4
Total	5	5	13	23

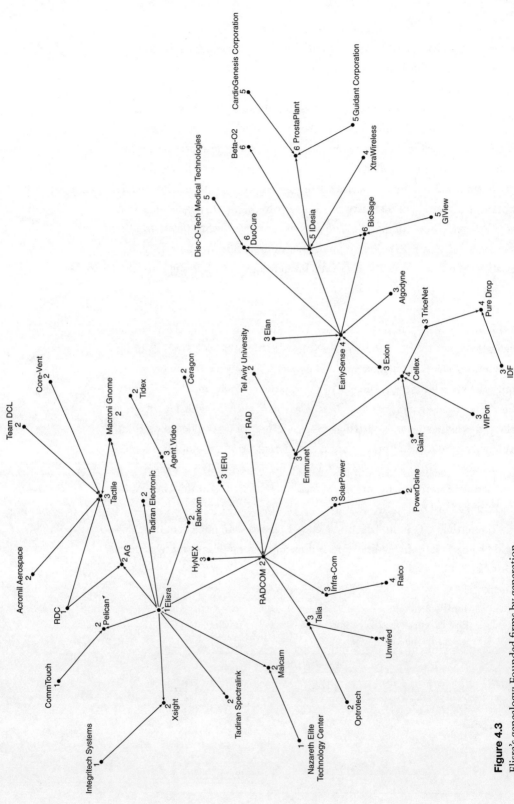

Figure 4.3

Elisra's genealogy: Founded firms by generation

Table 4.4

Orbit's genealogy: Distribution of de-novos as a function of generation and founding year

Generation	Founding year			Total
	1991–1995	1996–2000	2001–2005	
2	1	0	0	1
3	0	0	1	1
4	0	0	1	1
Total	1	0	2	3

Orbit Alchut Technologies (Orbit)

Orbit is the smallest of the nine genealogies explored in this study (see Exhibit 1, Table 4.4, and Figure 4.4). Its total reliance on the defense market differentiates it from the other genealogies. Orbit's specialization in military communication projects has provided the company with a stable market but, at the same time, has excluded it from the growing civilian ITC market. Although Orbit, as a private and later a public company, grew substantially over the years and acquired and spun off few firms, only two were founded by its ex-employees. An entrepreneur from Orbit founded Sagitta, and one entrepreneur from Sagitta left it and founded Sirica. Both ventures were established between 2000 and 2005 (Figure 4.4).

As noted in Chapter 3, the Orbit genealogy was expanded during 1985–2005 by a number of acquisitions and spinoffs (Orbit ACS and Orbit Communications). Few entrepreneurial activities were demonstrated by these genealogy members.

Motorola Israel (MIL)

MIL, a subsidiary of Motorola, Inc., has substantial operations in Israel, including sales, production, and R&D. In drafting its genealogy, we traced the founders who were affiliated with Motorola's various subsidiaries. As shown in Exhibit 1, Table 4.5, and Figure 4.5, individuals who left MIL founded a few de-novo firms, the first of these only about 20 years after Motorola had started its operations in Israel. In fact, MIL, which values its engineering manpower, does its best to channel its entrepreneurial energies toward intra-entrepreneurship—that is, pursuing its innovations within the company. Furthermore, it decided in 1999 to expand its activities to investments in Israeli start-ups. Motorola Venture Israel, Motorola's investment arm, searches for new venture opportunities—mainly in the fields of home networks, communications

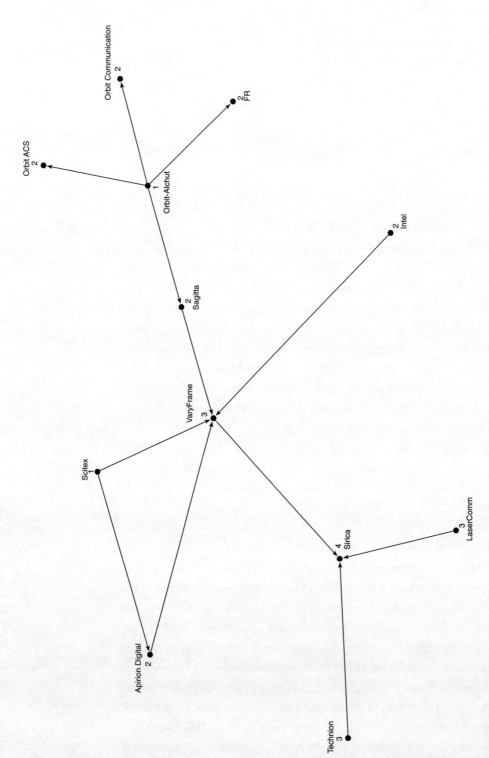

Figure 4.4

Orbit's genealogy: Founded firms by generation

Table 4.5

MIL's genealogy: Distribution of de-novos as a function of generation and founding year

Generation	Founding year					Total
	1981–1985	1986–1990	1991–1995	1996–2000	2001–2005	
2	1	1	1	3	2	8
3	0	1	1	3	4	9
4	0	0	0	1	2	4
5	0	0	0	0	1	1
Total	1	2	2	7	9	22

networks, and mobile solutions—that display technological and marketing synergy with MIL, which invests in these start-ups from product development to marketing and sales. Each year, three start-ups are chosen, with an average investment of three to five years' duration.

MIL's policy, though it contributes generally to the growth of the Israeli communication sector, inhibits the development of the MIL genealogy. Individuals having entrepreneurial potential or experience direct their activities inside MIL and not toward the general market.

ECI Telecom (ECI)

ECI was founded when the Israeli economy was still highly controlled by the government. A business group that viewed ECI as an essential product company owned it. However, over time and, particularly under the leadership of Mair Laiser during the 1980s, the company transformed itself into an R&D-oriented communications firm. Subject to the pressure of a competitive environment, ECI adopted practices that encourage innovation and entrepreneurship comparable to that of the thriving ITC community that had prospered since the late 1980s. The genealogy of ECI (see Exhibit 1, Table 4.6, and Figure 4.6) does not look like the genealogies founded during the cooperative economy period (see Chapter 3). Although its skeleton comprises relatively many M&As and spinoffs, it has also spun out more than 70 de-novos.

We identified two strategic turning points that marked ECI's shift toward becoming an innovative ITC firm. The first was the decision to change its focus from the defense to the civilian market through the development of "Telephone Line Doublers"; the second was the appointment of Mair Laiser as CEO. Orienting itself toward the competitive and innovative ITC market, ECI developed

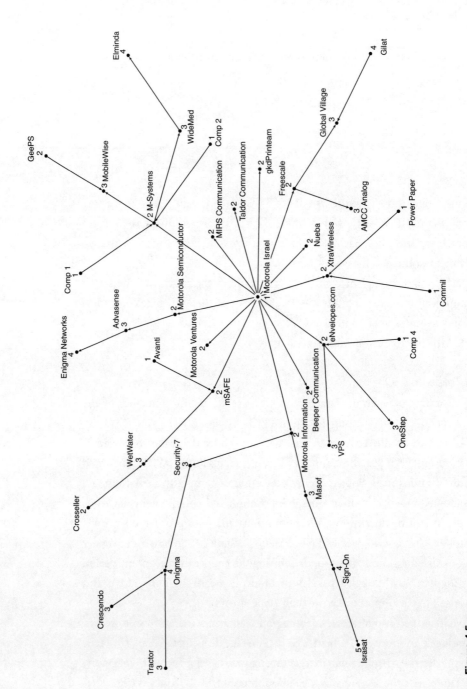

Figure 4.5

MIL's genealogy: Founded firms by generation

Table 4.6

ECI's genealogy: Distribution of de-novos as a function of generation and founding year

| Generation | Founding year | | | | Total |
	1986–1990	1991–1995	1996–2000	2001–2005	
1	0	1	0	0	1
2	2	1	12	8	23
3	0	1	11	14	26
4	0	0	2	6	8
5	0	1	1	7	9
6	0	1	0	0	1
7	0	0	1	0	1
Total	2	5	28	35	69

a business strategy that emphasized growth through strategic partnership both globally and locally. For example, ECI's strategic partnership with Deutsche Telecom led to establishing subsidiaries in West Germany and Panama and to the creation of new divisions/spinoffs (Innowave, Inovia, Enavis, Lightscape, and NGTS) as well as to the merging of Tadiran into ECI. The new organizational culture affected ECI's employees, and, since the 1980s, its ex-employees have been founding new firms. As Table 4.6 shows, 23 entrepreneurs left the company and established new start-ups. Furthermore, the first de-novos in the ECI genealogy were founded before the beginning of the Internet bubble period, which provided ample opportunities in Israel for initiating new ventures.

Finally, as with Telrad and Elisra, one may see many traces of the RAD genealogy in the ECI genealogy. Radnet was originated in Lightscape, and Broadlight was originated in RAD. Stage One was originated in Radwiz, and an ex-employee of RND and Axera co-founded Radlan and Flexlight. At least the first two start-ups created the most potent branches of ECI genealogy. In a way, the number of joint ventures between RAD and ex-employees of ECI also reflects the entrepreneurial spirit of ECI and the closeness of its culture to that of RAD.

Fibronics

The data presented in Exhibit 1, Table 4.7, and Figure 4.7 reveal a unique genealogy: zero ventures initiated by the founding parent but 85 de-novos. Entrepreneurs who left their organizations to establish their own start-ups founded

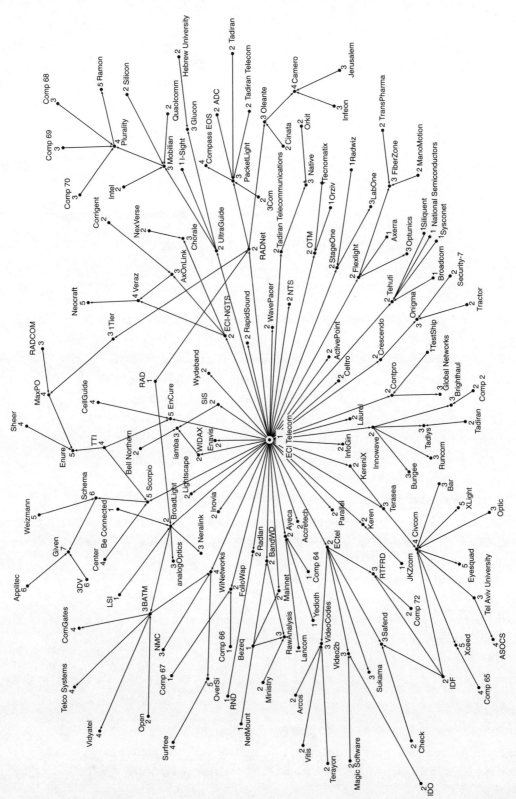

Figure 4.6

ECI's genealogy: Founded firms by generation

Table 4.7

Fibronics' genealogy: Distribution of de-novos as a function of generation and founding year

| Generation | Founding year | | | | | | Total |
	1976–1980	1981–1985	1986–1990	1991–1995	1996–2000	2001–2005	
2	1	1	3	8	3	6	22
3	0	0	1	5	6	4	16
4	0	0	0	0	11	9	20
5	0	0	0	0	5	11	16
6	0	0	0	0	0	6	6
7	0	0	0	0	0	4	4
8	0	0	0	0	0	2	2
Total	1	1	4	13	25	42	86

almost all the member firms of the Fibronics genealogy. In contrast to RAD and Comverse, Fibronics did not have an expansion strategy. It was established by Elron Electronic Industries as one of many new ventures within various technological domains. Fibronics' original idea was to develop connection parts for local communications networks based on fiber optics. After three years of failed attempts to generate potentially profitable ideas and on the verge of shutting down the new venture, a new development team led by a creative entrepreneur revitalized Fibronics and turned it into a success. That new CEO, Moti Gura, set an example not only with his resilience and innovative ideas; he founded a new firm, Adacom, when he was not selected as CEO of Fibronics International. Gura was able to attract many talented individuals to Fibronics, some of whom followed him to Adacom while others founded new firms. Adacom turned out to be one of the most potent branches of the Fibronics genealogy.

Beyond its creative environment and its intense fight to survive after a severe leadership crisis and environmental pressures, Fibronics became an excellent training ground for a new generation of entrepreneurs: 21 new ventures were founded by former Fibronics employees, and 85 in the whole genealogy between 1977and 2005. Finally, it should be noted that only one spinoff and five M&As were created. However, as opposed to other genealogies such as Tadiran, Telrad, and Comverse, these acquisitions were not initiated by the founding parent but by its offspring in later generations (four, five, and six). Thus, they do not reflect the genealogy's unique entrepreneurial character.

Comverse Technology (Comverse)

Comverse's genealogy has two founding parents—Efrat Future Technologies and Comverse Technology—that were founded almost at the same time. Efrat

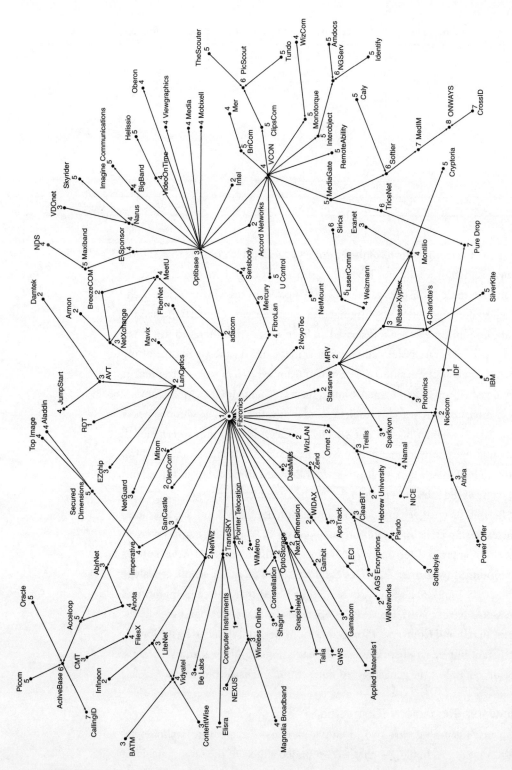

Figure 4.7

Fibronics' genealogy: Founded firms by generation

was registered first in Israel, and Comverse was registered later in the United States. This is why Efrat is listed in the genealogy map (Figure 4.8) as the first generation and Comverse as the second. The genealogy map displays the basic structure of Comverse: the two founding parents, Efrat Future Technologies and Comverse Technology, and four spinoffs: Comverse Network Systems, Verint Systems, Startel, and Starhome. Two branches look significantly more potent than the rest: Axis Mobile and Exalink, both of which originated from Comverse Technology and Comverse Networks.

Members of the Comverse genealogy founded only 67 new ventures. The relatively small number of de-novos is probably related to the company's strategy. Comverse evolved as a niche corporation. In the 1990s, nearly three-quarters of its revenues came from selling mobile mailboxes. Furthermore, its capacity to generate new activities was relatively limited. This led to the adoption of a business strategy based on aggressively pursuing acquisitions in order to capture significant value-added technologies that would expand and diversify Comverse's technologies, products, and services. Based on this rationale, Comverse completed several acquisitions, such as Boston Technology, Exalink, Startel, Ulticom, Alph Tech, StarHome, and Loronix Information Systems. Interestingly, the acquired firms established no spinoffs. As shown in Exhibit 1

Table 4.8

Comverse's genealogy: Distribution of de-novos as a function of generation and founding year

Generation	Founding year				Total
	1986–1990	1991–1995	1996–2000	2001–2005	
3	0	1	2	1	4
4	1	3	6	6	16
5	0	0	3	7	10
6	0	3	2	7	8
7	0	2	0	2	4
8	0	1	4	0	5
9	0	1	0	3	4
10	0	0	2	0	2
11	0	0	1	0	1
12	0	0	2	0	2
13	0	0	1	0	1
14	0	0	1	3	4
15	0	0	0	4	4
16	0	0	0	1	1
Total	1	11	24	30	66

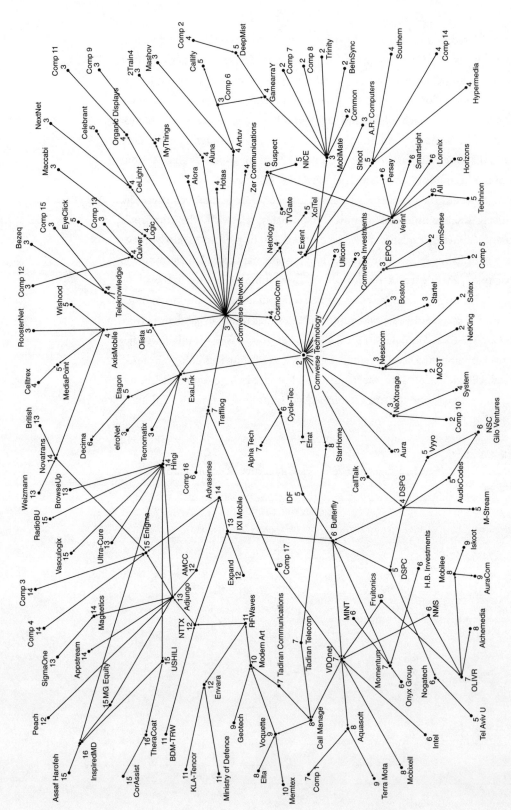

Figure 4.8

Comverse's genealogy: Founded firms by generation

and Figure 4.8, eight firms joined the genealogy as acquisitions of the founding parent company, Comverse (such as Boston Technology, Exalink, Startel, and Ulticom), and others (such as Alpha Tech, Star Home, Smartsight, and Loronix Information Systems) joined in later generations. It should be noted that the number of ventures affiliated with Comverse through acquisition was relatively larger than in other genealogies. Furthermore, Comverse and either its acquired firms or spinoffs carried out these acquisitions. Comverse's experience in acquiring firms and its knowledge of such strategy could hardly have served as an impetus for its employees or other members of the genealogy to establish new start-ups. Furthermore, Kobi Alexander, Comverse CEO, did not set an example of the enthusiastic entrepreneur but rather became a sophisticated business owner and financial wizard. Interestingly, one of Comverse's spinoffs, CallTalk, created an exceptionally potent genealogical branch. CallTalk was acquired in 1984 by David Gilo, who changed its name to DSP Group (DSPG). A serial entrepreneur, Gideon Barak, who worked at DSPG and founded DSPC with David Gilo, was actually the source for 27 de-novos of the Comverse genealogy. This branch of Comverse doesn't reflect the general growth strategy of this genealogy.

RAD Data Communications (RAD)

Like Comverse, RAD is a genealogy that has two related founding parents (run by two brothers): RAD Data Communications (RAD) and Bynet. Although Bynet, as noted in Chapter 3, was founded first, as an importing and distributing computer networking equipment company, in 1977, and RAD was founded a few years later as an ITC company, the entrepreneurial and business activities of the two can hardly be separated. The evolution of RAD's genealogy is closely intertwined with the business model developed by its founders, which has had an enduring impact on the genealogy as a whole. Unlike the founders of the others genealogies, RAD's founders, Zohar and Yehuda Zisapel, continued to be personally involved in the creation of new firms in the second and third and even later generations, and they are still involved today. The distribution of firms within the RAD genealogy according to affiliation type is presented in Exhibit 1. Table 4.9 displays the frequency of de-novos as a function of founding year and generation. The interrelations structure of the whole genealogy is presented in Figure 4.9.

The RAD genealogy stands out for its tremendous potency. It differs from Comverse, in that the latter expanded mainly through spinoffs or M&As while RAD expanded by founding new firms, consistently exhibiting entrepreneurial

Table 4.9

RAD's genealogy: Distribution of de-novos as a function of generation and founding year

| | Founding year | | | | | |
Generation	1981–1985	1986–1990	1991–1995	1996–2000	2001–2005	Total
2	0	0	0	1	1	2
3	0	0	2	5	3	10
4	1	0	3	10	8	22
5	0	0	0	16	11	27
6	0	0	1	7	11	19
7	0	1	1	3	13	18
8	0	0	0	0	10	10
9	0	0	0	0	2	2
Total	1	1	7	42	59	110

strategy. As noted in the previous chapter, the Zisapel brothers established 26 new ventures (excluding Bynet and its spinouts). Their entrepreneurial spirit triggered 10 of their employees and probably 100 additional entrepreneurs from across the genealogy to establish their own start-ups.

Effi Wachtel, the current president of RAD, says,

> When they leave us, we rarely have hard feelings toward them. And if these guys fail (and it happens, as we all know), we take them back to RAD. Few of them would try leaving us again in the future. (Interview, 2005)

RAD itself made just one acquisition (Packetlight in 2004). Only once did the two brothers divide a company (RND) into three spinoffs (Radware, Radwiz, and Radlan). According to Wachtel,

> RND [a company in the RAD genealogy] faced tremendous difficulties. We really didn't know how to cure the company and I was about to suggest closing it down. Yehuda Zisapel suggested dividing the company into three. To be honest, I did not understand how this move would change the situation. And it was like a miracle it worked! We now have three successful companies. I wish I had put some money in these companies. (Interview, 2005)

This example reflects a deep understanding of the ITC field and how the accumulation of the founding experience of the Zisapel brothers contributed to their success, not to mention to the acceleration and potency of the entire genealogy. It seems that their unique business philosophy was imprinted upon their descendants. Their method has been a proven success: establish a new

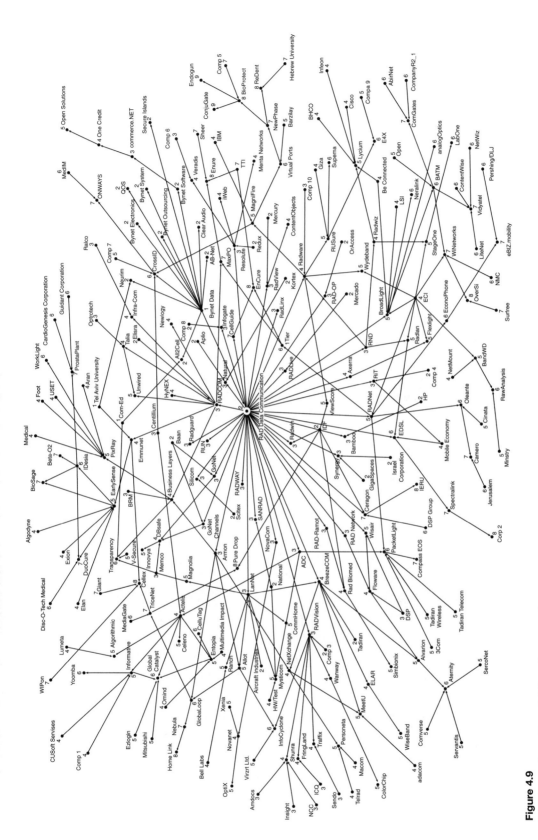

Figure 4.9

RAD's genealogy: Founded firms by generation

company whenever a promising market or technological opportunity is identified; match the innovative idea with a prospective founder; and provide the new firm with major resources and strategic guidance. RAD's expansion strategy of continuously founding firms, as opposed to conducting mergers, acquisitions, or strategic spinoffs, created an extremely potent genealogy. It seems that RAD's relatively large second generation played a mediating role for the knowledge and entrepreneurial inclinations of the Zisapel brothers toward the entire genealogy.

A Comparative Analysis of the Nine Genealogies: Entrepreneurial Inclination and Genealogical Potency

The genealogies that make up the Israeli ITC sector emerged from diverse founding conditions. These conditions, which can be characterized according to the economic policy that prevailed during founding, influence each genealogy's trajectory and potency. Generally, a competitive environment creates opportunities for entrepreneurs, and, accordingly, the genealogies founded between 1977 and 2005 grew quickly. Those founded during the cooperative economy period (1948–1976) grew rather slowly and by and large were less potent. Of all the genealogies founded in either period, however, we treat ECI as the exception. Although it was founded in the 1960s, during the cooperative period, ECI went through a major organizational and cultural change a decade later. We single it out as a genealogy whose founding spans the two periods. In fact, including ECI in either of these groups—pre- or post-1977—would not have changed the general pattern of the findings. Table 4.10 displays the distribution of firms according to type of affiliation and genealogy group—(1) the institutional-cooperative economy: Telrad, Tadiran, Elisra, Orbit, and MIL; (2) the competitive economy: Fibronics, Comverse, and RAD; and (3) the intermediate genealogy: ECI.

We measured the entrepreneurial potency of each of the nine genealogies using three variables: volume, growth pace, and resilience. The first variable, volume, represents genealogy size by the number of spawned start-ups founded by independent entrepreneurs who left their incumbent organizations (i.e., de-novos). This variable does not include spinoffs (new companies founded by incumbent firms) or firms in which the founding firms had business interests. As de-novo firms do not necessarily have any business relations with the founding firm or their own incumbents, they reflect the indirect impact of the founding parents on genealogical potency across generations.

Table 4.10

Ventures' frequency: Genealogy group by type of affiliation

| Type of affiliation | Genealogy group | | | |
	Institutional-cooperative	ECI	Competitive	Total
Founded by member	11	4	36	51
	1.10%	0.40%	3.60%	5.11%
Spinoff	22	7	14	43
	2.20%	0.70%	1.40%	4.30%
M&A	11	6	16	33
	1.10%	0.60%	1.60%	3.30%
Merger	2	1	4	7
	0.20%	0.10%	0.40%	0.70%
De-novo	149	69	263	481
	14.92%	6.91%	26.35%	48.10%
Founding parent	5	1	5	11
	0.60%	0.10%	0.50%	1.20%
Exogenous	96	68	208	372
	9.51%	6.61%	20.84%	37.27%
Total	296	156	546	998
	29.66%	15.63%	54.70%	100.00%

The second variable is the genealogies' growth pace. Genealogical potency reflects not only the number of its members but also the speed of genealogical evolution in terms of the number of new generations and the number of spawned start-ups in each generation or in each year. It is measured by (1) the number of years per generation (life duration/number of generations) and (2) the pace of growth in terms of the number of new independent ventures (de-novos) founded per year and per generation. The third variable is the genealogy's resilience, which is its tendency to found new ventures during times of environmental shock.

Volume

Table 4.11 shows that the nine genealogies differ in all three volume measures. The data show that RAD, Fibronics, and Comverse, which began as small start-ups in the early 1980s and encountered a competitive economy, spawned more de-novos per year and per generation than all the other genealogies—Telrad, Tadiran, Elisra, Orbit, MIL, and ECI—which were founded in the 1950s–1960s during the institutional-cooperative period. The three genealogies associated with the competitive period were more potent not only in the number of

Table 4.11

Potency measures of the nine genealogies: Volume and pace of growth

					Genealogy				
Potency measure	*Telrad*	*Tadiran*	*Elisra*	*Orbit*	*MIL*	*ECI*	*Fibronics*	*Comverse*	*RAD*
Volume									
Number of de-novos	15	85	23	4	22	69	86	67	110
Pace of growth									
Number of generations	4	8	6	4	5	7	8	16	9
Number of years	55	44	39	56	42	45	28	23	24
Number of years per generation	55/4 = 13.75	44/8 = 5.50	39/6 = 6.50	56/4 = 14.00	42/5 = 8.40	45/7 = 6.42	28/8 = 3.50	23/16 = 1.43	24/9 = 2.66
Number of de-novos per year	15/55 = 0.27	85/44 = 1.93	23/39 = 0.59	4/56 = 0.07	22/42 = 0.52	69/45 = 1.53	86/28 = 3.07	67/23 = 2.91	110/24 = 4.58
Number of de-novos per generation	15/4 = 3.75	85/8 = 10.62	23/6 = 3.83	4/4 = 1.00	22/5 = 4.40	69/7 = 9.85	86/8 = 10.75	67/16 = 4.19	110/9 = 12.22

spawned de-novos but also in their much higher pace of growth. As expected, the genealogies of the three companies—Fibronics, Comverse, and RAD—led the pack in the intensity of founding pace, with the shortest average number of years per generation and the highest number of de-novos per year and per generation.

Pace of Growth

Table 4.12 shows the effect of the different periods (cooperative and competitive) on genealogical potency. The data single out the competitive-economy genealogies over the other genealogies in terms of the first two potency measures—volume and pace of growth. More specifically, the genealogies of the competitive economy spawned more de-novos than did those of the cooperative economy (87.66 versus 29.80). Furthermore, they spawned these ventures at a faster pace than the other group: 3.50 versus 0.63 per year, or 7.96 versus 5.51 de-novos per generation. Whereas the mean life cycle of a genealogy's generation from the institutional-cooperative-economy category was 8.42 years, the mean life cycle of a generation in the competitive-economy category was only 2.14 years.

Tables 4.13 and 4.14 are similar to Tables 4.11 and 4.12, except for one difference: the values were computed without all the de-novos that are affiliated with more than a single genealogy. The analysis of this dataset shows that when all such de-novos are excluded from the analysis, the difference in potency between the genealogies of the cooperative period and those of the competitive period is even greater.

Table 4.12
Potency measures of the three genealogy groups

	Genealogy group		
Potency measure	Institutional-cooperative	ECI	Competitive
De-novos			
Mean volume	29.80	69.00	87.66
Pace of growth			
Mean generations	5.40	7.00	11.00
Mean years	47.20	45.00	25.00
Number of years per generation	8.42	6.42	2.14
Number of de-novos per year	0.63	1.53	3.50
Number of de-novos per generation	5.51	9.85	7.96

Table 4.13

Potency measures of the nine genealogies: Volume and pace of growth

Potency measure		Genealogy							
	Telrad	Tadiran	Elisra	Orbit	MIL	ECI	Fibronics	Comverse	RAD
Volume									
Number of de-novos	7	59	8	3	21	42	68	45	60
Pace of growth									
Number of generations	4	8	6	4	5	7	8	16	9
Number of years	55	44	39	56	42	45	28	23	24
Number of years per generation	55/4 = 13.75	44/8 = 5.50	39/6 = 6.50	56/4 = 14.00	42/5 = 8.40	45/7 = 6.42	28/8 = 3.50	23/16 = 1.43	24/9 = 2.66
Number of de-novos per year	7/55 = 0.12	59/44 = 1.34	8/39 = 0.20	3/56 = 0.05	21/42 = 0.50	42/45 = 0.93	68/28 = 2.42	45/23 = 1.95	60/24 = 2.50
Number of de-novos per generation	7/4 = 1.75	59/8 = 7.37	8/6 = 1.33	3/4 = 0.75	21/5 = 4.20	42/7 = 6.00	68/8 = 8.50	45/16 = 2.81	60/9 = 6.66

Note: De-novos with double affiliations are excluded.

Table 4.14

Potency measures of the three genealogy groups

| | Genealogy group | | |
	Institutional-cooperative	ECI	Competitive
Potency measure			
De-novos			
Mean	19.60	42.00	57.66
Pace of growth			
Mean generations	5.40	7.00	11.00
Mean years	47.20	45.00	25.00
Number of years per generation	8.74	6.42	2.27
Number of de-novos per year	0.41	0.93	2.30
Number of de-novos per generation	3.62	6.00	5.24

Note: De-novos with double affiliations are excluded.

The mean number of de-novos spawned in the competitive genealogies was 57.66, whereas the mean number spawned in the genealogies of the cooperative group was only 19.6. The former spawned these ventures at a faster rate than the latter group: 2.30 ventures per year in the competitive economy versus 0.41 in the cooperative economy. While the mean number of de-novos per generation founded in the competitive genealogies was 5.24, the mean number of de-novos per generation founded in the institutional-cooperative genealogies was 3.62. Whereas the mean life duration of a generation of a genealogy from the cooperative economy was 8.42 years, the mean life cycle of a generation in the competitive economy was much shorter—only 2.27 years.

Resilience

The third variable that differentiates the two groups (competitive and cooperative economies) relates to *genealogical resilience*. Tables 4.15, 4.16, 4.17, and 4.18 present the genealogies' potency in terms of the number of de-novos across the last 60 years—before the high-tech bubble era, during the bubble era, and after the burst of the bubble. The last period ranged from 2001 to 2005.

Tables 4.15 and 4.16 reveal quite clearly that the three genealogies of the competitive economy were more potent even in the bubble era. More important, the difference in potency trends of Fibronics, Comverse, and RAD, as compared with Telrad, Tadiran, Elisra, Orbit, and MIL, was also evident in the period after the high-tech bubble crisis (2000–2005). The growth of the five genealogies that were founded in the cooperative period did not proceed much during this time, whereas the genealogies founded during the competitive period continued to reproduce. Taking into account the size (number of

Table 4.15

Potency of the nine genealogies: Number of de-novos across years

Genealogy	Years					
	1932–1980	1981–1985	1986–1990	1991–1995	1996–2000	2001–2005
Telrad	0	1	0	1	4	9
Tadiran	1	0	3	11	37	33
Elisra	0	0	0	5	5	13
Orbit	0	0	0	1	0	2
MIL	0	1	2	2	7	9
ECI	0	0	2	5	28	35
Fibronics	1	1	4	13	25	42
Comverse	0	0	1	11	24	30
RAD	0	1	1	7	42	59

Table 4.16

Potency of the three genealogy groups: Number of de-novos across years

Genealogy group		Years					
		1932–1980	1981–1985	1986–1990	1991–1995	1996–2000	2001–2005
Institutional-cooperative	N	1	2	5	20	53	66
	Mean	0.2	0.4	1.00	4.0	10.6	13.2
ECI		0	0	2	5	28	35
Competitive	N	1	2	6	31	91	131
	Mean	0.33	0.66	2.00	10.33	30.33	42.66

Table 4.17

Potency of the nine genealogies: Number of de-novos across years

Genealogy	Years					
	1932–1980	1981–1985	1986–1990	1991–1995	1996–2000	2001–2005
Telrad	0	1	0	0	1	5
Tadiran	1	0	3	9	24	21
Elisra	0	0	0	4	1	3
Orbit	0	0	0	1	0	1
MIL	0	1	2	0	6	6
ECI	0	0	1	4	18	19
Fibronics	1	1	4	10	20	30
Comverse	0	0	1	8	15	19
RAD	0	1	1	2	26	27

Note: De-novos with double affiliations are excluded.

Table 4.18

Potency of the three genealogy groups: Number of de-novos across years

Genealogy group		Years					
		1932–1980	1981–1985	1986–1990	1991–1995	1996–2000	2001–2005
Institutional-cooperative	N	1	2	5	14	32	36
	Mean	0.20	0.40	1.00	2.80	6.40	7.20
ECI		0	0	2	4	19	18
Competitive	N	1	2	6	20	61	85
	Mean	0.33	0.66	2.00	6.66	20.33	28.33

Note: De-novos with double affiliations are excluded.

employees) of the six founding companies in 1990, the youngest three firms, RAD, Fibronics, and Comverse, appear to have been much more potent during the 2000–2005 period. Tables 4.17 and 4.18 display the same data but without the firms with double or even triple affiliations. The same effect is reflected in these tables: the strong resilience of the genealogies of the competitive period.

5 Founding and Genealogical Evolution

The Israeli high-tech industry, since it emerged during the 1960s, has succeeded because we discovered a successful recipe. The crucial ingredient is unconditional government support, and, in particular, the wisdom of a few, who invented the Chief Scientist's incentives scheme and the venture capital industry. Add to this the Israeli culture of entrepreneurship and innovation. The next ingredient stems from our smallness, the close network and our ability to tap it. So it doesn't matter who is in power or what regime you support; some things in Israel are at the heart of the consensus, and people in high-tech know how to mobilize the system and bond among themselves. We in the high-tech industry are living testimony to the idea that small is not only beautiful or well connected, but small also means strong affiliation with the country and its resources.

Nir, *founder of a successful communication technology*
start-up, June 2007

Studies of the Israeli information technology and communication (ITC) sector claim that the co-evolution of factors such as government policy, an innovative and entrepreneurial culture, and the growth of the venture capital industry explains the sector's astonishing growth. Like Silicon Valley, the Israeli ITC sector is based on the creation of a hub of institutions and services that facilitated the evolution of successful and innovative technologies and the start-up culture (Senor and Singer 2009). The Israeli ITC sector can be seen as an integrated "ecosystem" (e.g., Kenney and von Burg 2000), conceptualized as a bundle of institutions, policies, and practices that resulted in a distinct model of industrial growth (Avnimelech and Teubal 2004; Breznitz 2002, 2007; Carmel and de Fontenay 2004). These studies analyzed the sector from a cluster perspective, which is based on an entrepreneurial model that integrates the necessary conditions for a leading industrial technology sector and the creative innovation of state-of-the-art technologies.

The conceptual merit of the cluster approach is associated mainly with the institutional stimuli for founding start-ups. Given that more than 6,500 start-ups have been founded in Israel since the 1990s and the relatively small number of medium and large firms with more than 500 employees, the cluster approach supports the claim that the founding of start-ups is an Israeli "expertise." It reinforces the belief that Israel is a "start-up nation" (Senor and Singer 2009). Indeed, the cluster view is monolithic in the sense that it does not explain the diversity of business models and founding processes and, in particular, the historical roots of the industry prior to the emergence of the new telecommunications and Internet period in the early 1990s. Our genealogical approach is complementary to the cluster approach and attempts to understand the Israeli high-tech industry against the backdrop of its historical evolution. The ITC sector's growth during the 1990s and early 2000s can be explained by Israel's unique historical conditions and its social, economic, and public policies since independence. It is also due to the global surge in innovative communication technologies and infrastructure. The genealogical approach allows us to trace the evolution of the Israeli high-tech industry from its early founding. And by following the different genealogies, we reveal the different types of founding models and how they emerged, proliferated, and differentially shaped the ITC sector's growth trajectory.

Our main theme is that the structure and characteristics of the genealogies and ultimately their size are affected by the nature of their particular line of heredity and affinity. Initial conditions at the time of founding affect the ways in which parent organizations are shaped and evolve. This, in turn, affects their progenies and, indirectly, the evolution of the ITC sector as a whole. The founding parents transmit their accumulated knowledge (routines, norms, values, and initial assumptions) and entrepreneurial and managerial blueprints along heredity and affinity lines. Because genealogies are shaped by different initial conditions that evoke different entrepreneurial inclinations, they vary in their potency and size. In other words, the evolutionary paths of genealogies in a particular industry reflect the distinct entrepreneurial inclinations of their founding parents.

In this chapter, we formulate a conceptual framework to address the question that arises from our study: How and why are certain genealogies more potent than others? In doing so, we follow a theoretical framework, arguing that the historical sociopolitical and economic environments that shaped the initial conditions the parent firms met when they were founded, also affected the generational successions of their progenies.

This book develops a genealogical approach by analyzing data that trace the founding and affiliations of 731 firms in the Israeli ITC sector. The sector's growth has traditionally been attributed to the formation of highly effective clusters based on the co-evolution of industrial infrastructure and supporting institutions, including an entrepreneurial culture that stems from the defense establishment (see the Appendix). To understand the growth of the ITC sector from a genealogical perspective, we depart from the cluster approach, which focuses on the dynamics of industry emergence and growth, and look instead at the founding process of firms that constitute the ITC sector. Our goal in shifting the focus is to understand the emergence and evolutionary trajectory of industrial sectors. Our approach provides a complementary explanation to the extant literature on the dynamics of the Israeli high-tech industry.

This chapter is organized as follows. We start by providing a concise conceptual framework of genealogical dynamics and their major building blocks. The following sections discuss our major findings, probing their critical constructs: imprinting of environmental conditions on founding parents; inheritance and transmission; evolutionary trajectory and potency; and, finally, convergence. The last section provides a summary and some implications for studying the emergence of a new industrial sector.

General Principles of Genealogical Evolution

Genealogical evolution refers to the process of spawning new ventures along generational lines. One might say that start-up opportunities reside within the "DNA" of a genealogy—its entrepreneurial tendencies, knowledge, and routines. Genealogical evolution also encompasses the process through which progenies inherit certain characteristics from their parents—such as knowledge, values, organizational capabilities, and managerial practices—and how this inheritance process affects the genealogies' potency (Phillips 2002, 2005). Genealogical evolution implies that every firm is a repository of knowledge and entrepreneurial capabilities for all firms in its genealogy (e.g., Wiewel and Hunter 1985).

The process of genealogical evolution is highly linked to the environment and the initial conditions at founding—the "genesis events" that shape the character of the founding parent firms and, ultimately, the character of the genealogy. These environmental conditions include size of markets, technology, values, and particular economic or political crises (Agarwal et al. 2004; Baron, Burton, and Hannan 1999; Baron and Hannan 2005; Bhide 2000). The external environment at the time of founding is highly influential in shaping character-istics that are imprinted upon organizations, including policies, programs, and structure of the labor market (Stinchcombe 1965). The resulting characteris-tics, which are passed on through the heredity process described previously, affect how and why capabilities for founding new firms are persistent in certain genealogies and not in others.

We have argued that imprinting and inheritance through parent-progeny relations explain the evolutionary trajectory of the Israeli ITC sector. Because the subsequent growth of each genealogy is the result of those relations, un-derstanding the genealogical trajectory depends on recognizing organiza-tional characteristics that parents possess—such as values and managerial blueprints—and that their progenies employ in constructing their own firms. Note that the generational trajectory may blur the imprinting and inheritance of these characteristics (Burton and Beckman 2007; Beckman and Burton 2008) for several reasons: (1) Over time, firms encounter environmental and organizational changes that affect their acceptance of certain characteristics and their rejection of others; (2) organizational elements transmitted through parent-progeny relations may be "diluted" along generations; and (3) there is a tendency in later generations toward conversion or co-founding of new firms by members of two or more genealogies. Still, we show that the extent to which specific characteristics and values persist along generations is a strong indication of their ongoing effect on a genealogy's evolution, growth, and potency.

Environmental Imprints on Founding Parents

To test the imprinting argument, we identified two constitutive periods that might have shaped the entrepreneurial tendencies, the capabilities of the found-ing parents' organizations, and, later, the evolution of two groups of genealo-gies. The first period, before 1977, was marked by an ideology that elevated the collective above individual interests and harnessed the resources of both for the goal of nation building. This period was associated with high involve-ment of the government and other national institutions in the formative years of the state, as well as institutional intervention in economic and industrial activities. We call this the *institutional-cooperative period*. The second period was marked by political upheaval, a shift toward a neoliberal economy, and substantial growth of the private sector. We call this *the competitive period*. We then examined the characteristics of the genealogies that were founded during these two periods.

Our analysis of nine founding parent organizations revealed that firms that emerged during the two distinct periods developed different strategies regarding knowledge creation versus knowledge acquisition, as well as different choices of target markets—local and institutional versus competitive and international. RAD, Fibronics, and Comverse, which were founded during the competitive period, based their strategy on knowledge creation and an entrepreneurial orientation, whereas Tadiran, Telrad, Orbit, MIL, and Elisra, which were founded during the institutional-cooperative period, and most of them focused initially on knowledge acquisition. Founding parents of genealogies in the competitive group began as young start-ups led by founders who were oriented toward both business and R&D in order to survive and prosper in the competitive environment. The vision of founding parents of the institutional-cooperative group, however, was nation building, social responsibility, and survival; these firms operated in a centralized, institutionalized communication sector of the Israeli market until the late 1970s. Firms in the institutional-cooperative group were practically free from external competition and did not have to invest in R&D beyond the needs of their institutional clients. One genealogy, ECI, which was founded during the institutional-cooperative period but went through a major leadership and organizational change, exhibited characteristics typical of the two periods and was considered a hybrid.

Inheritance: Transmission of Knowledge, Values, and Blueprints

Zohar Zisapel, one of the two founders of RAD's genealogy, in a forum of managers and founders of the Israeli high-tech industry several years ago, humorously stated,

> Every year new talented young engineers join RAD. They work with us and after two or three years they realize that what my brother [Yehuda] and I can do, they can do better . . . and leave our company to create their own start-up. This is why our genealogy is so big.

What Zohar Zisapel meant in this statement is that he and his brother represented a hotbed of entrepreneurship. Those who are groomed by such an encounter develop the perception, understanding, and skills needed for founding new ventures. Over time, all of those who worked at RAD also came to represent hotbeds for subsequent generations of entrepreneurs. This is the central idea behind our genealogical framework: the founding parents' entrepreneurial capabilities, values, and practices were transmitted to progenies through generational lines of affiliation and helped determine a genealogy's growth and potency. It is quite hard, or even impossible, to exactly detect which values, capabilities, or blueprints are transmitted from founding parents to their progenies and from generation to generation. However, our historical analysis points to several indicators supporting several theoretical arguments.

I. Founding parents' direct influence on firms across generations varies. A parent firm can have a *direct* influence on its progenies only if it still exists, but even firms that operate for a short time can create powerful genealogies. Only the founding parents of RAD, Comverse, and Orbit could have exerted a direct influence on their genealogy from the founding day until the end of 2005 (see Table 3.1). Most of the successors of the founding parents in other genealogies did not have the opportunity to even know them. However, the continued existence of parent firms is not necessary for the potency of a genealogy. For example, RAD, Comverse, ECI, and Telrad, all of which still exist, differ on all potency measures. Tadiran's genealogy, the founding firm of which ceased to exist in its original form in the early 1990s, remained relatively potent through 2005. Fibronics, which existed for only 17 years, created one of the most potent genealogies, demonstrating that a parent firm that has a relatively short time to operate as a model for newer generations can still accomplish this. Once the parents' values, characteristics, and blueprints have been transferred, their actual existence may not be necessary for potency and growth. Yet the continued presence of active founders who create relationships with offspring, as in the case of RAD, is likely to increase potency.

II. Founding parents' influence dominates within, but not across, genealogies. One might argue that, since the founding parents of three potent genealogies, RAD, Fibronics, and Comverse, were influential figures in the Israeli high-tech industry, they could have set an example not only for their own genealogies but also for firms in others. The Google citation numbers of these founders— Uziah Galil (Fibronics, 34,000), Zohar Zisapel (RAD, 37,000), and Kobi Alexander (Comverse, 133,000)—demonstrate their potential influence. However, the fact that we found differences in characteristics and potency among the nine genealogies, especially between the two genealogy groups, indicates that the founding parents were more likely to exert influence on the behavior of their own genealogy.

III. Founding parents of potent genealogies exhibit different models of growth that are inherited by their progenies. The unique characteristics of each of the three most entrepreneurial genealogies (RAD, Comverse, and Fibronics) reflect the unique entrepreneurial characteristics of their founding parents, and these characteristics played an important role in shaping their genealogical structures. RAD, for example, was founded by two brothers, one of whom was a technological entrepreneur and the other a business-oriented entrepreneur. Both based their growth strategy on initiating "satellite" firms that covered diverse areas within the ITC sector. In addition to being the initiators of technological ideas, they were also serial entrepreneurs who founded 36 new ventures in 23 years—more than the founders of all the other genealogies combined.

In contrast to RAD, the founding parents of Comverse created a different entrepreneurial model for their genealogy. Three entrepreneurs, two technological experts, and one financial expert created Comverse, channeling their efforts into development and control of a particular technological niche: voicemail and surveillance. They invested in R&D, but also acquired a relatively large number of firms to gain competitive knowledge and reduce competition. Whereas RAD and Fibronics consistently employed an entrepreneurial strategy based on the creation of new start-ups, Comverse opted to defend its niche through mergers and acquisitions (M&As) of competitors in addition to developing new technologies. Comverse affiliates that were brought into the genealogy through M&As outnumbered the M&As in each of the other genealogies.

The third potent genealogy, Fibronics, which was founded during the competitive period as well, also mirrors the character of its legendary founding parent, Uziah Galil. Galil was not very active in the firm's daily management, and Moti Gura, its CEO, shaped its unique character. When he left Fibronics in 1984 to found Adacom, Gura persuaded a large group of talented engineers (almost 10 percent of Fibronics' employees at its peak) to follow him. We traced 23 companies that were founded by these former Fibronics employees between 1984 and the end of 2005. Fibronics did not initiate and did not acquire even a single firm during its 17 years of existence; neither did its followers in the next generation.

IV. Direct channels of inheritance vary. The founding parents of RAD, Fibronics, and Comverse created more channels that could be used for direct transmission of routines and blueprints to their progenies than the other genealogies did. For example, first-generation firms continued to spawn new ventures similarly to firms from younger generations in other genealogies, but only RAD, Fibronics, and Comverse spawned de-novos in each generation. These de-novos proved to be the channel through which routines and blueprints were disseminated more easily to progenies. One channel that allows a quicker transmission of blueprints is opened by a genealogy's serial entrepreneurs. Fifty-six entrepreneurs in the RAD genealogy, 37 in Comverse, and 30 in Fibronics were involved in founding more than one new venture. In contrast, only 11 serial founders operated in Telrad, 25 in Tadiran, 8 in Elisra, 11 in Motorola, 1 in Orbit, and 24 in ECI. The potential influence of the founding parents' values on their genealogies through this channel has been stronger in RAD, Fibronics, and Comverse than in the other genealogies.

Furthermore, RAD and Comverse engaged in cross-generational founding. That is, it founded new ventures with entrepreneurs from companies representing later generations. Such co-founding allows the founders from early generations to transfer values and blueprints directly to firms in much newer generations. We counted a total of 8 and 5 such cross-affinity relations in RAD and Comverse, respectively. .

Transmission via serial entrepreneurship or cross-affinity relations that led to higher potency may be considered tautological. On the one hand, the higher the potency, the denser the inter-entrepreneurial networks and the more channels that are opened for transfer of entrepreneurial blueprints and routines. On the other hand, more channels mean higher potential potency. In other words, it is not clear whether the transfer channels are the cause or the effect of potency. In evolutionary terms, it is possible that potency at one time affects the genealogy's structure, which in turn facilitates the transmission of capabilities at the next time. This argument is consistent with our implicit assumption that potency, which is the ability to spawn new firms, drives both the structural characteristics and the malleability of a genealogy. Once a certain potency rate is achieved, it affects the genealogy's structure and its reproductive model. Each genealogy exhibited a different composition of potency, which drove certain genealogical configurations. For example, Fibronics, Tadiran, and ECI witnessed growth in their potency following a decline in their business activities. New firms that were founded following this period of decline altered the basic structures, practices, and managerial blueprints of the founding parents and of those progenies that were founded before the crisis.

V. Mechanisms exist for transmitting values, practices, and routines across generations. The different genealogies are the carriers of respective routines, practices, and managerial blueprints. We detected different mechanisms, which enable the transfer of distinct organizational traits across generations. We begin by addressing the dominant processes and structures through which such transfers occur within genealogies, and provide anecdotal evidence for what was actually transferred.

A. First-generation parent-progeny transfer. The first transfer mechanism is the unmediated parent-progeny relations within a certain genealogy.

For example, the founder of one of the companies who was formerly employed at Lannet, an early RAD-initiated venture that merged with another RAD-originated start-up, says,

> Merging with them was highly facilitated by our [founders'] common background in working with Zohar [RAD founder]. We brought ourselves into the planning of the merger on [an] equal footing regarding what was needed to be done first. Together we analyzed our two respective markets and designed a strategy how to align our technologies and services with each other's market. It is easier said than done, but we found ourselves using Zohar's logic and planning methods during our pre-merger deliberations. (Interview, 2007)

In addition to the application of planning methods that originated at their former employer and these founders' close association with the founder of RAD, at the heart of the post-merger integration processes was the ability to create a compatible organizational culture (Drori, Wrzesniewski, and Ellis 2012). The founders of both firms emphasize the fact that these organizations were utterly different, one being focused on market and sales and the other on R&D and technology. According to the second partner to this merger,

> However, working in Lannet and with Zohar [RAD founder], resembled working the way we did in the army, under Zohar's command. We learned from him how to push the limit and connect the unconnectable. This ability or knowledge, if you like, made the merger successful. Yes, the organizations are different, but we, the founders, have a common heritage of making things happened. (Interview, 2007)

Uri and Noam, founders of two third-generation start-ups, respectively of the Fibronics genealogy, provide more evidence for what gets transferred, and how, across generations in their genealogy. Uri, a software engineer, notes,

> Our CEO would never take "no" for an answer. When someone blocks his way with a tall fence, he would jump over it. If the fence is too tall, he would dig under it; if he can't dig, he would run as much as needed to bypass the fence . . . nothing can stop him. I don't know where he acquired this character, maybe in the special unit in which he served in the army. We, his employees, don't have any choice but to follow him. Although I don't have his military experience, I do believe that if you want to succeed, this is the way you must do it. . . . I am quite sure that if and when I try to found my own start-up, I will behave in the same way. . . . (Interview, 2009)

Noam, a hardware engineer in the same genealogy, adds:

My boss is a serial entrepreneur. Our start-up is his third. I watch him and say to myself: Oh God, from where does he take the energy, the power to cope with all the problems and difficulties? He is very stubborn, never quits, and will never take a break. I know that he is not one of the Israeli heroes who served in the special military unit. I think that after founding two start-ups you become such a guy. You learn what it takes to found a start-up. I have friends who intend to establish a new start-up. They try to imitate him in every way. I don't think that I have the internal strength to do it. . . . (Interview, 2009)

B. Heredity dynamics endure across generations. The second mechanism of unmediated transfer of routines, practices, and blueprints is the heredity dynamics of cross-genealogical lines—in particular, the prominence of the founding parents of certain genealogies, their substantial social capital, their reputation, and their embeddedness in the industry (Shane and Stuart 2002). As we demonstrate, the influence of such prominent founders endures along the generational line and affects the potency and survival of the organizations within the genealogy (Burton, Sorensen, and Beckman 2002). Founders who possess a well-established position within the ITC sector enhance their ability to seek and exploit business opportunities through various models of founding such as serial entrepreneurship or by teaming up with other promising entrepreneurs. For example, prospective entrepreneurs highly appreciate the reputation, business clout, and knowledge and experience of the Zisapel brothers, and they seek their involvement in their new ventures. Founding models such as serial entrepreneurship or cross-generational founding enhance direct transfer of managerial blueprints. In such models, the presence of an established founder with proven experience enables the creation of blueprints, which are transferred directly, regardless of the "generational gap."

Consider the following example. A prominent, self-assured serial entrepreneur describes the process of founding a new start-up:

My first exit during the height of the Internet boom changed my agenda. I'm not interested in growing up firms but founding them. This is a risky strategy and maybe not so popular or correct. But this is my way and it fits me. How do I go about it? Very simple, by looking for ideas and people among those who work in other companies that I founded. These people are hungry entrepreneurs—like me. Some would claim that cloning is not such a good thing, but it works for me. (Interview, 2008)

Furthermore, we learned from anecdotal evidence collected in interviews with founders that there is a common "DNA" for those who are affiliated with certain genealogies and that it is transferable. Our interviewees said that what is transferable are the core features of identity, which are distinctive to certain genealogies. For example, upon launching our study we interviewed numerous founders based on their prominence in the Israeli high-tech industry regardless of their genealogical affiliation. Analyzing these interviews by aggregating founders according to their genealogical affiliation, we discovered that in many cases they attribute key identity features of their organizations to what they learned and inherited from their incumbent firms. We identified the origin of these key features in the founding firms of certain genealogies, mainly RAD, Comverse, Fibronics, and, to lesser extent, ECI and Tadiran. In particular, founders highlighted features such as focus on certain technology development protocols and procedures, criteria and processes of founding, and procedures for recruiting key technological and management personnel. In a few firms associated with RAD, the founders said that their founding model starts with the recruitment of only those who are alumni of their military unit. This is because they appreciate the alumni's creativity, loyalty, and endurance. The importance of what is transferred along a generational line rests with the genealogy's distinct features. Founders render these features as tangible and essential to obtain recognition, legitimacy, and access to necessary resources.

Genealogical composition and structure affect not only the scope and pace of reproduction of new ventures; they signal unique features that are transferable along a genealogy. New organizations can benefit not only from the skill of employees in founding and maintaining new firms but also from their genealogical affiliation, which itself signals their "good stock" (Burton 2001) to the external environment. Take, for example, the comments of a partner of one of the leading venture capital (VC) companies in Israel. After presenting our genealogical framework, he tried to persuade us to start a venture based on our research findings. He claimed that our research on the potency of the different genealogies could serve as a powerful selection tool.

> You can provide people like me and the HR [human resources] managers with the necessary information regarding the underlying culture and traits that are associated with the potential founder's employment history. For example, if he was trained in a company which is potent and entrepreneurial, he may well be bestowed with entrepreneurial tendencies. (Interview, 2005)

The HR manager of the same firm added:

> Furthermore, if I want to recruit a CEO for a relatively big company, I will never recruit her or him from the genealogies of RAD or Fibronics because they are

genealogies comprised of small firms. I will go and find what I am looking for in a genealogy such as Tadiran. People in this genealogy have values, practices, and routines of big companies. (Interview, 2009)

C. Co-founding. A third mechanism of transfer of organizational practices and values is co-founding—namely, members of two or more firms from the same genealogy teaming up to found new firm. This mechanism can facilitate the transmission of organizational practices and values not only within genealogies but also between them. Our anecdotal evidence based on interviews with such founders reveals that entrepreneurial values and practices are usually associated with members of the more potent genealogies, which were founded mostly during the competitive era. This observation is important because it may explain the reproduction of traits and practices that are conducive to founding new firms. More generally, such cross-genealogy interaction suggests that the convergence of genealogies goes hand in hand with the transfer of tangible entrepreneurial skills and the ability to scan and exploit business opportunities, which many believe has been the competitive advantage of the Israeli high-tech industry (see also Senor and Singer 2009). For example, in reviewing how firms present themselves on their official websites, we found evidence of the enduring characteristics of the founding parents and the resilience of certain shared values throughout generations.

Organizations in the Tadiran and Elisra genealogies, which were founded in the institutional-cooperative period, focus in their self-descriptions on the links between them and the country, embedding their mission within the national-security and nation-building narratives. Interestingly, in contrast to members of Tadiran and Elisra, organizations that belong to the RAD genealogy feature in their self-descriptions the importance of the founders' and managers' excellence and employment history in acquiring high-quality human capital, which provides a competitive edge. This indirect evidence supports our argument that values characterizing the founding parents are transmitted from generation to generation along genealogical lines. However, in generations of later periods, when Israeli society adopted individualistic and competitive values, we observe a decreasing representation of "nation-building" values and a stronger representation of values associated with entrepreneurship, innovation, and technological excellence. These are much more dominant in the genealogies of the competitive period.

In sum, our claim regarding what is being transferred along generational lines, and how, is based on two sets of well-established arguments: The first, organizational routines, practices, or values are transferable within parent-progeny relations (Phillips 2005) and founders' affiliation with incumbent employers (Klepper 2009; Burton, Sorensen, and Beckman 2002). Second, in line with imprinting theory (Stinchcombe 1965), the initial conditions prevailing at the time of founding of the parent of a particular genealogy shape the founding structures of generations of firms and their potential for further genealogy expansion. This is carried out mainly by reproduction of DNA of the kind that embodies practices and values of entrepreneurship.

VI. Potency varies during harsh times. We observed differences in potency between the two groups of genealogies, even during the 1990s bubble era in which all firms in the different genealogies felt the impact of the competitive and entrepreneurial environment. Our observations suggest that original characteristics are durable and inherited across generations even during periods of environmental jolts.

Our analysis suggests that the genealogies' parent firms, molded in a particular environment and shaped by specific initial conditions, pass their particular DNA to future generations. The high potency rate of these genealogies indicates that their respective entrepreneurial capabilities have indeed been transmitted.

Evolutionary Trajectory and Potency

Genealogies whose parent firms emerged during the competitive period scored high on all measures of potency, as compared with those whose founding firms originated during the institutional-cooperative period. The former spawned more de-novos than did firms affiliated with genealogies that had started 20 years earlier and that enjoyed the privilege of institutional markets in a socialist, centralized economy. The more potent genealogies differ from the others in the sheer number of their new ventures (de-novos) as well as in their embedded reproduction structure. They evolved at a faster pace than the less potent did—that is, the number of years per generation was smaller. They also had longer generational lines. Furthermore, genealogies that originated during the competitive period spawned more progenies per year and per generation than did those from the institutional-cooperative era.

Finally, the difference in potency trends between the two groups—RAD, Fibronics, and Comverse on the one hand and Tadiran, Telrad, Elisra, Orbit, and Motorola on the other—was also apparent in the period following the high-tech bubble crisis (2000–2005). The latter five, which were founded in the institutional-cooperative period, did not grow between 2001 and 2005, whereas those of the competitive period continued to reproduce more firms. This is noteworthy because companies in the older genealogies were larger than those in the new genealogies. Therefore, it appears that the dominant influence of the founding parents on their genealogy's potency depends on the historical environment and heredity. Studying the genealogical development of the Israeli ITC sector clearly shows that the genealogies founded during the institutional-cooperative period have been less potent than those founded during the competitive environment period. Genealogies carry their cumulative capabilities, including those formed at birth, to ensure their survival (Helfat and Lieberman 2002).

From Genealogy Evolution to Industrial Sector Evolution: Genealogy Convergence

We observed many cases in which entrepreneurs from a firm in one genealogy teamed up with entrepreneurs from another to establish a new venture. Furthermore, many of these ventures were established by entrepreneurs from the two genealogy groups founded, respectively, during the two different economic periods. Note that our analysis shows that differences in potency measures are larger when we ignore all the firms with double affiliations. Such firms facilitate the transfer of knowledge and capabilities from one genealogy to another, thus blurring their boundaries. Firms that are affiliated with the less potent genealogies exploit entrepreneurial opportunities by tapping into the capabilities and resources of those who have experience in initiating a new business. An entrepreneur who worked at Tadiran until the late 1980s reflects on his experience there:

> I was doing a challenging work in Tadiran, and then came the crisis, and many people were laid off. Luckily, I knew Gadi [his partner] from my working relations with RAD, and when he came with the offer for a start-up, I agreed immediately. I'm a very good technological person, but he knows how to make business happen. This is what the Zisapel brothers [RAD founders] are teaching them out there. (Interview, July 2004)

As noted earlier, employees who left Telrad or Tadiran after the company experienced a major crisis came away with a much technological knowledge but did not feel prepared to create a start-up. Many of these potential entrepreneurs preferred to spend several years in other start-ups to absorb the relevant blueprints, appropriate values, and entrepreneurial spirit needed to establish successful new ventures.

We also found that a few branches of genealogies from the institutional-cooperative era, such as Telrad and Elisra, started as joint ventures that were created by two or more entrepreneurs affiliated with genealogies of the competitive period, such as RAD and Fibronics. These branches were more potent and spawned more generations consisting of more companies than all of the other branches.

One of the factors that contributed to the creation of joint ventures and, ultimately, to the surge of potency in the ITC sector was the permeability of the genealogies' boundaries—that is, the ease of moving from one to another—mainly after 2000. Zohar Zisapel, one of the founding fathers of RAD, says,

> I know what to do; I have the ideas. What I need are good managers [who] will turn these ideas into a successful start-up. . . . I know how to find them. . . . Usually I need only one step to locate them in the high-tech sector. (Interview, 2009)

Any venture co-founded by Zohar Zisapel and an individual from another genealogy served as a bridge between the entrepreneurial networks of their genealogies. Consequently, the entrepreneurial tendencies expanded beyond RAD's, Fibronics', and Comverse's boundaries.

In short, the knowledge spillover and capabilities of founders who were affiliated with potent genealogies provided the crucial impetus for exploiting entrepreneurial opportunities (e.g., Helfat and Lieberman 2002). In addition, since the 1980s the hospitable institutional environment and the emergence of new communication technologies have created opportunities for new start-ups, even for those that did not inherit entrepreneurial capabilities and knowledge from their industry incumbents.

The culture of entrepreneurship inherent in the genealogies founded in the competitive period has enabled founders to share their entrepreneurial capabilities through cross-genealogy ventures. This explains why we may see potency within the high-tech industry's *entire* genealogical configuration. The convergence process manifested in the founding of new ventures by mixed-genealogy teams has provided the necessary resources and conditions for growth via knowledge and information transfer (Shane 2000; Burton, Sorensen, and Beckman 2002); better networking (Shane and Cable 2002; Wiewel and Hunter 1985); technological know-how and first-hand experience in the development of technology at the start-up stage; and the realization of entrepreneurial opportunities (Shane 2001).

Summary

Genealogy, as a demonstration of path-dependent organizational evolution, has received relatively little attention in the literature. Scholars have rarely studied genealogies beyond two-generation parent-progeny relations (e.g., Phillips 2002, 2005). Our study contributes to the understanding of organizational evolution by examining the influence of genealogical potency on the growth of an entire industrial sector along many generations.

We presented the dynamics associated with founding new firms through two interrelated processes. The first involved the initial conditions present (cultural, social, political, and technological) at the time of the founding of the parent firms. These conditions contributed to characteristics of the genealogy's founding parents—characteristics that have persisted through their genealogical lines. Imprinting theory provides us with a framework to deal with these enduring economic, institutional, and sociocultural characteristics that influence and predict how and why different organizational histories shape firms' evolutionary trajectories (e.g., Dobrev and Gotsopoulos 2010; Johnson 2007; Marquis 2003; Marquis and Huang 2010; Stinchcombe 1965).

The second process involved parent-progeny inheritance dynamics (Klepper 2002; Phillips 2002, 2005): the transfer of entrepreneurial capabilities and other characteristics in direct and nonmediated ways through learning and socialization. As spinouts evolve from the founding parents, their "genetic content" is made available to succeeding generations. Our study expands on Klepper's (2001) and Phillips' (2005) notions of inheritance relations and elaborates on the ideas of transmission of traits, values, and blueprints (see also Burton 2001; Burton, Sorensen, and Beckman 2002; Burton and Beckman 2007; Dencker, Gruber, and Shah 2009). A genealogy that transmits norms and values conducive to entrepreneurial initiatives tends to retain its tenacity along generational lines (cf. Jaffee and McKendrick 2006).

The mechanisms that govern the extent and content of knowledge inherited by progenies from parents may explain the growth potential of each genealogy. Prospective founders have both explicit and tacit knowledge about entrepreneurial opportunities and how to exploit the relevant values and routines acquired while working in a parent firm (e.g., Klepper 2001, 2009). Genealogies in which the founding parents have a strong entrepreneurial culture develop various ways to spawn new firms, essentially by lowering the barrier to spawning. It is easy to start new ventures if both external conditions and internal mechanisms exist that support entrepreneurship, leading to more potent genealogies. The tenacity of the conditions at founding in the competitive period encouraged potency, imprinting similar values along the genealogical line. This fits the structural inertia argument (Hannan and Freeman 1984) in the sense that the entrepreneurial spirit is the source of path dependence through which progenies in a genealogy are imprinted with similar values. This does not mean that adaptive processes are mute. It is more likely that the convergence of the two is part of the imprinting process, but the genealogical path is strongly affected by the conditions at the time of founding.

Some genealogies are less potent because they were formed during the institutional-cooperative period. In addition, the growth of an entire genealogy is constrained by the nature of ownership, as is the case when founders are a part of a business group (such as Telrad or Elisra). Furthermore, a strategic orientation toward a more exploitative stance results in less potency. Indeed, our findings show that the genealogies founded during the institutional-cooperative period, and that focused more on acquiring knowledge than on creating it, were less potent.

This book contributes to our knowledge of the mechanisms that shape diverse genealogies founded in different periods and in different environments. It also contributes to our understanding of the nature of the interdependencies between such genealogies. Our point of departure is based on Stinchcombe's imprinting theory (1965), which essentially argues for the enduring effects of the societal environment during founding. New organizations founded in a given environment adopt that environment's prevailing structures and values, and these imprints tend to persist along time. We identified two distinct periods in Israel's economic history and two types of genealogies that emerged from them. The first type consists of parent companies founded during the institutional-cooperative period; the second consists of parent companies founded during the competitive period. Tracing these genealogies provides a perspective on their different characteristics, potencies, and evolutionary trajectories. As our findings show, these two types evolved in separate generational lines and exhibited different structural characteristics and potencies. The notable exception is ECI, which was founded during the institutional-cooperative period. However, as a result of changes in its management and strategy early in its history, its evolutionary trajectory came to be more consistent with that of the genealogies of the competitive period. As the genealogies continued to evolve along time, the boundaries between them started to blur.

Israel, a very heterogeneous society, is considered a melting pot of various groups and cultures. Merging of the various groups into a more cohesive society is carried out informally in schools and especially in the military. For many years, the melting pot was an official governmental doctrine for assimilating immigrants from various immigration waves—from those who came to Israel from Eastern Europe in the pre-state era (starting in the 1920s) through those who came from Asia and Africa in the 1950s to the huge immigration wave from Russia in the 1990s. Israeli society is a unique blend of norms and values that originated in the Communist regimes of Eastern Europe, the totalitarian regimes of Asia and Africa, and the democratic societies of the West—Europe, the United States, and Canada.

One might argue that Israel's high-tech community is a kind of melting pot of two sets of values leading to a unique blend that evolved into the two genealogy groups we studied. The first set of values emerged from the ideological combination of nation building, economy, and society that evolved through the 1950s and 1960s, during the institutional-cooperative period. In that period, many important values and capabilities were shaped, such as cooperation, commitment, creativity, improvisation, and the willingness to forego personal gratification for the sake of the collective. The second set of values, which evolved during the past 35 years, originated in Western ideologies such as self-realization, competition, and individual goal orientation. On the one hand, the earlier value set—embodied in the institutional-cooperative movement, the national labor unions, and the Labor Party—have given way to a new value set (Yaar-Yuchtman and Shavit 2001). This emergence of new values triggered the takeoff of the Israeli ITC industry in the 1980s. On the other hand, we, along with authors such as Senor and Singer (2009), assert that the secret of Israeli high-tech's great success is embedded in the unique blend of values and capabilities of Israeli society and its focus on cooperation. This is true both in the micro sense of behavior within a group as opposed to competition between groups and in the macro sense of cooperation among organizations within Israel as opposed to competition in the global environment. The exact cultural blend is probably one determinant of success of the Israeli high-tech industry in general and of the ITC sector in particular.

The process of cultural socialization within the ITC sector is accomplished through three distinct mechanisms:

1. The young generation of engineers who were already a product of the cultural melting pot and who populated the old and new ventures in the two genealogy groups.

2. The many engineers who left their founding parents' organizations in the 1990s, such as Tadiran and Telrad, and are now working in young start-ups. These employees are equipped with knowledge, capabilities, and values acquired during many years of working in organizations inspired by the institutional-cooperative ideology. As shown

in Chapter 3, many of them were not prepared to start new ventures unless they could absorb the values and entrepreneurial capabilities embedded in the second group of genealogies.

3.   Joint ventures or the co-founding of new ventures by entrepreneurs who have double affiliations—that is, with old and new genealogies.

The last two mechanisms might be referred to as cross-implementation of entrepreneurial knowledge, tendencies, or capabilities.

The salient difference in size and structure between the two genealogy groups demonstrates that it is quite difficult for firms in the old genealogies to adapt to the new competitive world. This is why the implantation of entrepreneurs carrying another set of capabilities or values may seem like an "invasion," but they eventually contribute to growth and future prosperity. This "implantation" enriches the entrepreneurs' repertoire of entrepreneurial values and capabilities, and will facilitate the spillover of entrepreneurial values, skills, and knowledge between genealogies in the future.

Recognizing the different historical periods and their effects on the culture of newly founded firms reinforces the strong link between historical context and genealogical structure. Studies of the emergence of the Israeli ITC sector have focused on opportunity structures, capabilities, and geography (Avnimelech 2008; Breznitz 2007; Carmel and de Fontenay 2004; de Fontenay and Carmel 2001). The genealogy approach allows us to draw attention to the dynamics of the sector's evolution while relating the effects of structures and social ties. We suggest that genealogical evolution is a key mechanism for understanding the rate and extent of the founding of new organizations. Furthermore, we show how the social structure of certain genealogies facilitates founding, growth, and survival of progenies by enabling social ties, parental imprinting of values, and channeling of blueprints and knowledge.

The Israeli high-tech industry is considered a success story, and it has gained fame for its innovative and entrepreneurial spirit as well as its technological ingenuity (Senor and Singer 2009). The recent global economic turbulence has been a mixed blessing for the Israeli high tech, which has experienced periodic fluctuations, including a severe slowdown in the founding of new firms, scarcity of resources, and competitive threats from companies in countries such as China and India. Some already eulogize the so-called "engine of the Israeli economy" and the tangible and symbolic miracle of Israel's unique contributions and leading technological world position. However, the industry has always made a comeback and sparked new optimism. Strong periods have followed weak ones. The creative fountain of Israeli technology entrepreneurs has never dried up. New companies spawn and sprout as new technologies are developed and seek new markets.

In this book, we told the story of the lasting effect of historical legacy on genealogical evolution, in spite of radical changes in the institutional environment. We traced the evolution of the ITC sector to two periods that influenced the founding of varied genealogies possessing different structural characteristics and entrepreneurial tendencies. We showed how genealogies founded during the institutional-cooperative environment exhibit lower potency in the number of spawned start-ups. In contrast, we showed that the genealogies founded during more favorable conditions for ITC sector development during the late 1980s benefited from an institutional environment that heavily supported the industry through incentive policies and ITC sector arrangements. This environment impacted not only the evolutionary trajectory of the genealogies but also their specific structural and cultural characteristics and, eventually, their capabilities for spawning new firms. Mechanisms such as serial entrepreneurship and "incest" founding led, in the long run, to the relatively high potency rates of these genealogies.

6

Concluding Remarks

New organizations, especially new types of organizations, generally involve new roles, which have to be learned. In old organizations former occupants of roles can teach their successors, communicating not only skills but also decision criteria, responsibilities to various people who have relations to role occupants, devices for smoothing over persistent sources of tension and conflict, generalized loyalty to the organization, what sort of things can go wrong with routine procedures, and so on.

Arthur Stinchcombe, *"Social Structure and Organizations"*

This book developed a genealogical approach by analyzing data that trace the founding affiliation of 731 firms in the Israeli information technology and communication (ITC) sector. The growth of this sector is traditionally attributed to the formation of highly effective clusters based on the co-evolution of industrial infrastructure and supporting institutions, including an entrepreneurial culture that stemmed from the defense establishment (see the Appendix).

In describing the growth of the ITC sector from a genealogical perspective, we expanded on the cluster approach for explaining the dynamics of industry emergence and growth, and focused on the founding process of the sector's firms. By shifting our attention to the genealogical perspective, our main goal was to understand the emergence and evolutionary trajectory of industrial sectors through their genealogical structure and characteristics. Our approach provides a complementary explanation of the Israeli ITC sector's dynamics.

In studying genealogical evolution in which historical conditions at founding vary, this book enhances our knowledge of the mechanisms that shape diverse genealogies founded in different periods or in different economic environments. It also furthers our understanding of the nature of interdependencies among genealogies. New organizations founded in any given environmental context adopt structures and values that prevail at the time of founding, and these founding imprints tend to persist along time. We argue that the interaction between environment and internal organizational founding processes, based on parent-progeny relations, is the building block of genealogical evolution. For the Israeli ITC sector, genealogical growth involved (1) environmental factors during the time of founding such as policy, culture, market, and technology, all of which had a substantial impact on the sector's genealogical evolutionary trajectory; and (2) inheritance processes of entrepreneurial capabilities based both on values associated with the founding parents of the respective genealogies and on organizational elements transmitted along the generations through different spawning models. These interrelated mechanisms led to the emergence of varied genealogies that differed in terms of their potency, structure, and growth trajectory.

In this chapter, we summarize our major concepts and provide ideas for further research. We address the key topics covered in the book: those that consist of the major components of the genealogical perspective—imprinting, heredity, and potency. We then offer a concise conceptual framework of our genealogical approach and suggest several possibilities for future study. We conclude by suggesting that the Israeli ITC sector evolved as a result of complex institutional environments and intra-genealogical processes that influenced the trajectory paths of the various genealogies.

Imprinting and Heredity

Throughout the book, we showed how the ITC genealogies were shaped by the historical circumstances at the time of their founding. Different historical periods provided different resources for the founding parent firms. Following the imprinting hypothesis, we argued that, once founded, the various genealogies embarked on an evolutionary trajectory that resulted in the spawning of new firms, which relied to a certain extent on those values and structures already laid down by their founding parents. Inertial forces such as certain values and ideologies, the dominance of government policies, and organizational arrangements endured along generational lines. Our study provides ample evidence for the continuous effects of the genealogies' founding parents on spawning patterns, genealogical potency, and, consequently, the genealogies' structures and evolutionary trajectories.

Imprinting dynamics affected the genealogies in two ways. First, the environment during the time of founding that imprinted on the founding parents proved to be an enduring factor that influenced the spawning activities of subsequent generations. Second, the imprinting process served as the basis for inheritance dynamics—that is, the processes through which the transfer of entrepreneurial capabilities between parents and progenies takes place along generational lines. Ecologists have long studied the tendency of organizations to survive through inertial mechanisms, which produce enduring structures (Hannan and Freeman 1984). In the same vein, neo-institutional theory emphasizes the role of isomorphism and legitimacy in preserving organizational structures and practices (DiMaggio and Powell 1983; Scott 2001). Such ideas lead to a natural introduction of a genealogical approach.

In line with imprinting theory, the respective institutional-cooperative and competitive economy periods influenced the founding parents of the genealogies we studied. Values (such as nation building) that originated during the institutional-cooperative economy period dominated Israel's high-tech industry development, including during the formation of its cluster. The genealogies founded during the competitive economy period drew on their distinct entrepreneurial values, but also reinforced the cultural legacy of the early days of the state. Beginning with Israel's transformation into a competitive economy, genealogical evolution took place against the backdrop of imprinting one set of cultural values (associated with the institutional-cooperative period), which existed alongside the repertoire of entrepreneurial values that fit the spirit of the new ITC sector (e.g., Murray 2011).

As we illustrated in Chapters 3 and 4, two groups of genealogies founded, respectively, in the institutional-cooperative and competitive periods have characterized the Israeli economy since the country's independence (1948). One genealogy (ECI) exhibits distinct characteristics of the two periods and is considered conceptually as a sequence that evolved from both. We contend that those genealogies founded during the institutional-cooperative environment (Telrad, Tadiran, Elisra, Orbit, MIL) exhibited less potency because of the nature of the institutional and policy environment that prevailed during the formative days of the Israeli state. The genealogies founded after the late 1970s (RAD, Fibronics, Comverse) were born in a period in which substantial changes brought to the fore governmental policies and activities aligned with two major forces: the emergence of a new communication technology and Israel's political shift toward liberalism and the consequent economic move toward privatization and a liberal market economy.

From a broader perspective, during the era of globalization and the rise of the importance and distribution of technological innovation, Israel was well suited to enhance its competitive advantages in the high-tech business. As numerous studies illustrate, existential threats, geopolitical position, and internal resources led policy makers to place a high priority on the development of a national education system and to promote technological self-sufficiency by formulating highly supportive incentive policies (Breznitz 2007). Because of these processes, the Israeli high-tech industry evolved in a manner consistent with the varied institutional environments and historical legacies of two major systems—socialism and capitalism. However, because of the initial conditions during their founding, the younger genealogies, which were also characterized by their entrepreneurial capabilities, proved to be more potent and overall spun off more firms than did the old and established genealogies.

Furthermore, the evolutionary trajectory of the ITC sector stemmed from cohort-based influences. The older genealogies that originated in the institutional-cooperative economy, such as Telrad and Tadiran, were characterized by templates closely associated with their founding legacy as state-sponsored and worker-oriented organizations. These mature genealogies, for most of their existence, operated in a stable and sheltered environment (Aharoni 1976, 1991; Brookfield et al. 2012; Maman 2004). The ability of firms in these genealogies to exploit business opportunities during the competitive institutional-cooperative period suggests that they could still adjust somewhat to a competitive environment.

Consistent and broad-based founding activity can be seen in the younger genealogies and can be attributed to the influence of their founding parents, which remain active as private firms (e.g., RAD). Note that the firms affiliated with the older genealogies (Telrad, Tadiran, ECI) were able to depart somewhat from the legacies they inherited from their ancestors. The break from such rigidity by developing capabilities for founding new firms or by getting rid of the inertial forces that were deeply rooted in the institutional-cooperative environment was driven both at the institutional and at the individual level. Institutional change during the transformation to a free-market economy and globalization created founding opportunities in technology-related fields through the provision of necessary resources by the government, aimed at creating a vibrant high-tech industry.

Note that the evolutionary trajectories of the genealogies during the competitive period exhibited certain "interbreeding," or convergence, tendencies among genealogies such as RAD and Telrad. This convergence included all the firms, which their founding parents had originated from two different genealogies, and it resulted in a cross-genealogical accelerated rate of founding, mainly in the less potent genealogies.

Identifying the founding parents of a genealogy in the ITC sector and tracing the structure of their generational lines reveal different founding models. The idea that these models were based on the initial conditions at founding departs from the view that populations of organizations emerge, grow, and decline as a corollary to concentration (Hannan and Carroll 1992), entry rate (Hannan and Freeman 1989), or competition over resources (Baum and Singh 1994). In our study, we outline the dynamics of the creation of divergent founding models as conditioned to a great extent on imprinting processes echoing the environment and its characteristics during the time of founding. Contrary to a common intuition, which assumes a steady decay of the influence of the imprinting associated with the founding parents of a genealogy over its progenies, we have found that such influence does not vanish under certain initial conditions, and that entrepreneurial values remain consistent along generational lines.

Potency

Unlike earlier genealogical researchers who viewed parent-progeny relations within a single-generation time frame (e.g., Phillips 2002, 2005), we reveal the complexity of affinity of intergenerational relations and its connection to potency. We identify complex patterns of affinity, which represent different genealogical potencies and consequently shape genealogical structures. Thus, genealogical potency, in terms of the spawning rate of new firms, might influence the degree to which parents' "genetic code" is transmitted from generation to generation. For this reason, older genealogies that were less inclined to spawn new ventures, and founded relatively few firms during the institutional-cooperative period, were influenced by the newer genealogies that were founded in the competitive period and spawned more firms during this time.

The basic entrepreneurial model of genealogies assumes that transmission of capabilities to spawn new ventures is manifested in the potency of genealogies, which, in turn, influences their structure and reproductive models. The genealogical trajectory shows that more potent genealogies exhibit a fairly rapid pace of generational evolution (see, e.g., Tables 4.12 and 4.14). Generational potency dynamics appears to influence the structure of the different genealogies and the configuration of their network and founding model. Furthermore, the more potent genealogies, in particular RAD, had more serial entrepreneurs and more companies founded through what we term *incest relations*, where the founding parents were still founding new ventures with younger members.

The growth rate and potency of the entire ITC sector were enhanced during the competitive economy, not only through the founding activities of the younger genealogies but also as a result of cross-genealogical founding activities. By teaming with founders originating from the younger genealogies, founders that affiliated with the older ones reconfigured around an invigorated founding process. This process was identified with the competitive period, after years of stagnation in terms of founding among incumbents of older genealogies. For this reason, our genealogical model challenges the previous literature of spinoff and imprinting by addressing the temporal gap of the founding process. We reveal that the various mechanisms of genealogical evolution enable employees of incumbent firms to break past inertial forces. Based on a model of genealogical evolution, which is nested not only in initial conditions of ancestor founding but also in transmission of entrepreneurial capabilities, we demonstrate how variations among our genealogies emerged and influenced the potency of the entire ITC sector.

On the Nature of Genealogical Evolution

Various studies on the spinout process have suggested that the pre-entry experience of founders shapes their entrepreneurial decisions (Klepper 2009). Some have emphasized the nature of inheritance between parents and progenies (Phillips 2002, 2005); others have focused on what is transmitted (Baron and Hannan 2005; Burton 2001). Our genealogical analysis claims that the genealogical evolution of the Israeli high-tech industry exhibits substantial variations, expressed by different rates of potency—that is, the ability of incumbent firms to spawn new firms within or between genealogies. These variations stem from differences in the initial conditions and genesis events during founding, while the founding legacy of genealogical ancestors and their inheritance capabilities influence incumbent firms and their progenies along generational lines. Studies on imprinting already reveal that different founding contexts yield variations in structure and practices (Tucker, Singh, and Meinhardt 1990). But imprinting alone only partially explains genealogical evolution because intra-genealogical heredity processes are not accounted for (Johnson 2007). Our approach claims that heredity processes stretched along genealogical lines transmit those elements imprinted from the environment (i.e., rules, policy, beliefs, norms) and reflected in practices, routines, values, or entrepreneurial capabilities drawn from parent-progeny relations. In turn, as we show, the capability for spawning new firms, and its extent (potency), tends to persist and eventually shape the growth trajectory of each genealogy and, consequently, of the entire industrial sector.

This book started with a focus on the ancestral origin and intergenerational evolution of diverse genealogies in Israel's ITC sector. Each one presented a different reproductive process, and eventually a different potency rate stemmed from the variations that existed within and between the various genealogies. Furthermore, the ancestry origin of a genealogy and the process of heredity affected the nature of future organizational creation. In this book, we argue that the founding contexts of genealogies serve as mechanism for introducing variation among them, which, in turn, leads to different spawning models of creating new firms. Thus, variation reflects an evolutionary process that stems from the historical circumstances of genesis and founding events, which influence various variables and patterns that eventually constitute distinct and varied populations of organizations occupying the ITC niche (e.g., Aldrich and Ruef 2006; Hannan and Freeman 1977, 1984, 1989). In addition, the source of this variation resides within individual genealogies. Firms in a genealogy's generational line create offspring, which may be either similar or different or may be more or less potent than it is. The potency of a genealogy and sometimes the centrality of certain actors within it (such as serial entrepreneurs or incest relations) have a direct bearing on the new venture's possibilities for transferring entrepreneurial capabilities.

Thus, the genealogical evolutionary process that characterized the Israeli ITC sector indicates that genealogical variations shaped in different historical stages exhibit a variety of possibilities for founding new firms. The variations in genealogical trajectory, and in particular in the genealogies' potency and structure, resulted in uneven growth of the ITC sector. In the case of the older genealogies, the historical legacy and patterns of heredity led, for example, to low fitness for the start-up environment and eventually to a lower potency rate. This is in contrast to the newer genealogies.

But along the trajectory of generational growth, genealogies tend to converge; consequently, both variation and convergence contribute to the potency of the larger entity, the Israeli ITC sector. Thus, our main assertion is that the context of the founding of each genealogy and the nature of its particular line of heredity and affinity resulted in a different evolutionary path shaped by both internal dynamics and interrelationships within the genealogy and with external genealogies. The latter serve as the source of an entrepreneurial "genetic pool" for the respective genealogy. The "interbreeding" between genealogies resulted in an increase in overall potency. Thus, firms originated in two different genealogies contribute to the number of new firms founded by each genealogy and eventually by the entire ITC sector. These, in turn, affected the ITC sector's development. The variations and convergence produced heterogeneous genealogies that portrayed different selection and adaptation mechanisms in varied environments. This heterogeneity was the key reason for genealogical resilience, and it eventually shaped the Israeli ITC sector's survival and successes in achieving a competitive edge in global markets.

Future Research

We built our framework on the assumption that routines and values are transferred along genealogical lines, but we did not measure what exactly was transferred. In the study of the emergence of new organizational forms over a long period of time, such material may not be easy to obtain. Future research should focus on situations where more genealogies can be identified and where the content transmitted along genealogical lines can be measured. Also, after several generations (and especially in a small country such as Israel), genealogies begin to merge. That is, members of two or more genealogies co-found new ventures. On the one hand, this phenomenon may blur the boundaries between genealogies; on the other, it may provide clearer information about the real entrepreneurial nature of the genealogies. Further research on the evolution of this industrial sector should specifically focus on the links between genealogies and whether and how members of genealogies that are more entrepreneurial will succeed in influencing those that are less entrepreneurial. Our initial findings reveal that they can have such an influence only if the founders spend a few years in an entrepreneurial genealogy, absorb its routines, and adopt its culture. The nature of such conversion along generational lines is a promising avenue for genealogical research.

Summary

The Israeli high-tech industry is considered to be a success and has gained fame for its innovative and entrepreneurial spirit as well as for its technological ingenuity (Senor and Singer 2009). However, the recent global economic turbulences are a mixed blessing for its future.

In this book, we tell the story of the lasting effect of the Israeli high-tech industry's historical legacy on genealogical evolution in spite of radical changes in the institutional environment. We attribute this evolution to two periods that influenced the founding of varied genealogies, which possessed different structural characteristics and entrepreneurial tendencies. We show how genealogies founded during the institutional-cooperative environment influenced their offspring. These offspring exhibited distinct spawning potencies that created difficulty in the development of entrepreneurial tendencies and did not contribute substantially to the growth of the sector or to its innovative vitality. In contrast, genealogies that were founded during more favorable conditions for high-tech development, during the late 1980s, benefited from an institutional-competitive environment that heavily supported the industry both through incentive policies and developed cluster arrangements. This environment impacted not only the evolutionary trajectory of the genealogies but also their specific structural and cultural characteristics and eventually their capabilities for spawning new firms. Mechanisms such as serial entrepreneurship and "incest" founding led to their relatively high potency rates.

Early in our research, we interviewed Zvi, the CEO of a company known as the "wireless broadband pioneer." Referring to the competitive edge of both his company and the ITC sector, Zvi commented,

> We are outsourcing to companies in Romania, China and India. We transfer [out] programming jobs and knowledge, [but] that is not so important. What we have here [in Israel], beyond the technological knowledge, the hunger for success, and the collective inclination towards entrepreneurship is the know-how for identifying an opportunity and putting it into practice—[this is] what is needed to create new ventures. The moment we transfer this to others, we lose our competitive edge as a leading high-tech country. (Interview, 2008)

Zvi started at Tadiran, moved to one of RAD's start-ups, and only then founded his own venture. No wonder that he expressed his deep concern regarding the potential transfer of entrepreneurial inclinations from Israel to its potential competitors. This book attributes the potency of the Israeli high-tech industry to its genealogical history and characteristics, which constantly nurture the knowledge of entrepreneurship. As reiterated by Zvi, ". . . high-tech is [the] locomotive of growth because the art of founding companies is essentially shared knowledge and aspiration."

What does Zvi's comment imply for our understanding of the story of Israel's high-tech industry? In line with our genealogical perspective, our findings suggest that knowledge and entrepreneurial tendencies grow further along genealogical lines. The development of strong inter- and intra-genealogical networks influenced by Israel's historical legacy and drive for self-reliance is associated with entrepreneurial capabilities generated through the industry's unique genealogical configuration.

Reference Matter

Appendix:
History of the Israeli High-Tech Industry

Often, we've had a typical phenomenon that you're probably familiar with here: we sprout many, many ideas and these ideas go through the start-up phase; they go into an initial development; they're bought; and those companies move abroad. And that's a natural process that will continue. We understand that. But we want to create governmental incentives to have more of these companies stay in Israel.

Benyamin Netanyahu, Israeli prime minister, in an address to the
High-Tech Industry Association Annual Conference, June 2010

This appendix provides an overview of the Israeli high-tech industry by presenting the major theories that explain its historical evolution, the formation of policy around it, and the socioeconomic factors that have shaped its success. Our goal is to provide an integrated conceptual framework to account for the dynamic nature of the industry's emergence and success. This evolution was influenced by the interplay between targeted policy that provided incentives for innovation and historical and societal developments in Israel. We argue that the driving force behind Israeli high-tech's success can be explained by the strategies and structures embedded in policy to promote innovation and R&D and to provide a breeding ground for pioneering high-tech entrepreneurship. Furthermore, the peculiar history of Israel, and its geopolitical situation, compelled its founding fathers to harness and shape industrial policies for the purpose of nation building, while transcending considerations of efficiency and market.

Theoretical Orientation
Reviewing the history of industrial evolution requires a theoretical and analytical conceptualization that takes into account a complex set of factors, including the social, economic, and political aspects of a system in transition. High-tech industries in countries such as India, China, Taiwan, Ireland, and Israel are examples of the importance of creating such a comprehensive analytical framework for analysis (Breznitz 2007; Saxenian 2006). Consider, for instance, favorable government policies, such as China's high-tech parks, which are specifically designated for returning emigrants. These parks attract experienced entrepreneurs capable of exploiting the opportunities created by such policies. Chinese entrepreneurs also take advantage of new opportunities provided

by globalization, regardless of direct government support. Israel's high-tech industry is marked by an evolutionary path based on its historical and social development along with global technological trends such as the emergence of the information technology and communication (ITC) industry in the 1980s. In what follows, we explore the evolution of Israeli high-tech against the backdrop of its particular historical conditions and the adaptive and competitive processes that shaped its growth. We consider the "path-dependent" nature of the emergence of the Israeli high-tech cluster, as well as the institutional and cultural factors that allowed it to adapt to environmental changes. This integration allows us to introduce our genealogical approach in historical and cultural contexts.

State Intervention and the Formation of a Cluster

The emergence of the Israeli high-tech industry occurred in line with a number of societal changes—in particular, the transition of Israel's economic and political systems from a socialist, interventionist to a privatization and market-based regime (Aharoni 1976, 1991). Over time, these trends contributed to the liberation of capital markets and the massive privatization of large state banks and corporations. A salient result of this liberalization was an opening up of the Israeli economy to global corporations that eventually triggered the rise of a technological and knowledge-intensive industry and the decline of labor-intensive industries in the 1990s. The rapid development of Israeli high-tech during the 1980s and 1990s can be attributed to the policy and societal context in which the industry was spawned, as well as to the specific mechanisms that created a unique founding model for new high-tech organizations.

Many of the numerous studies on the emergence of the Israeli high-tech industry in general, and the ITC, software, and Internet sectors in particular, begin by describing a "cluster" of social and political conditions. Cluster theory attributes the development of an industrial sector to the contextual and spatial configuration of a certain locale (Piore and Sabel 1984; Porter 1998). In a well-known study, Saxenian (1994) demonstrated that the different evolutions of Silicon Valley in California and Route 128 in Massachusetts could be explained by looking at regional differences, which included aspects such as co-operation and competition, size of companies, the influence of business structure on innovation and production composition, diversity of networks, and vertical and horizontal linkages with various organizations and institutions (such as research universities).

The formation of the cluster, as the narrative goes, originated in the early days of the Israeli state (founded in 1948), during which urgent national concerns about security and nation building guided industrial and economic policies. These policies targeted industries that directly contributed to the development of the emerging nation (Levi-Faur 2001). Aharoni (1991) observes that during these formative years, government intervention and tight regulation were cornerstones of the state's economic policies. Consequently, government interference and direction were highly influential in shaping almost every facet of industrial development, including industry structures, patterns of ownership and entrepreneurship, and the level of government incentives. A high degree of government involvement and a sense of mission associated with the notion of nation building thus characterized the formative days of the Israeli state, shaping the nature and scope of its high-tech industry.

The success of Israeli high-tech attracts both academic and nonacademic observers, who provide several major reasons for its abrupt emergence as a global player. The most notable reasons tie the sector's success to numerous sources: the necessity to rely on modern industry as the economic foundation for a resource-starved, newly founded country (which led to innovative governmental policies); the relative strength of Israeli technology and science higher-education institutions; the technological and entrepreneurial legacy of the military; the absorption of skilled immigrants, mainly from Russia; returnee entrepreneurs from the United States and, consequently, the establishment of R&D centers of technology in Israel; the availability of modern infrastructure; and a "national culture" that supported risks, innovation, and entrepreneurship (see, e.g., Senor and Singer 2009).

Furthermore, scholars of the Israeli high-tech cluster (e.g., Breznitz 2007; de Fontenay and Carmel 2001; Avnimelech and Teubal 2004) have long held that its competitive advantage stemmed from the combination of human capital and targeted incentive policies that were consistent with specific historical circumstances, ones that made the cluster prone to easy exploitation of its innovative potential. For example, major cluster effects are associated with the following:

Strong network ties.   There are personal and professional networks. The former originate, for instance, in the army or the university, among expatriates, or in social and familial relations. The latter consist of various services needed for the maintenance of the high-tech industry, including suppliers and intermediaries in the fields of human resources (HR), law, accounting, and the like.

A robust venture capital industry.   Israel's venture capital (VC) industry has about 70 active venture capital funds, of which 14 are international with Israeli offices. In the years 2000–2009, 4,374 Israeli high-tech companies raised $16.6 billion.[1]

Specialized institutional and policy mechanisms.   Under the auspices of the government's Office of the Chief Scientist (OCS) of the Ministry of Industry, Trade and Labor, various policies for industrial R&D and support for entrepreneurship were implemented. The OCS currently operates on an annual budget of about U.S. $300 million (2009), which is spent on about 1,000 projects undertaken by 500 companies. Its main program (the R&D Fund) supports R&D projects of Israeli companies by offering conditional grants of up to 50 percent of the approved expenditure. If the project is commercially successful, the company is obligated to repay the grant through royalty payments. The OCS policy tools also include a variety of specialized programs that are intended to provide a competitive edge through financial and infrastructure-related incentives to entrepreneurs and investors.

Linkages with major sources of demand and timely integration into the technological globalization of the high-tech industry.   The Israeli high-tech industry is closely linked to the United States, in terms of market, capital, information, and business relations. A notable example of this linkage is the extent of merger and acquisitions (M&As) of Israeli high-tech companies. Between 2000 and 2009, there were 673 M&As in the Israeli market, worth a total of U.S. $43.7 billion.[2]

Human and social capital. This is evident through the highly skilled engineering- and science-related labor force, including trained managers and serial entrepreneurs. Furthermore, Israeli academic institutions in the fields of science and technology forge close ties with Israeli high-tech.

Entrepreneurial culture. This encourages innovation and the founding of new ventures. Also, it seems that creativity, improvisation, and quick response are characteristics that dominate the high-tech organizational culture in Israel (Senor and Singer 2009).

The process of cluster formation might best be understood as a concerted national effort directed toward growing industry while also mobilizing wide institutional support. The prevalence of highly effective R&D work within academia and the military is considered to have been the prime lever for technological innovation (Breznitz 2005a). Accordingly, the emergence of a vibrant, highly-innovative information and communication sector with enormous growth potential and a global reach provided a unique opportunity for the emergence of Israeli high-tech—which reached its heyday during the 1990s.[3] The emerging global ITC market increased the demand for Israeli technologies and channeled foreign capital and VC investment into the country. This made Israel an attractive destination for major technological powerhouses wanting to acquire Israeli technology and firms and establish R&D centers.

Breznitz's (2002, 2005a, 2005b, 2006, 2007) analysis of the historical development of the Israeli ITC sector reveals that government R&D policy overemphasized innovation diffusion at the expense of building infrastructure capabilities. Such policies drew on the already abundant R&D skills at the universities and in the military, and the state-led capacity-diffusion policy instigated more activities in the civilian industrial R&D sector. Furthermore, the policy sought to expand reach and provide universal criteria for incentives aimed at encouraging various R&D activities that would result in a competitive advantage, not necessarily at identifying specific technological or industrial preferences. The government initiated mainly horizontal policies, which were generalist in nature with regard to market, products, or technology. This is useful in situations where industry is not fully developed and must consolidate and crystallize. Horizontal policies allow for bottom-up innovation. Provided they satisfy certain criteria, entrepreneurs can select the field in which they want to work. These policies—open in principle to all firms regardless of sector and to all projects whatever the product class and technology—allowed for market-friendly R&D support programs and bottom-up, innovative entrepreneurial activity. They were structured to facilitate collective learning as well as to promote and encourage technological entrepreneurship (Avnimelech and Teubal 2008). According to Avnimelech and Teubal (2008), there are three objectives to such policies. The first is generating and diffusing R&D/innovation capabilities throughout the business sector; the second is promoting technological entrepreneurship; and the third—through experience with alternative innovative areas—is identifying and "selecting" those with potential for sustainable competitive advantage.

The historical path of the Israeli ITC sector's evolution reflects the extent to which competitive advantage and local external effects—both direct, such as in inter-firm cooperation, and indirect, such as in the availability of inputs and infrastructure—were the prime movers of rapid growth during the 1990s (see Bresnahan, Gambardella, and Saxenian 2001). Bresnahan and colleagues (2001) studied the emergence of new high-tech clusters in several locations, including Ireland, India, Israel, and Taiwan. They found that, in order for a high-tech industry to emerge successfully, there are some critical, necessary factors. The first is a link to sizable demand, in Israel's case the American market and the VC industry. The second is skilled labor, developed in Israel through substantial investments in education and the military, as well as through the influx of educated immigrants. The third involves firm- and market-building capabilities that in Israel have been developed by government policies and initiatives like the Technological Incubators Program.

Furthermore, de Fontenay and Carmel (2001) argue that the route to cluster technological opportunities, firm capability, educated labor, and flow of entrepreneurs with a record number of start-ups[4] is evidence for the following:

> First, traditional forces of comparative advantage were gradually drawing activity to the region, and each newly established firm contributed to cluster effect, [and] second, there were major exogenous forces at work, including the Internet boom, which dramatically increased the number of firms, and reinforced certain types of cluster effects. (p. 31)

Yet our review suggests that the new Israeli technologies offered impressive complementarities to existing ITC in terms of innovative products. Complementary technology, together with close links to the U.S. (and, to a lesser extent, European and Asian) markets, enabled the Israeli ITC sector to exploit its competitive advantages. These advantages stemmed from the co-evolution of an innovation-oriented industrial policy; the emergence of new global opportunities in the technological VC industry; and high skills and network capabilities. In particular, the unique clustering capabilities and processes of the ITC sector were closely related to the nature of Israel's human capital (Carmel and de Fontenay 2004). The ample pool of educated and highly skilled ITC professionals came from a variety of sources: the technological and science faculties of the country's research universities; immigrants from the former Soviet Union; graduates of the military's technological and R&D units; and expatriates. Economic, social, and policy processes associated with this reservoir of human and social capital enabled the sector to take advantage of previously unexploited technological and market opportunities. For example, the government's Technological Incubators Program provided comprehensive institutional support in the forms of finance, infrastructure, business connections, and training for Russian immigrants who were planning to spin off their own start-ups (Carmel and de Fontenay 2004; Yerushalmi 2002).

The Legacy of Defense and the Role of the Military

Start-up firms initiated many of Israel's high-tech innovations. The Israeli start-up industry is described as resilient and innovative (e.g., Senor and Singer 2009) and perfectly poised to exploit a highly skilled labor force of scientists and engineers. It benefited from sound infrastructure in the form of supportive policies and available finance. Both popular and academic literature has devoted a great deal of effort in explaining the origin and impact of start-ups on the Israeli high-tech "miracle." The Caesarea Forum (2009, 9) summarized the main factors responsible for the growth of the industry as follows: a highly developed science and technology ethos; an excellent higher-education system; the availability of human capital; a highly developed defense R&D system that contributed to creation of the knowledge base and trained a skilled labor force; innovative governmental policies; an effective VC industry; a mature global market for ITC technologies; and an entrepreneurial spirit. Thus, innovative R&D and technological developments also became linked to national-security concerns, and consequently, the institutional environment in Israel; its civilian as well as military establishment provided incentives for innovation and entrepreneurship.

Senor and Singer (2009) claim that the proliferation of innovative start-ups (more than 6,000 since the early 1990s) can be attributed to both the culture and the history of nation building, which they describe as a mix of survival and a visionary outlook toward social and economic development. In particular, they see Israel's military legacy as a key driver of the high-tech industry (see also Breznitz 2007). The embodiment of this legacy is Gil Shwed, who, upon finishing his army service, built on his military experience to invent the *firewall* and, with comrades from the same unit, founded Checkpoint, the most successful software company in Israel—and globally prominent. Shwed and others like him—a group of adventurous and savvy entrepreneurs—are responsible for many of the industry's success stories. These entrepreneurs generally served in the army's elite intelligence-technology units, which select the brightest young high school graduates (mandatory military service in Israel starts at age 18). Known for encouraging experimentation, giving responsibility, and using state-of-the-art technology, these units are both a hotbed of technological innovation and a breeding ground for Israel's unique organizational culture. Avi, a serial entrepreneur who served in such unit, says,

> In 8200 [an Israeli Defense Force intelligence unit], you are encouraged to experiment, to think out of the box, to be critical, to raise the most difficult questions and provide the most creative answers. You are working with the best minds, all committed to the objective of performance against all odds. So when you have a technological idea that is worthy for a start-up, you already have a network of friends who are willing to go with you and are the best. (Interview, 2007)

Eventually, products and technologies that originated from Israel's military-industrial complex—for example, Rafael (the Armament Development Authority) and IAI (Israel Aircraft Industries)—became the foundation for its prosperous military-industrial exports. In particular, of the IDF's (Israeli Defense Force's) specialized technical units, the most notable are MAMRAM, the central IT center, and the more secretive 8200 (see also Honig, Lerner, and Raban 2006), which became the source of both "converted" technologies and the entrepreneurs who founded the majority of the most successful Israeli IT companies, including Checkpoint, RAD, Gilat, and Nice.

The infrastructure for technological innovation is embedded in the army's recruitment and organizational practices. The army locates the brightest and most gifted youths and recruits them for several key units, where they undergo intensive training in science and engineering and eventually become the nation's technological elite.

Even after mandatory long periods of service, they often stay with their units afterwards. Once they leave, however, these youths represent a valuable labor resource: highly skilled, innovative, and well versed in state-of-the-art technology. Such a reservoir of human capital played a significant role in shaping the high-tech industry that exists today, for a number of reasons. First, because the Israeli military is at the forefront of high-tech development, especially in wireless communications, networks, data security, and cryptography, privatized industries were able to capitalize on this innovation and excel in these fields. With the exception of cryptography, the army does not restrict soldiers and officers from working in their area of technological specialization after leaving. For example, electro-optics was first developed by military R&D in the 1960s and subsequently spawned privatized organizations. By the 1990s, there were about 150 Israeli firms specializing in this sector (de Fontenay and Carmel 2001).

Second, there is a functional benefit to army experience. Even though the military is an enormous organization, different units may act independently, thus offering recruits the opportunity to operate within a small- to medium-sized entity, much like the organizations they will go on to found or work in later in life. Officers in the army's special units not only develop the technical skills they need for future business ventures and entrepreneurial activity; they also assume great responsibility at a young age and take it upon themselves to essentially manage their units. These soldiers work long hours and learn to respond quickly to problems, approaching them creatively and becoming flexible and able to improvise when needed. They understand that they must find a solution and do whatever is necessary to get the job done. They learn to think broadly about overall strategy and mission, not just about specific tasks. They learn to work within a hierarchy, but with informal communication so that they can voice their own opinions. And they learn how to work in and coordinate teams, adopting the qualities of good leadership early on.

Finally, recruits gain networking skills and social capital during their service. Indeed, it has become a truism that mandatory military service in the Israeli army—especially in certain technological units—germinates innovative start-ups (Senor and Singer 2009). But beyond the individual skills just discussed, the service provides "social" input to prospective entrepreneurs. First, there are the personal networks recruits develop, which not only provide resources and information but also serve as a kind of affiliation that resembles a family or an order of devotees with a lifelong commitment to each other. Members of these networks have full trust in one another, share similar values, and count on their relationships as strong bonds of mutual help.

Many graduates of the army's technological units have noted the various benefits of this socialization, including the empowerment of its members through designating authority and encouraging autonomy, experimentation, and creative thinking. A start-up founder and graduate of the famous 8200 technological intelligence unit, explains:

> I served in the army's renowned technological unit for 15 years. My strategic and managerial logic is overshadowed by my military service. It was a secured and abundant environment. You get whatever resources you want and the best people. At the age of 20, you find yourself running huge and speculative projects on your own. There is no sense of risk or uncertainty. You

are encouraged to experiment as much as you like—there is no external or internal pressure. The need and motivation to perform originates from you and from the fact that you are surrounded by the brightest people you can imagine, and they perform. The system is tolerant to failures. In my time, there was not much accountability in terms of money or work plans. What mattered most [was] a drive to succeed, the personal pride of succeeding against the brightest. You were recognized by your successes, and so at an early age, I was moving up fast in the ranks and got the most challenging and technologically advanced projects. (Interview, 2005)

This culture of commitment and creativity encouraged many founders of new start-ups to search for both partners and employees among the graduates of their old units. One of the most successful entrepreneurs we spoke with, whose start-up was acquired by a large multinational for more than $300 million, describes why, in the early days of his firm, he recruited mainly workers from his ex-army unit:

I consciously decided that the first batch of employees would come from my military unit—people that I know and they know me. People that I can fully trust and by serving at the "unit," I could tell that they would do the job. We recruited every person who had served in the "unit" regardless of the expertise. We didn't define roles or build an organizational structure. We didn't do anything orderly; we didn't have a clue of the tasks at hand and the proper organizational structure to support them. We counted on people. We knew them along the years. We knew how they confront pressure. The people from the "unit" are not only talented, but they learn fast, can master various technologies, and are loyal. They think in terms of production and effectiveness. With such a group at founding, you don't need formal structure. (Interview, 2007)

Founders who had graduated from the army's elite technological units did not rely solely on their culture of "challenge and determination," characterized by accomplishing tasks through autonomy and creativity. They also borrowed their work routines and blueprint practices. In contrast to the standard "by the book" army model—overly hierarchical and structured with a strict chain of command—these units were extremely flexible and unstructured. One of the founders we interviewed, a graduate of the 8200, describes how this translated to the private sector:

In the firm, we use our army model. We don't have a structured way of doing things. Although we are composed of three work groups—hardware and integration, software, and components—we all are interdependent and closely integrated with one another. We the founders are sucked into operational roles, actively helping out in cases of bottlenecks. Strategic decisions concerned with development and market are taken first among the founders and then presented to the management. Allocation of crucial tasks [is] to the most competent people, regardless of their managerial status, and more than anything else, as in the "unit," we the founders have an open-door policy and spend time with programmers to debate and solve even the most trivial problem. (Interview, 2007)

In short, the legacy of these particular army units is their remarkable pool of talent, which gives entrepreneurs and founders a major incentive for establishing start-up companies. The technology developed for military purposes easily translates into ample opportunities for civil application and commercialization. Moreover, because army service in these units often involves a certain strategic and identity trajectory, it becomes the bedrock for a continual selection process in which those who are recruited are quite likely to become an important part of the Israeli start-up scene.

Networks

The Israeli high-tech industry is highly dependent on strong, tight social networks, which are crucial for mobilizing key resources needed in a firm's nascent days (Aldrich, Rosen, and Woodward 1987; Hite and Hesterly 2001; Saxenian 2002). Network connections may be particularly helpful in explaining the magnitude and scope of opportunity structures as well as of social and cultural capital (Hoang and Antoncic 2003). Analyzing the corporate social capital of Israeli software firms by applying network centrality and cohesion measures, Gabbay, Talmud, and Raz (2001) argue that the two elements of social structure—network position and geographical proximity—provide a dual gain of corporate social capital. The first gain is recognition, and the second is global bridging capacity. Gabbay and colleagues (2001) also demonstrate that the key players in the Israeli high-tech industry are in fact the linking agents for Israeli software firms and global capital and external markets. They serve as key identifiers for other firms of worthwhile investment and technological solutions in a highly uncertain market, operating according to the rules of the "new economy." A key position in the central clique thus provides corporate social capital. In this way, Israeli ITC entrepreneurs are benefiting from the fact that the cluster facilitates a wide range of accessible resources and services needed for both founding and operating new ventures.

The Israeli entrepreneurial networks' characteristics—their relational and structural composition, content, and strength—all influence the emergence and outcomes of the ITC sector. For example, the existing degree of relational embeddedness may affect the rate at which new ventures are established, as one cohort of successful firms spawns successive generations. As we noted earlier (and in Chapters 4 and 5), there is a pronounced tendency among Israeli high-tech entrepreneurs to recruit members of their former military units into their management or technology teams, facilitating high levels of trust in cross-border relationships (cf. Breznitz 2007). Leveraging ties developed in places such as the army and the university facilitates access to skilled experts and capital, including establishing relationships with critical actors such as suppliers and customers. Thus, through their dense networks, Israeli entrepreneurs are able to expand the trust base of their social and business relations (Lorenzoni and Lipparini 1999; Saxenian 2006), which provides them with critical information and advice (Hoang and Antoncic 2003), as well as legitimacy from the reputation of their network linkages (Shane and Cable 2002; Stuart, Hoang, and Hybels 1999).

Israel's high-tech networks consist of both local and overseas linkages. Following immigration, networks of destination provide primordial affinity that yields social capital in the form of affection and trust. This enhances business possibilities and cross-national partnerships, alleviating risk and uncertainty stemming from the complexity and unpredictability of global markets. For example, the so-called "bamboo networks" of loosely structured Chinese transnational businesses reflect the Confucian value system of familial affinity, which mandates solidarity, cooperation, harmony, and trust, and provides an environment conducive to the building of inter-network support for the members of a particular network (Fukuyama 1996; Weidenbaum and Hughes 1996). Similarly, Israeli entrepreneurs exploit their networks to leverage economic opportunities and resources for the establishment of their ventures. Many entrepreneurs whom we interviewed emphasized the width and depth of their network, which typically transcends national boundaries and reaches across different social spheres. The following scenario described by a high-tech entrepreneur is a case in point:

> When I just started, I got help from my army mates. Then another colleague, from the firm [at which] I work now, became a partner in a venture capital firm. The chief technology officer [CTO] joined this firm because he is friend of a friend—also from the army. I know the CEO of the biggest electronic firms in Israel; he is a remote relative of my father. He knew someone who immigrated to Israel from the United States and is well connected. At one time, he worked for an American laser company, representing them also here. He made a good impression on me. Here is someone that I can pay an Israeli salary, and he is an American who can work also in America. (Interview, 2008)

The dense networks—although providing accessibility of information, resources, and labor—are not always viewed as universally beneficial but sometimes as posing a burden to access. Thus, despite the supportive role of social networks, the social sphere also has a "dark side"—namely, the propensity to overlook efficiency or other important factors in favor of kin recruitment, nepotism, or favoritism. This is explained by a start-up founder as follows:

> I was recruiting people from the "unit" [8200]. It came to a point when I wasn't called to reserve service because my commanding officers complain[ed] that like the "Piper from Hamlin," people [were following] me and they [were] losing them. But as the company grew, I needed other people, more business-oriented and not just a bunch of tech enthusiasts. Then I had to let go many of those from the "unit." Their relative advantage in a start-up became a liability when we became a more established, larger firm. (Interview, 2007)

Evolutionary Perspectives on the Emergence of the High-Tech Industry

Numerous studies have reviewed the emergence and growth of the Israel high-tech industry by employing an evolutionary perspective to understand the policies that led to its unique development. The main thrust of this perspective is the assertion that initial organizational and institutional patterns follow a certain path that proves to be beneficial to the industry.

The Industry Life-Cycle Model

An influential stream of research on the evolution of the Israeli ITC sector has focused mainly on the policy process and its economic determinants. In this vein, Avnimelech along with Teubal and his associates (Avnimelech 2008; Avnimelech and Teubal 2003a, 2006, 2008; Justman and Teubal 1996; Teubal and Andersen 2000; Teubal 1993, 1997, 2002) have developed an integrative evolutionary life-cycle policy model and system approach that views the Israeli high-tech industry as essentially embedded in innovation-restructuring phases. These phases reflect a policy sequencing that predicts certain path dependencies of knowledge-based restructuring that co-evolves with local external effect.

Avnimelech (2008) and Avnimelech and Teubal (2006) present a five-phase cluster development model based on a case study of the development of the Israeli ITC cluster. The *background* phase begins with the appearance of high-tech activities; it is a period of experimentation by various agents in which capabilities and other relevant recourses are gradually accumulated. The *pre-emergence* phase, a distinctive part of the creation of background conditions, begins with the appearance of start-up companies, followed by extensive *variation* within this category. The accumulation of start-up-related experience enables *selection* of start-up-related features, which involves extensive structural changes in the cluster, including creation of new start-up forms of organization, new technological competencies, clear technological focal points, and cultural changes oriented toward increased acceptance of entrepreneurship. In turn, this process creates the preconditions for the cumulative growth process in the next phase. In the *emergence* phase, the VC industry emerges, and the start-up-intensive cluster grows rapidly. Emergence is generally followed by a *restructuring process* in order to reach *maturity*. Finally, the ability of the cluster to retain a significant level of diversity in terms of knowledge, types of agents, networks, and sources of new technologies determines its chances for undertaking a *renewal* process—that is, avoiding lock-in and decline.

Industry life-cycle perspectives assume change processes that guide industry evolution through a predetermined sequence of stages. Industries imminently evolve from start-up through growth and harvest to termination as a result of specific event sequences and generative mechanisms. For example, innovation life-cycle theory (Abernathy and Utterback 1978) identifies three stages of industry evolution that correspond to major shifts in industrial innovation, market structure, and competition. In the early (fluid) stage, intense product innovation leads to radical designs and technological diversity, with rapid entry of specialized competitors that respond to emerging opportunities and low entry barriers. In the intermediate (growth) stage, a dominant design emerges and the industry gradually grows through output and process innovation. The number of competitors declines with the increasing focus on product differentiation. Finally, in the maturity stage product innovation becomes incremental, with process innovation leading to cost reduction. Avnimelech and Teubal use life-cycle theory in numerous studies to claim that the Israeli case exhibits a unique model of start-up clusters, which co-evolved in phases that can be explained through the processes of variation, selection, and retention (e.g., Aldrich and Ruef 2006). The evolution of the industry represents a cumulative process, which is path-dependent. Path-dependent theory assumes that the strategic choices of key actors are responsible for the nature of new-industry evolution, including the prospects that an industry can become locked in to less than optimal ways (David 1994; Hargadon and Douglas 2001; Sydow, Schreyögg, and Koch 2009). Certainly, external shocks of an economic, political, or technological nature can alter these less than optimal directions; when the shocks take place, new investment paths may be taken up and old ones abandoned (Vergne and Durand 2010). Thus, path dependence implies that initial patterns persist into the future, while environmental shocks determine the nature and content of change. Path dependence is influenced mainly by the initial conditions that shaped the early days of the industry and by environmental intervention in the form of governmental policies that stimulated the growth of the Israeli start-up cluster. Avnimelech (2008) contends that, in Israel's case, the evolutionary model is defined as a transition from phase to phase determined by "selection and production" of certain variables:

> In the Israeli case, these include the identification of some technological areas with [the] potential competitive advantage of Israeli companies such as data security, enterprise software, computer networking, IC design, DSP and other communication-related technologies, the creation of some key companies that would eventually become significant source[s] of spin-off and imitation, the selection of the LP VC organizational form as the dominant design, experience with IPOs in NASDAQ, and the first IPOs of very young Israeli startups in NASDAQ. (p. 33)

Thus, the industry life-cycle perspective relates industry evolution to time-dependent changes rather than to contextual events that shape industries at their embryonic stage. Industry characteristics are assumed constant during each stage and do not account for industry heterogeneity. The prospects of organizations are ascribed to their ex ante capabilities, and even if managing to develop optimal strategies, the organizations' actions are considered independent.

The Takeoff Perspective

Fiegenbaum (2007), utilizing a strategic *takeoff* paradigm, also attempted to understand the emergence of the Israeli high-tech industry. The Israeli high-tech takeoff occurred in line with numerous factors that intersected during the 1990s. These included Israel's incorporation into the global economy and the transformation of its society and economy—in particular, policy changes oriented toward privatization and neoliberalism. These policy changes also encouraged technology-based multinational corporations (MNCs) to establish subsidiaries in Israel and take advantage of the country's highly technological skilled labor force. Furthermore, the shift toward privatization and market-oriented economic policy created a competitive environment for Israeli high-tech, including several business opportunities that improved the competitive potential of many Israeli industries in international markets. Fiegenbaum (2007) summarizes this process as follows:

> The strategic position of foreign firms was superior to that of local firms; hence, the inferior position of Israeli firms motivated them to search for new strategic solutions. In summary, such changes on the global level as increasing globalization, the entry of foreign firms and privatization of government corporations exposed inchoate Israeli High-Tech industries into a new international environment whose challenges clearly stimulated the industry's takeoff. (p. 21)

The success of Israeli high-tech, then, was highly contingent on a global prevalence of new technologies and maturity of the markets. Takeoff is dependent on reaching a certain degree of maturity that allows the industrial sector to take advantage of global integration. However, it should be noted that the dominance of the start-up model, the overwhelming founding of start-ups that either die or remain small or medium size, is considered a constraint on the growth of high-tech to a mature stage. In this stage, companies may better exploit their initial innovation by achieving a competitive position in the market. Thus, the Israeli high-tech model is based on innovative breakthroughs and technological leadership in niche markets. However, it sidesteps the issues associated with operational management and the tedious task of building organizations that integrate well in the global economy with its complex structures and strategies. As Orna Berry, the former head of the OCS, comments:

> I think that establishing "built-to-last" companies in Israel is difficult because of management problems and low operational capabilities. We are better in short-term issues. Innovation is relatively short-term. It involves lots of adrenalin and, sometimes, quick results. When you finish with discovering [one thing], you move on to a new idea. The tedious work of production, infrastructure, logistics, or sales is less attractive to us. (Interview, 2007)

Policy Mechanisms That Shape the Industry Evolutionary Path

The emergence of Israel's high-tech industry[5] is embedded in the country's industrial policy, which, in turn, is related to Israel's strive for self reliance and pursuit of global opportunities for its emerging high-tech industry.

The Formation of R&D Policy

Since the early days of statehood Israel's policies have been designed to harness available resources for the creation of a competitive edge in areas considered vital—primarily national security and nation building. Thus, institutional building of technology policy during the 1990s provided ample industrial R&D funds for innovation restructuring and, to a lesser extent, for technological infrastructure (Breznitz 2006; Teubal 2002; Trachtenberg 2001). This policy acted as a powerful moderator in promoting the development of the ITC and Internet sectors and their subsequent success in the global market.[6] The backbone of this policy was the development of local innovative capabilities, the creation of a local VC industry, and various incentive programs for entrepreneurs.

For example, the focus on R&D-based technological entrepreneurship makes the Israel ITC sector an innovative force that harnesses resources from a number of areas: academia, the defense industry, army technological units, skilled engineering-oriented immigrants from Russia, and a score of returnees, including Israeli technological entrepreneurs who have returned from the United States. In addition, as Breznitz (2007) contends,

> The focus on R&D motivates the industry to develop specific business models based on a particular relationship with advanced countries. In the case of Israel, this over-reliance on R&D and the state's drive to develop a particular relationship with the American market are the reasons for its spectacular success in the 1990s, as well as some will argue the main source of its weakness. (p. 148)

Indeed, the ITC sector has been able to capture a big chunk of Israeli R&D capacity, as virtually every prominent technology powerhouse in the United States, including giants such as IBM, Cisco, Google, and Microsoft, has an R&D subsidiary in Israel.

The Venture Capital Industry

The history of the Israeli venture capital industry began in a unique government policy that provided seed capital for financial institutions that expressed interest in investing in the emerging high-tech industry.[7] Avnimelech and Teubal (2008) assert that in Israel the VC-start-up co-evolution had already begun in the early 1980s, with the emergence of the modern ITC and software industries. The availability of global capital intersected with policy mechanisms created by the Israeli government, fostering emergence of the VC industry, which strongly supported Israeli high-tech's start-up activities. VCs not only provided capital but also disseminated knowledge regarding technology and markets using connections between founders and professional managers. Furthermore, the establishment of the VC industry intersected with the high demand for capital from the ever-growing number of start-ups during the 1990s, also it and benefited tremendously from hospitable government policies, a calmer geopolitical environment, and neoliberal, market-oriented policies coupled with privatization and easing currency regulations.

The Office of the Chief Scientist

The policy framework consisted of two components. First, it provided financial incentives for individual investors and entrepreneurs regardless of their industrial priorities. Second, it promoted (mainly defense-oriented) R&D in higher education and at national laboratories, and established technological incubators. Breznitz (2007) claims that the thrust of this policy's framework resulted in the development of R&D capabilities, routines, and cultures that are restructuring the entire economy (p. 146). Championed by the OCS, the policy evolved during the 1970s and was integrated into a set of tools that boosted national innovation by catering to the supply of and demand for R&D and enhancing technological and development capabilities and skills. The result, as Breznitz (2007) demonstrates, "created a base of sophisticated customers side by side with an IT industrial base. In turn, this change triggered a process of self reinforcing sequences, both strengthening and demanding more R&D-based products as well as products to solve R&D-related issue[s]" (p. 1467).

The OCS is considered a source that is readily available and "democratic," in the sense that it applies the same meritocratic criteria for its grants based on the feasibility of business and technological plans. For young start-ups, grants from the OCS served as a signal of legitimacy to other potential investors, underwriting their feasibility and appropriateness. In addition, OCS support lowered the risk associated with founding a new venture, as the return model for its grants was connected to royalties and only tied to revenues. From a series of interviews with various founders in the ITC sector, we can conclude that placing the risk with the OCS and not with the entrepreneurs was a dominant factor in the Israeli start-up boom. For new ventures, these grants not only enabled "gambling with government money," as one of the founders comments, but also—and perhaps more important—moved scarce resources from R&D to other purposes, such as marketing and business development. The latter activities are crucial to the survival of young ventures, especially during the early stages of the life cycle (Ruef 2005). As a founder who established his company with OCS grants explains:

When we started, the OCS was our first option. We got money for our R&D activities, including money for wages. The fact that we got the grant helped us to raise additional funds from VCs and to finish relatively uninterrupted the prototype of our product. For us, it was risk-free money. I liked the incentives model, including the return of royalties following the generation of revenues. If the OCS's grant had been based on even a comfortable loan, we would not have taken it. The fact that the OCS was paying for R&D created a kind of partnership. The OCS complements the VCs. Today [2007], the OCS money is essential, as other sources are drying up. During the late 1990s, when VC money was abundant, the OCS money was considered "bad money," with too many obligations attached. Today, and usually in times of crisis, firms, including the big ones, are returning to the OCS for grants or participating in one of the joint programs with other industries or with academia, like Magnet. (Interview, 2007)

In spite of the OCS's contribution to the ITC sector, founders still encountered numerous policy-related and bureaucratic obstacles. Over the years, the allocated budget of the OCS dropped and, in accordance, the terms of its grants worsened. This included the lowering of the percentage of support for R&D projects from 50 to 30 percent. One of the CEOs of an ITC firm contends,

Over the years, the bureaucracy become more and more disconnected from what we as a company needed. So when we submitted grants, their evaluation was farfetched. From my experience, the OCS lost its idealism and drive and what remains is "grey." They canceled a few of our projects, and eventually, we gave up on them. Anyhow, we were acquired by an American company. (Interview, 2006)

Another constraint mentioned by recipients of OCS grants concerns the limitation placed on disseminating and transferring knowledge outside Israel. Generally, the CEOs we interviewed claim that this legal limitation hampered their competitive advantage, especially with regard to competitors from China and India. Many interviewees noted that, contrary to constraints placed on certain partnerships outside Israel—including production—the OCS did not place any substantial constraints on Israeli companies acquired by foreign entities or on those that registered at stock exchanges outside Israel. A CEO of a major ITC firm that is also production-oriented, testifies:

I don't understand the OCS logic. The moment we are starting to grow, we are required to return the money we received and we have to comply with a series of constraints regarding the sharing of knowledge or production. We are a global village, and constraints on knowledge sharing leave us in an inferior position vis-a-vis our competitors. We are witnessing the trend of moving the R&D elsewhere, mainly to India and China. We shouldn't do it. This is going to hit us in our soft spots and ruin the crucial advantage we have here. If we move our R&D, and even our production, outside, and the government is not helping to create a supportive policy environment, as was done in the 1990s, companies like Comverse will leave [for] China. (Interview, 2009)

OCS perceives the lowering of risk as a requirement for encouraging innovations. Practically speaking, it operates in two modes—on the one hand, providing funds according to VC principles and risking its return on investment; on the other, assuming the role of meeting national objectives for developing innovation and R&D. Reconciling the two is justified, according to a senior officer of the OSC:

> Our purpose is lowering the firm's risk and not to allocate money. This makes us sensitive to the idea that we are willing to take the burden of loss, because on the national level, the knowledge developed still remains in the country. People are moving from one place to another and are using it. Although this is our attitude, still we are responsible for the public and the government, and we want to put our meager resources to the best . . . use and not be a source of income for those who know how to exploit the support we give. We are looking not only at the benefit for the individual firm but also attempting to design policies that will enhance the high-tech global competitive advantage. This is why we put such a strong emphasis on innovation. (Interview, 2009)

The firms, however, have different priorities: They are more concerned with their business development than with only R&D. The CEO of an ITC firm explains:

> The OCS wants innovation and to see new developments, but it is not always our main priority. Sometimes, we need funds to develop in a direction that the OSC doesn't see as the state of the art but that means business opportunities for us. For example, taking a product and enhancing its performance requires lots of resources, but the OCS doesn't see this as innovative enough to support. But doing it means improving the products and even lowering the cost. For this, the OCS won't give money. This is problematic, because we suffer from an excess of ideas but little capacity for implementation. After you are done with the technology, you need to succeed in the market. Success is not necessarily developing new technology—it is also in marketing and quality. We are good in ideas, innovation, and searching for new directions, but less good in quality and marketing. (Interview, 2009)

Returnees

Many Israeli expatriates worked for global multinationals such as Intel, IBM, Motorola, Microsoft, and Cisco, in leading ITC clusters such as Silicon Valley. These transnational entrepreneurs became a crucial bridge between the local ITC industry and the global market. Consider the testimony of an Israeli entrepreneur who situated the R&D division of his business in Israel and the operations and sales office in New York:

> Luckily enough, I'm familiar with the American sales culture, since I have a silk-tie business in San Francisco and have to manage an army of salespersons. I know that, although my main business is in Israel, I still have to be hands-on with my sales force here in the United States if I want to see results. So I'm not only a bridge between these people and their clients and the technical geeks back in Israel, but I also bring in aggressive sales techniques, which have served me well in my tie business. (Interview 2007)

Changes in the county's legal, regulatory, and policy regimes significantly enhanced the social capital of the Israeli high-tech industry. In Israel, immigration policy granting immediate citizenship to Diaspora Jews allowed the country to absorb nearly 1 million immigrants from the former Soviet Union (Remennick 2007). This policy of absorption and initiatives for developing the high-tech industry led to the implementation of special programs such as the "incubator" program that provided Russian engineers and scientists with employment and business opportunities (Wylie 2011; Yerushalmi 2002). The high number of skilled engineers among the Russian immigrants provided the human capital needed for an emergent high-tech industry. Thus, Israeli transnational entrepreneurs could benefit from two types of state policies: a national, ideological immigration policy concerning the absorption of skilled engineers from the former Soviet Union and economic incentives and policies.

Furthermore, the clustering process was facilitated by a strong VC industry, which co-evolved with the ITC sector and developed the ability to link with global markets. The availability of infrastructure, skilled technological labor, and access to capital and markets thus attracted Israeli high-tech entrepreneurs, who re-established their base in Israel. One "returnee" describes this process:

> I was cushioned when I came back. I became a partner in one of the government-subsidized technological incubators, which were founded for the sake of absorbing the Russian immigration. So I had access to highly skilled engineers, at a lower cost, as well as a grant from the [Office of the] Chief Scientist. My first business deal from Israel was with the company I worked for in Texas. (Interview, 2009)

The institutions and structures of Israeli high-tech provided the ideal environment in which to exploit the knowledge and expertise of skilled immigrants in founding and managing firms—in particular, the ability to mobilize readily available local resources (Stinchcombe 1965; Aldrich and Fiol 1994). The *availability of resources*, mainly through government incentives and the societal conditions that prevailed between the 1970s and the 1990s, provided a competitive advantage that enabled Israelis like Dov Frohman (a co-founder of Intel) to initiate high-tech businesses while creating a new model based on complementary tasks and resources both in Israel and abroad. A returnee who founded the communication infrastructure for broadband service explains:

> A huge contribution to the development of the Israeli high-tech [industry] should attribute to people like Dov Frohman [the founder of Intel Israel] and the like. We started in the United States, where the seeds of knowledge and founding firms were planted. When we moved back to Israel, we tailored our knowledge and experience to the Israeli context. There is no better school than working in an established American company to learn to do things correctly, to adapt appropriate business models, and then immigrate with it to Israel. The atmosphere in Israel changed. Six years ago, I would have been considered *Yored* a Hebrew word with a bad connotation for those who immigrate. Now we bring in our experience, connections, and our ability to create business opportunities. Don't be mistaken—it's not only us (the technology people), but you also see returnees who are bankers, accountants, and marketing people. We bring huge value-added by bridging the needs of the American market with the Israeli high-tech capabilities. We know how to harness the Israeli creativity and translate it to the American standards and market. So, now my business spans countries and there's an allocation of tasks. Here in Israel, we are doing mainly R&D and technical support and, in the U.S., business development and marketing. I could say that the real headquarters are here, but I spend lots of time in the United States, where our customers are. (Interview, 2009)

Crisis and Decline

Recently, there have been several critics who questioned the survival chances of the Israeli high-tech industry given the global financial crisis. *The Marker*, a leading economic Israeli newspaper, describes the crisis this way:

> The big question is whether Israel is willing to lose this industrial sector, which produced not only a positive image as an innovative state, but was also a sector that nourished the rest of the [h]igh-tech industry, beyond its direct production. This is a sector in which the laid-off workers move away to work for foreign R&D centers that believe in the extraordinary Israeli qualities. This is a sector in which its workers return to work in more established companies if the start-up fails. This is a sector that has paid, over the last years, billions of IS in state taxes. Ladies and gentlemen, the start-up nation is decaying. (*The Marker–IT Computerworld*, June 29, 2010)

During the 1990s, the high-tech industry became the major powerhouse of the Israeli economy.[8] However, the industry's strengths and rapid growth are also seen as the reason for the general weakness experienced by non-high-tech industrial sectors. As high-tech grew five times as fast as the rest of the economy, the country experienced wide-ranging disparities, including the creation of a "dual economy." On the one hand, a well-developed, modern high-tech industry, with its own set of incentive policies, employment criteria, salaries, and spatial-cluster concentration, benefited the more affluent (mainly central) regions of the country. On the other hand, the rest of the country's industrial sectors came to be perceived as less technologically advanced, less efficient, and, consequently, less privileged in terms of policy priorities, employment, and salaries. This state of affairs contributed to rising socioeconomic inequality, which remains high on the Israeli public agenda. Furthermore, the success of high-tech is based on exporting its innovation and technology, so the benefit is realized mostly abroad with only some internal spillover. The Israeli start-up culture has sought short-term gains, mostly by selling off to U.S.-based corporations.[9]

Israel's entrepreneurial culture of exit is blamed on shortsightedness and a focus on immediate monetary return—with less attention to other important facets of business development, especially marketing and formulating strategies for growth and sustainability. In a time of crisis, start-ups also suffer from the "liability of smallness." In other words, companies lack the resources, legitimacy, and resilience necessary for survival, which renders them more vulnerable to market and economic fluctuations (Aldrich and Ruef 2006). In times of crisis, VCs tend to engage in "wholesaling" to save their investment, regardless of the long-term prospects or the quality of the start-ups in which they had invested. As Y. Oron, founder and partner of the VC Vertex, claims, "We see typical VCs' reaction to a crisis situation. There are many companies with superb technology, but [they] require lots of money from us to become profitable or even balanced. In this situation, we prefer to sell our holdings and lose money" ("The Sad Wholesale of the Israeli High-Tech," *Kalkalist*, November 22, 2009, p. 8). The VCs' rationale is that many start-ups are prone to go bankrupt in a crisis, imposing an excessive financial burden in terms of employee compensation or servicing operational debt. Furthermore, the start-up culture, which is built on strong networks, competitiveness, and a distinct task-oriented employment model (Baron and Hannan 2005), tends to crack under pressure. According to the CTO of one start-up that is being acquired by a large U.S. corporation,

> This is my third start-up, and I'm burning out. On the face of it, you work with people who are [as] competitive as you, highly motivated by success and highly committed—they can't bear a situation of not achieving their goal. It is a culture of promise, even if you can't deliver at the point of promise. But with the crisis, the solidarity evaporates—no compassion, no care for the worker, not a word about their contributions. For the founders, the people are disposable; what they care about is how much they can make out of their sinking boat. (Interview, 2009)

The recent financial crisis (2007–2010) has brought to the fore the need to support technology and innovation based on their own merits. This is seen as the fundamental aspect of the Israeli government's latest policy ethos and as the major competitive advantage of Israeli high-tech. Additionally, it accentuates the fact that, from 2000 through 2010, R&D policies underwent very minor modifications and the budget allocated to high-tech through government incentives was stalled (Cohen 2009).[10] Alarmed, the government has declared a new set of policies to provide a "lifeboat for the high-tech" ("Lifeboat for the High-Tech," *Kalkalist*, July 9, 2010). Some observers focus mainly on tax exemptions for various investments and sustainability activities, such as improving technology-related education; encouraging the build-up of medium and large companies; supporting innovative technologies for service sectors such as finance; reducing the OCS's financial return on its support in certain cases; providing guarantees for institutional investors; and consolidating the polices of the various government R&D agencies.

In sum, this appendix has sought to answer the question: How did the Israeli high-tech industry emerge and evolve? Three predominant answers have come out of the existing literature: (1) the process of cluster formation; (2) the co-evolution of the industry as a series of stages; and (3) the consequences of planned policy. Our review of this industry has presented the social and historical conditions and the major factors that shaped its nature and structure, including the role of the army's special technological units, which bred a virtually perfect labor force. We have also traced the context and evolution of government policies that influenced the high-tech industry, explaining how entrepreneurs were able to create space for a start-up culture built on Israel's state-specific societal and geopolitical conditions.

Notes

Chapter 1

1. On the process of spawning and its different models, see Klepper (2009) as well as Chapter 3 of this book.

Chapter 2

1. Although various studies see the institutional and ecological theories as competing or at least engaging in understanding different organizational aspects (DiMaggio and Powell 1983; Scott 2001), there are some that see them as complementary (see, e.g., Suchman, forthcoming) claims that, although organizational ecology focuses on operational resources (raw material that supports organizational survival) and institutional theory focuses on constitutive information (basic roles that determine organizational structure), both are consistent with the organization's institutional ecology. Both resources and information flows co-evolve, and an understanding of the evolution of a certain community of organization would need the integration of these two flows.

2. For example, the composition of top management teams can be an indicator of "position imprints"—that is, the past organizational positions of top management teams that consequently shape management blueprints, practices, or norms (Beckman and Burton 2008; Burton and Beckman 2007).

3. The issue of pre-entry, or pre-founding, experience is discussed extensively in the spinoff literature. For example, Klepper (2001) distinguishes between founders who gain their experience working in the same industry and those who acquire experience in a different industry. Furthermore, Klepper (2001, 2009) terms new ventures founded by experienced entrepreneurs *de alio* and those founded by inexperienced entrepreneurs (without work experience in a related area of their new venture) *de novo*. In this vein, liability of newness (Stinchcombe 1965) can be curtailed by a founding team with pre-entry experience, meaning that the team's skills, knowledge, or routines are a corollary of work experience in a related field of their new venture.

Chapter 3

1. This threefold ideology actually dictated the objectives of the labor movement institutions (the Histadrut—the General Federation of Labor and its economic arm—Hevrat Ha'Ovdim), which actually controlled and navigated the economic and political

paths of the pre-born country. For example, the first goal of Hevrat Ha'Ovdim dealt with national and economic elements—participation in the establishment of the de-mographic and economic territorial infrastructure of the Jewish settlements in Israel (Palestine) by expanding its geographical spread, accelerating the development of the local economy, and creating employment opportunities for Jewish immigrants. The second goal, in contrast, was social—the advancement of the working class by reduc-ing equalities in income and private ownership of property. This was accomplished by preventing worker exploitation and advancing the development of welfare, educational, and, cultural services.

2. Ha Histadrut HaKlalit shel Ha Ovdim B'EretzYisrael (General Federation of Labor in the Land of Israel), known as the Histadrut, is Israel's the Israeli organization of trade unions. Established in December 1920 during the British Mandate for Palestine, it has become one of Israel's most powerful institutions. The Histadrut was founded in December 1920 in Haifa to look out for the interests of Jewish workers. It is now a mainstay of the Labor Zionist movement and, aside from being a trade union, its state-building role has made it the owner of a number of businesses and factories and, for a time, the largest employer in the country. Membership in the Histadrut grew from 4,400 in 1920 to 1,600,000 in 1983 (including dependents), accounting for more than one-third of the total population of Israel and about 85 percent of all wage earners. Ap-proximately 170,000 Histadrut members are Arabs (who were admitted to membership starting in 1959). In 1989, the Histadrut was the employer of approximately 280,000 workers. With the increasing liberalization and deregulation of the Israeli economy since the 1980s, the Histadrut's role and size have declined, although it still remains a powerful force in Israeli society and the nation's economy.

3. Through its economic arm, Hevrat Ha'Ovdim (Society of Workers), the His-tadrut owns and operates a number of enterprises, including the country's largest in-dustrial conglomerates (Solel Boneh, Koor) as well as its largest bank (Bank Hapoalim).

4. In his extensive review of the political influence on early industrialization in Israel, David Levi-Faur (2001) contends that in the mid-1950s the ownership struc-ture of industry was composed as follows: 60 percent private sector, 20 percent union (Histadrut and Hevrat Ha'Ovdim, respectively), and 20 percent government (see also Barkai 1990).

5. At the Constitutional Convention of Hevrat Ha'Ovdim in 1923, David Ben Gu-rion attempted to define the goals of the Public Works Office in utilitarian terms—namely, that administrative enterprises are tools for the achievement of economic goals, are socially oriented toward the future, and are a method of increasing workers' ability to manage their work by themselves.

6. Over the years, Bynet developed other domains of specialization such as telecom, computing, and networking. Maintaining a high level of technological expertise in mul-tiple disciplines enabled the company to deliver specialized solutions that are unique to each business area. Today, Bynet provides a comprehensive range of end-to-end solu-tions and professional services that meet the rapidly evolving IT and telecom needs of companies in Israel and across the globe.

Chapter 4

1. We have cases where the founders had rich employment histories before founding their own firms. For the purpose of building the genealogy, we referred only to the last employment. In the case of employment information missing from the founders' bios (provided by the IVC data), we personally contacted the founder or used other sources, such as Web searches, for filling in the necessary information.

Appendix

1. According to the government's Investment Promotion Center. ("Venture Capital in Israel," Invest in Israel, Investment Promotion Center, http://www.investinisrael.gov .il/NR/exeres/A19A138D-87A7-416B-8D62-1C968E035E13.htm.)

2. http://www.investinisrael.gov.il/NR/exeres/A19A138D-87A7-416B-8D62-1C968E035E13.htm.

3. Various reports discuss the growth indicators of the Israeli high-tech industry during the 1990s in terms of exports, employment, investments, or number of start-ups or IPOs on the NASDAQ, all of which demonstrate impressive and unprecedented growth in comparison with other industrialized nations (Cohen 2009; Caesarea Forum 2009). For example, during the 1990s, the industry attracted approximately $13 billion in VC investment, second only to that in the United States (Caesarea Forum 2009, 13). Furthermore, 43 percent of engineers and scientists are employed in foreign R&D centers established by major U.S. technology firms and European giants, such as Microsoft, Google, Cisco, Motorola, Applied Material, and Siemens.

4. The number of start-up companies in Israel during the period 1999–2000 was estimated at 3,500 to 4,000 (Carmel and de Fontenay 2004).

5. The sector consists mainly of software, data communications, electro-optics, hardware design, and Internet technologies and content.

6. In 2000, the Israeli high-tech industry employed 148,000 people (one-third of whom were scientists and engineers), generated $15 billion, and contributed 71 percent of the country's GDP growth (Carmel and de Fontenay 2004). Furthermore, Israeli firms listed on the NASDAQ outnumbered any other country's, excluding the United States and Canada (Carmel and de Fontenay 2004).

7. The formation of the Israeli VC industry, as we know it today, can be traced back to 1993, when the government decided to establish a Fund of Funds known as the Yozma Program ("Initiative" in Hebrew). Prior to 1993, there was only one VC fund operating in the country. The Yozma Program caused a dramatically positive change in the perception of foreign VC investors and their attitude toward investing in Israel. Under the program, ten new VC funds were formed that managed $20 million. Yozma's share of each was 40 percent; the foreign investors', 60 percent. Yozma also directly invested $20 million through a government-owned Yozma 1 Fund, which started operating in 1993 (it was privatized in 1997). Six were founded in 1993: Gemini, Star, Concord, Pitango, Walden, and Invantech; one in 1994: JVP; two in 1995: Medica and EuroFund; and one in 1997: Vertex. The total capital raised by Yozma funds was about $250 million ($100 million out of its government capital), which invested in over 200 start-up companies.

8. The potency of the Israeli high-tech industry is always presented through a series of performance statistics. For example: Israel is second in the world (after California) in founding start-ups (on average, more than 200 a year); Israel is the world's fourth in U.S. patents per capita (a total of 7,652 between 1980 and 2000); Israel has the world's highest R&D expenditure as a percentage of GDP (4.9 percent in 2009—although most of it comes from the business sector, while the government's R&D contribution has steadily declined from 2001 through 2010); Israeli high-tech accounted for 50 percent ($21 billion) of total industrial exports in 2008, while employing only 6.8 percent (approximately 70,000) of the labor force in 2007; in terms of VC investment, Israel is third in the world in VC-funded start-ups (378); and finally, but not least, relative to the size of the population, Israel has more engineers per capita (135 engineers per 10,000 people) than the United States (85 per capita) (Getz et al. 2005).

9. Some of the most notable acquisitions by U.S. corporations are summarized in the following table:

Acquisition price (in millions of dollars)	Year	Israeli company	Acquirer
407	1998	Mirabilis	America Online
1,600	1999	DSP	Intel
4,800	2000	Chromatics	Lucent
2,700	2000	Galileo	Marvel
780	2000	Visiontech	Broadcom
620	2005	Shopping.com	eBay Inc.
4,500	2006	Mercury	Hewlett-Packard
1,550	2006	M-Systems	SanDisk

10. For example, the budget of the OCS was cut from IS 1.62 billion in 2010 to IS 1.3 for 2011.

Government of Israel, ministry of Industry, Commerce and Employment, The Office of Chief Scientist: Ongoing Programs (Hebrew). http://www.moital.gov.il/NR/rdonlyres/F03510EF-4C99-4AD7-8E99-92827A0F1809/0/nochnit2011.pdf.

References

Abernathy, W., and J. M. Utterback. 1978. "Patterns of Industrial Innovation." *Technology Review* 80 (7): 41–47.

Agarwal, R., R. Echambadi, A. M. Franco, and M. B. Sarkar. 2004. "Knowledge Transfer through Inheritance: Spinout Generation, Development and Survival." *Academy of Management Journal* 47 (4): 501–522.

Aharoni, Y. 1976. *Structure and Performance in the Israeli Economy*. Tel Aviv: Cherikover Press.

———. 1991. *The Political Economy of Israel*. Tel Aviv: Am Oved.

———. 1993. *The Israeli Economy: A Retrospective View*. IASPS Policy Study 16. Tel Aviv: Institute for Advanced Strategic and Political Studies.

———. 2007. "New Business Elites." In *New Elites in Israel*, edited by E. Ben-Rafael and Y. Sternberg, 80–113. Jerusalem: Bialik Institute.

Akzin, B. 1955. "The Role of Parties in Israeli Democracy." *Journal of Politics* 17 (4): 507–545.

Aldrich, E. H., and M. C. Fiol. 1994. "Fools Rush In? The Institutional Context of Industry Creation." *Academy of Management Review* 19 (4): 645–670.

Aldrich, E. H., B. Rosen, and B. Woodward. 1987. "The Impact of Social Networks on Business Founding and Profit: A Longitudinal Study." In *Frontiers of Entrepreneurship Research*, edited by N. Churchill et al., 154–168. Wellesley, MA: Center for Entrepreneurial Studies.

Aldrich, E. H., and M. Ruef. 2006. *Organizations Evolving*. 2nd ed. London: Sage.

Aldrich, E. H., and G. Wiedenmayer. 1993. "From Traits to Rates: An Ecological Perspective on Organizational Foundlings." In *Advances in Entrepreneurship, Firm Emergence, and Growth*, edited by J. Katz and R. Brockhaus, 145–195. Greenwich, CT: JAI Press.

Anton, J. J., and D. A. Yao. 1995. "Start-Ups, Spin-Offs, and Internal Projects." *Journal of Law, Economics, and Organization* 11 (2): 362–378.

Arthur, W. B. 1989. "Competing Technologies, Increasing Returns, and Lock-In by Historical Events." *Economic Journal* 99 (394): 116–131.

———. 1994. *Increasing Returns and Path Dependence in the Economy*. Ann Arbor: University of Michigan Press.

Avnimelech, G. 2008. "A Five-Phase Entrepreneurial Oriented Innovation and Technology Policy Profile: The Israeli Experience." *European Planning Studies* 16 (1): 81–98.

Avnimelech, G., and M. Teubal. 2003a. "Evolutionary Venture Capital Policies: Insights from a Product Life Cycle Analysis of Israel's Venture Capital Industry." Working Paper Series, Science, Technology, and the Economy Program (STE), Samuel Neaman Institute for Advanced Studies in Science and Technology, Technion–Israel Institute of Technology, Haifa.

———. 2003b. "Israel's Venture Capital Industry: Emergence, Operation and Impact." In *The Growth of Venture Capital: A Cross-Cultural Comparison*, edited by D. Cetindamar, 207–240. Westport, CT: Praeger.

———. 2004. "Venture Capital Start-Up Co-evolution and the Emergence and Development of Israel's New High Tech Cluster." *Economics of Innovation and New Technology* 13 (1): 33–60.

———. 2006. "Creating VC Industries Which Co-evolve with High Tech: Insights from an Extended Industry Life Cycle (ILC) Perspective to the Israeli Experience." *Research Policy* 35 (10): 1477–1498.

———. 2008. "From Direct Support of Business Sector R&D/Innovation to Targeting Venture Capital/Private Equity: A Catching-Up Innovation and Technology Policy Life Cycle Perspective." *Economics of Innovation and New Technology* 17 (1): 153–171.

Bankman, J., and R. J. Gilson. 1999. "Why Start-Ups?" *Stanford Law Review* 51 (2): 289–308.

Bank of Israel. 2005. *Bank of Israel Annual Report—2004*. Jerusalem: Bank of Israel.

———. 2006. *Bank of Israel Annual Report—2005*. Jerusalem: Bank of Israel.

———. 2007. *Bank of Israel Annual Report—2006*. Jerusalem: Bank of Israel.

Barak, B. 1987. "The Measures of Success." *Tadiran Monthly Newsletter*, May 22–23.

Barkai, H. 1990. *The Early Days of the Israeli Economy*. Jerusalem: Bialik Institute.

Baron, J. N., M. D. Burton, and M. T. Hannan. 1996. "Road Taken: Origins and Evolution of Employment Systems in Emerging Companies." *Industrial and Corporate Change* 5 (2): 239–275.

———. 1999. "Building the Iron Cage: Determinants of Managerial Intensity in the Early Years of Organizations." *American Sociological Review* 64 (4): 527–547.

Baron, J. N., and M. T. Hannan. 2002. "Organizational Blueprints for Success in High-Tech Start-Ups: Lessons from the Stanford Project on Emerging Companies." *California Management Review* 44 (3): 8–36.

———. 2005. "The Economic Sociology of Organizational Entrepreneurship: Lessons from the Stanford Project on Emerging Companies." In *The Economic Sociology of Capitalism*, edited by V. Nee and R. Swedberg, 168–203. Princeton, NJ: Princeton University Press.

Baum, J. A. C., and H. Rao. 2004. "Dynamics of Organizational Populations and Communities." In *Handbook of Organizational Change and Innovation*, edited by M. S. Poole and A. H. Van de Ven, 212–258. Oxford: Oxford University Press.

Baum, J. A. C., and J. V. Singh. 1994. "Organizational Niches and the Dynamics of Organizational Founding." *Organization Science* 5 (4): 483–501.

Beckman, C. M. 2006. "The Influence of Founding Team Company Affiliations on Firm Behavior." *Academy of Management Journal* 49 (4): 741–758.

Beckman, C. M., and M. D. Burton. 2008. "Founding the Future: Path Dependence in the Evolution of Top Management Teams from Founding to IPO." *Organization Science* 19 (1): 3–24.

Ben-Bassat, A. 2002. "The Obstacle Course to a Market Economy in Israel." In *The Israeli Economy, 1985–1998: From Government Interventions to Market Economics*, edited by A. Ben-Bassat, 1–60. Cambridge, MA: MIT Press.

Bernstein, J. 1990. "Big Catch for Small Fry." *Newsday*, May 18, p. 47.

Bhide, A. V. 2000. *The Origin and Evolution of New Business.* Oxford: Oxford University Press.

Blum, A., and A. Tishler. 2000. "Security Needs and the Performance of the Defense Industry." Working Paper, Israel Institute of Business Research, Graduate School of Business, Tel Aviv University.

Boeker, W. 1988. "Organizational Origins: Entrepreneurial and Environmental Imprinting at the Time of Founding." In *Ecological Models of Organizations*, edited by G. R. Carroll, 33–52. Cambridge, MA: Ballinger.

———. 1989. "Strategic Change: The Effects of Founding and History." *Academy of Management Journal* 32 (3): 489–515.

———. 1997. "Executive Migration and Strategic Change: The Effect of Top Management Movement on Product-Market Entry." *Administrative Science Quarterly* 42 (2): 213–236.

Bonen, Z. 1995. "The Defense Industry: The Horse of Shalom Aleicem?" In *Discussions in National Defense*, edited by M. Arens, G. Steinberg, S. Sadeh, R. Shalom, Z. Bonen, and O. Tov, 37–41 [in Hebrew]. Ramat Gan, Israel: Begin-Sadat (BESA) Center for Strategic Studies, Bar Ilan University.

Bonne, A. 1958. "Entrepreneurial Problems in Israel." *Middle East Journal* 12: 89–95.

Braun, E., and S. MacDonald. 1982. *Revolution in Miniature: The History and Impact of Semiconductor Electronics.* 2nd ed. Cambridge: Cambridge University Press.

Bresnahan, T., A. Gambardella, and A. Saxenian. 2001. "'Old Economy' Inputs for 'New Economy' Outcomes: Cluster Formation in the New Silicon Valleys." *Industrial and Corporate Change* 10 (4): 835–860.

Breznitz, D. 2002. "Conceiving New Industrial Systems: The Different Emergence Paths of High-Technology Companies in Israel and Ireland." Working Paper Series, Science, Technology, and the Economy Program (STE), Samuel Neaman Institute for Advanced Studies in Science and Technology, Technion–Israel Institute of Technology, Haifa.

———. 2005a. "Collaborative Public Space in a National Innovation System: A Case Study of the Israeli Military's Impact on the Software Industry." *Industry and Innovation* 12 (1): 31–64.

———. 2005b. "An Iron Cage or the Final Stage? Intensive Product R&D and the Evolution of the Israeli Software Industry." Working Paper, Georgia Institute of Technology, Atlanta.

———. 2006. "Innovation-Based Industrial Policy in Emerging Economies: The Case of the Israeli IT Sector." *Business and Politics* 8 (1): 1–38.

———. 2007. *Innovation and the State: Political Choice and Strategies for Growth in Israel, Taiwan and Ireland.* New Haven, CT: Yale University Press.

Brookfield, J., S. J. Chang, I. Drori, S. Ellis, J. Lazzarini, G. J. Siegel, and J. P. von Bernath-Bardina. 2012. "The Small Worlds of Business Groups: Liberalization and Network Dynamics." In *The Small Worlds of Corporate Governance*, edited by Bruce Kogut, chap. 3. Cambridge, MA: MIT Press.

Burt, R. S. 2000. "The Network Structure of Social Capital." In *Research in Organizational Behavior*, edited by R. Sutton and B. Staw, 345–423. Greenwich, CT: JAI Press.

Burton, M. D. 2001. "The Company They Keep: Founders' Model for Organizing New Firms." In *The Entrepreneurship Dynamics*, edited by C. B. Schoonhoven and E. Romanelli, 13–39. Stanford, CA: Stanford University Press.

Burton, M. D., and C. M. Beckman. 2007. "Leaving a Legacy: Position Imprints and Successor Turnover in Young Firms." *American Sociological Review* 72 (2): 239–266.

Burton, M. D., J. B. Sorensen, and C. M. Beckman. 2002. "Coming from Good Stock: Career Histories and New Venture Formation." In *Research in the Sociology of Organizations*, edited by M. Lounsbury and M. J. Ventresca, 229–262. New York: Elsevier Science.

Cabral, L., and Z. Wang. 2008. "Spin-Offs: Theory and Evidence." Working Paper 08-15, Economic Research Department, Federal Reserve Bank of Kansas City.

Caesarea Forum. 2009. *The Future of Growth Promotion in Israel: A Return to Boosting Avant-Garde Industries and Scientific-Technological Innovation.* Jerusalem: Israeli Democracy Institute.

Campbell, D. T. 1965. "Variation and Selective Retention in Socio-Cultural Evolution." In *Social Change in Developing Areas: A Reinterpretation of Evolutionary Theory*, edited by H. R. Barringer, G. I. Blanksten, and R. W. Mack, 19–48. Cambridge, MA: Schenkman.

Carmel, A., and C. de Fontenay. 2004. "Israel's Silicon Wadi: The Forces behind Cluster Formation." In *Building High Tech Clusters: Silicon Valley and Beyond*, edited by T. Bresnahan and A. Gambardella, 40–77. Cambridge: Cambridge University Press.

Carroll, G. R. 1984. "Organizational Ecology." *Annual Review of Sociology* 10 (1): 71–93.

Carroll, G. R., L. S. Bigelow, M. D. Seidel, and L. B. Tsai. 1996. "The Fate of de Novo and de Alio Producers in the American Automobile Industry, 1885–1981." *Strategic Management Journal* 17 (2): 117–137.

Carroll, G. R., and M. T. Hannan. 2000. *The Demography of Corporations and Industries.* Princeton, NJ: Princeton University Press.

Castilla, E. J., H. Hwang, E. Granovetter, and M. Granovetter. 2000. "Social Networks in Silicon Valley." In *The Silicon Valley Edge: A Habitat for Innovation and Entrepreneurship*, edited by C. M. Lee, W. F. Miller, M. G. Hancock, and H. S. Rowen, 218–247. Stanford, CA: Stanford University Press.

Chatterjee, S., and E. Rossi-Hansberg. 2008. "Spinoffs and the Market for Ideas." Working Paper 08-26, Federal Reserve Bank of Philadelphia.

Chatterji, A. K. 2009. "Spawned with a Silver Spoon: Entrepreneurial Performance and Innovation in the Medical Device Industry." *Strategic Management Journal* 30 (2): 185–206.

Christensen, C. M. 1993. "The Rigid Disk Drive Industry: A History of Commercial and Technological Turbulence." *Business History Review* 67 (4): 531–588.

Cohen, E. 2009. *The Israeli High-Tech: Lack of Future Thinking.* Jerusalem: Carmel.

Cooper, A. 1985. "The Role of Incubator Organizations in the Founding of Growth Oriented Firms." *Journal of Business Venturing* 1 (1): 75–86.

Daniel, A. 1976. *Labor Enterprises in Israel.* New Brunswick, NJ: Transaction.

David, P. A. 1994. "Why Are Institutions the 'Carriers of History'? Path Dependence and the Evolution of Conventions, Organizations and Institutions." *Structural Change and Economic Dynamics* 5 (2): 205–220.

de Fontenay, C., and E. Carmel. 2001. "Israel's Silicon Wadi: The Forces behind Cluster Formation." In *Building High-Tech Clusters: Silicon Valley and Beyond*, edited by T. Bresnahan, A. Gambardella, and A. Saxenian, 2–36. Cambridge: Cambridge University Press.

Dencker, J. C., M. Gruber, and S. Shah. 2009. "Individual and Opportunity Factors Influencing Job Creation in New Firms." *Academy of Management Journal* 52 (6): 1125–1147.

de Nooy, W., A. Mrvar, and V. Batagelj. 2005. *Exploratory Social Network Analysis with Pajek.* Cambridge: Cambridge University Press.

DiMaggio, P. J., and W. W. Powell. 1983. "The Iron Cage Revisited: Institutional Isomorphism and Collective Rationality in Organizational Fields." *American Sociological Review* 48 (2): 147–160.

———. 1991. "Introduction." In *The New Institutionalism in Organization Analysis*, edited by W. W. Powell and P. J. DiMaggio, 1–38. Chicago: University of Chicago Press.

Dobrev, S. D., and A. Gotsopoulos. 2010. "Legitimacy Vacuum, Structural Imprinting, and the First-Mover Disadvantage." *Academy of Management Journal* 53 (5): 1153–1174.

Drori, I. 2000. *The Seam Line: Arab Women and Jewish Managers in the Israeli Textile Industry.* Stanford, CA: Stanford University Press.

Drori, I., and D. Landau. 2011. *Vision and Change in Institutional Entrepreneurship: From Science to Commercialization.* New York: Berghahn Books.

Drori, I., A. Wrzesniewski, and S. Ellis. 2012. "Symbolic Boundaries and Boundary Work during Post-Merger Integration." Working Paper, Faculty of Management, Tel Aviv University.

Durkheim, E. 1933. *The Division of Labor in Society.* New York: Free Press.

Dvir, D., and A. Tishler. 1999. "The Changing Role of the Defense Industry in Israel's Industrial and Technological Development." Working Paper, Israel Institute of Business Research, Graduate School of Business, Tel Aviv University.

Dyck, B. 1997. "Exploring Organizational Family Trees: A Multigenerational Approach for Studying Organizational Births." *Journal of Management Inquiry* 6 (3): 222–233.

Eckhardt, J. T., and S. Shane. 2003. "Opportunities and Entrepreneurship." *Journal of Management* 29 (3): 333–349.

Eilam, Y. 1974. *A Time to Build.* Tel Aviv: Am Oved/Tarbut Vechinuch.

Eisenhardt, K. M., and C. B. Schoonhoven. 1996. "Resource-Based View of Strategic Alliance Formation: Strategic and Social Effects in Entrepreneurial Firms." *Organization Science* 7 (2): 136–150.

Eisenstadt, S. N. 1969. *Israeli Society.* New York: Basic Books.

Fiegenbaum, A. 2007. *The Take-Off of Israeli High Tech Entrepreneurship in the 1990s: A Strategic Management Research Perspective.* Oxford: Elsevier.

Florida, R., and M. Kenney. 1988a. "Venture Capital, High Technology and Regional Development." *Regional Studies* 22 (1): 33–48.

———. 1988b. "Venture Capital–Financing Innovation and Technological Change in the U.S." *Research Policy* 17 (3): 119–137.

Fox, R. 1984. *Kinship and Marriage: An Anthropological Perspective.* Cambridge: Cambridge University Press.

Franco, A. M. 2005. "Employee Entrepreneurship: Recent Research and Future Directions." In *Handbook of Entrepreneurship Research*, edited by S. A. Alvarez, R. Agarwal, and O. Sorenson, 81–97. New York: Springer.

Franco, A. M., and D. Filson. 2006. "Spin-Outs: Knowledge Diffusion through Employee Mobility." *RAND Journal of Economics* 37 (4): 841–860.

Freeman, J. H. 1986. "Entrepreneurs as Organizational Products: Semiconductor Firms and Venture Capital Firms." In *Advances in the Study of Entrepreneurship, Innovation, and Economic Growth*, edited by G. Libecap, 1:33–52. Greenwich, CT: JAI Press.

Freeman, J., G. R. Carroll, and M. T. Hannan. 1983. "Liability of Newness: Age Dependence in Organizational Death Rate." *American Sociological Review* 48 (5): 692–710.

Fukuyama, F. 1996. *Trust: The Social Virtue and the Creation of Prosperity.* New York: Free Press.

Gabbay, S. M., I. Talmud, and O. Raz. 2001. "Corporate Social Capital and Strategic Isomorphism: The Case of the Israeli Software Industry." *Social Capital of Organizations* 18: 135–150.

Galai, D., and Y. Schachar. 1993. *Technology Transfer and Projects Conversion in the Israeli Defense Industry* [in Hebrew]. Jerusalem: Israel Democracy Institute.

Ganco, M., and R. Agarwal. 2009. "Performance Differentials between Diversifying Entrants and Entrepreneurial Start-Ups: A Complexity Approach." *Academy of Management Review* 34 (2): 228–253.

Garvin, D. 1983. "Spin-Offs and New Firm Formation." *California Management Review* 25 (2): 3–20.

Getz, D., H. Mansour, D. Peled, and M. Shumaf-Tehawkho. 2005. "Science and Technology Indicators in Israel: An International Comparison." National Policy Research Paper Series, Samuel Neaman Institute for Advanced Studies in Science and Technology, Technion–Israel Institute of Technology, Haifa.

Goel, A. 2007. "Success Is Fulfilling One's Objectives." www.itmagz.com.

Gompers, P., A. Kovner, J. Lerner, and D. Scharfstein. 2006. "Skill vs. Luck in Entrepreneurship and Venture Capital: Evidence from Serial Entrepreneurs." NBER Working Paper, National Bureau of Economic Research, Cambridge, MA.

Gompers, P., J. Lerner, and D. Scharfstein. 2005. "Entrepreneurial Spawning: Public Co-operation and the Genesis of New Venture, 1986–1999." *Journal of Finance* 60 (2): 577–614.

Granovetter, M., and P. McGuire. 1998. "The Making of an Industry: Electricity in the United States." In *The Laws of the Markets*, edited by M. Callon, 147–173. Oxford: Blackwell/Sociological Review.

Greenberg, Y. 1987. *From Workers' Society to Workers' Economy: Evolution of the Idea of Hevrat Ha'Ovdim in the Years 1920–1929* [in Hebrew]. Tel Aviv: Papyrus.

Hannan, M. T., M. D. Burton, and J. N. Baron. 1996. "Inertia and Change in the Early Years: Employment Relations in Young, High Technology Firms." *Industrial and Corporate Change* 5 (2): 503–536.

Hannan, M. T., and G. R. Carroll. 1992. *Dynamics of Organizational Populations: Density, Legitimation and Competition*. New York: Oxford University Press.

Hannan, M. T., and J. H. Freeman. 1977. "The Population Ecology of Organizations." *American Journal of Sociology* 82 (5): 929–964.

———. 1984. "Structural Inertia and Organizational Change." *American Sociological Review* 49 (2): 149–164.

———. 1989. *Organizational Ecology*. Cambridge, MA: Harvard University Press.

Hargadon, A. B., and Y. Douglas. 2001. "When Innovation Meets Institutions: Edison and the Design of the Electric Light." *Administrative Science Quarterly* 46 (3): 476–501.

Haspel, B. 1990. "In the Beginning There Was a Dream." *Tadiran Company Magazine*, pp. 13-16.

Helfat, C. E., and M. B. Lieberman. 2002. "The Birth Capabilities: Market Entry and the Importance of Prehistory." *Industrial and Corporate Change* 11 (4): 725–760.

Helfat, C. E., and M. A. Peteraf. 2003. "The Dynamic Resource-Based View: Capability Lifecycles." *Strategic Management Journal* 24 (10): 997–1010.

Higgins, M. C., and R. Gulati. 2003. "Getting Off to a Good Start: The Effects of Upper Echelon Affiliations on Inter-Organizational Endorsements." Working Paper, Harvard Business School, Boston.

Hite, J. M., and W. S. Hesterly. 2001. "The Evolution of Firm Networks: From Emergence to Early Growth of the Firm." *Strategic Management Journal* 22 (3): 275–286.

Hoang, H., and B. Antoncic. 2003. "Network-Based Research in Entrepreneurship: A Critical Review." *Journal of Business Venturing* 18 (2): 165–187.

Honig, B., M. Lerner, and Y. Raban. 2006. "High-Tech Companies and the Israeli Military Defense System." *Small Business Economics* 27 (4/5): 419–437.

Horowitz, D., and M. Lissak. 1989. *Trouble in Utopia: The Overburdened Polity of Israel*. Chicago: University of Chicago Press.

Ito, K. 1995. "Japanese Spinoffs: Unexplored Survival Strategies." *Strategic Management Journal* 16 (6): 431–446.

Ito, K., and E. L. Rose. 1994. "The Genealogical Structure of Japanese Firms: Parent-Subsidiary Relationships." *Strategic Management Journal* 15 (Summer): 35–51.

Jaffee, J., and D. G. McKendrick. 2006. "The Cumulative and Temporal Effects of Spin-Outs on the Performance of Parent Firms (Progenitors) in the Hard Disk Drive

Industry." Working Paper, Durham University, Durham, UK.Johnson, V. 2007. "What Is Organizational Imprinting? Cultural Entrepreneurship in the Founding of the Paris Opera." *American Journal of Sociology* 113 (1): 97–127.

Justman, M., and M. Teubal. 1996. "Technological Infrastructure Policy (TIP): Creating Capabilities and Building Markets." *Research Policy* 24 (2): 259–281.

Kenney, M., ed. 2000. *Understanding Silicon Valley: Anatomy of an Entrepreneurial Region.* Stanford, CA: Stanford University Press.

Kenney, M., and U. von Burg. 2000. "Institutions and Economies: Creating Silicon Valley." In *Understanding Silicon Valley: Anatomy of an Entrepreneurial Region*, edited by M. Kenney, 218–240. Stanford, CA: Stanford University Press.

Klepper, S. 1996. "Entry, Exit, Growth, and Innovation over the Product Life Cycle." *American Economic Review* 86 (3): 562–583.

———. 2001. "Employee Startups in High-Tech Industries." *Industrial and Corporate Change* 10 (3): 639–674.

———. 2002. "The Capabilities of New Firms and the Evolution of the US Automobile Industry." *Industrial and Corporate Change* 11 (4): 645–666.

———. 2009. "Spinoffs: A Review and Synthesis." *European Management Review* 6 (3): 159–171.

Klepper, S., and S. D. Sleeper. 2005. "Entry by Spin-Offs." *Management Science* 51 (8): 1291–1306.

Klepper, S., and P. Thompson. 2010. "Disagreements and Intra-Industry Spinoffs." *International Journal of Industrial Organization* 28 (5): 526–538.

Klieman, A. 1992. *Double-Edged Sword: Israel Defense Exports as an Instrument of Foreign Policy* [in Hebrew]. Tel Aviv: Am Oved.

Kraatz, M. S., and J. H. Moore. 2002. "Executive Migration and Institutional Change." *Academy of Management Journal* 45 (1): 120–143.

Lavie, D., U. Stettner, and M. L. Tushman. 2010. "Exploration and Exploitation within and across Organizations." *Academy of Management Annals* 4 (1): 109–155.

Levav, A. 1998. *Shevavim-shel-tikva: The Story of the Birth of Israel's High-Tech Industry.* Tel Aviv: Zemorah-Bitan.

Levi-Faur, D. 2001. *The Visible Hand: State-Directed Industrialization in Israel* [in Hebrew]. Jerusalem: Yad Ben-Zvi.

Lorenzoni, G., and A. Lipparini. 1999. "The Leveraging of Inter-Firm Relationships as a Distinctive Organizational Capacity: A Longitudinal Study." *Strategic Management Journal* 20 (4): 317–338.

Lounsbury, M., and M. A. Glynn. 2001. "Cultural Entrepreneurship: Stories, Legitimacy, and the Acquisition of Resources." *Strategic Management Journal* 22 (6/7): 545–564.

Maman, D. 2004. "Business Groups in the Israeli Economy: Factors of Formation/Consolidation and Strengthening." In *The Power of Property: Israeli Society in the Global Age*, edited by D. Filc and U. Ram, 113–160. Tel Aviv: Van Leer Jerusalem Institute/Hakibbutz Hameuchad.

March, J. 1991. "Exploration and Exploitation in Organizational Learning." *Organizational Science* 2 (1): 71–87.

Marquis, C. 2003. "The Pressure of the Past: Network Imprinting in Intercorporate Communities." *Administrative Science Quarterly* 48 (4): 655–689.

Marquis, C., and Z. Huang. 2010. "Acquisitions as Exaptation: The Legacy of Founding Institutions in the U.S. Commercial Banking Industry." *Administrative Science Quarterly* 53 (6): 1441–1473.

McGahan, A. M. 2004. *How Industries Evolve: Principles for Achieving and Sustaining Superior Performance*. Boston: Harvard Business School Press.

Meyer, J. W., and B. Rowan. 1977. "Institutionalized Organizations: Formal Structure as Myth and Ceremony." *American Journal of Sociology* 83 (2): 340–363.

———. 1983. "Institutionalized Organizations: Formal Structure as Myth and Ceremony." In *Organizational Environments Ritual and Rationality*, edited by W. Meyer, B. Rowan, and T. E. Deal, 21–44. Beverly Hills, CA: Sage.

Michalson, E. 1985. "Tadiran." *Tadiran Company Magazine*, pp. 34–36

Mohney, D. 2007. "Zohar Zisapel, Founder and Chairman, the RAD Group." *VON Magazine*, May 22, pp. 21–23.

Murray, F. 2011. "The Oncomouse That Roared: Hybrid Exchange Strategies as a Source of Distinction at the Boundaries of Overlapping Institutions." *American Journal of Sociology* 116 (2): 341–388.

Naor, M. 1977. *Keshet Deruchah: Friends Tell about Moshe Kashti*. Tel Aviv: Milo.

Neck, H. M., G. D. Meyer, A. C. Cohen, and A. C. Corbett. 2004. "An Entrepreneurial System View of New Venture Creation." *Journal of Small Business Management* 42 (2): 190–208.

Nelson, R. R., and S. G. Winter. 1982. *An Evolutionary Theory of Economic Change*. Cambridge, MA: Harvard University Press.

Netanyahu, B. 2010. "Address by PM Netanyahu at the High Tech Industry Association Annual Conference." http://www.htia.co.il/images/stories/Pdf/PM_Netanyahu_HTIA_Conf.pdf.

Nonaka, I., G. Von Krogh, and S. Voelpel. 2006. "Organizational Knowledge Creation Theory: Evolutionary Paths and Future Advances." *Organization Studies* 27 (8): 1179–1208.

Phillips, D. 2002. "A Genealogical Approach to Organizational Life Chances." *Administrative Science Quarterly* 47 (3): 474–506.

———. 2005. "Organizational Genealogies and the Persistence of Gender Hierarchies: The Case of Silicon Valley Law Firms." *Administrative Science Quarterly* 50 (3): 440–472.

Piore, M. L. J., and C. F. Sabel. 1984. *The Second Industrial Divide: Possibilities for Prosperity*. New York: Basic Books.

Plunkett, M. 1958. "The Histadrut: The General Federation of Jewish Labor in Israel." *Industrial and Labor Relations Review* 11 (2): 152–155.

Podolny, J., and T. Stuart. 1995. "A Role-Based Ecology of Technological Change." *American Journal of Sociology* 100 (5): 1224–1260.

Porter, M. E. 1998. "Cluster and the New Economic of Competition." *Harvard Business Review* 76 (6): 77–90.

Powell, W. W., K. Packalen, and K. Whittington. Forthcoming. "Organizational and Institutional Genesis: The Emergence of High-Tech Clusters in the Life Sciences." In *The Emergence of Organization and Markets*, edited by J. Padgett and W. Powell, Princeton, NJ: Princeton University Press.

Powell, W. W., D. R. White, K. W. Koput, and J. Owen-Smith. 2005. "Network Dynamics and Field Evolution: The Growth of Inter-Organizational Collaboration in the Life Sciences." *American Journal of Sociology* 110 (4): 1132–1205.

Remennick, L. 2007. *Russian Jews on Three Continents: Identity, Integration, and Conflict.* New Brunswick, NJ: Transaction.

Ringer, R. C., and K. C. Strong. 1998. "Managerial Perceptions of Change at a National Laboratory." *Leadership and Organization Development Journal* 19 (1): 14–21.

Rogers, E. M., and J. Larsen. 1984. *Silicon Valley Fever: Growth of High-Technology Culture.* New York: Basic Books.

Romanelli, E., and C. B. Schoonhoven. 2001. "The Local Origin of New Firms." In *The Entrepreneurship Dynamics: Origin of Entrepreneurship and the Evolution of Industries*, edited by C. B. Schoonhoven and E. Romanelli, 40–67. Stanford, CA: Stanford University Press.

Rose, E., and K. Ito. 2005. "Widening the Family Circle: Spinoffs in the Japanese Service Sector." *Long Range Planning* 38 (1): 9–26.

Ruef, M. 2005. "Origins of Organizations: The Entrepreneurial Process." *Research in the Sociology of Work* 15: 63–100.

Sadeh, S. 1995. "The Process of Recovery of the Defense Industries." In *Discussions in National Defense*, edited by M. Arens, G. Steinberg, S. Sadeh, R. Shalom, Z. Bonen, and O. Tov, 15–29 [in Hebrew]. Ramat Gan, Israel: Begin-Sadat (BESA) Center for Strategic Studies, Bar Ilan University.

Saxenian, A. 1994. *Regional Advantage: Culture and Competition in Silicon Valley and Route 128.* Cambridge, MA: Harvard University Press.

———. 2002. "Transnational Communities and the Evolution of Global Production Networks: The Cases of Taiwan, China and India." *Industry and Innovation* 9 (3): 183–202.

———. 2006. *The New Argonauts.* Cambridge, MA: MIT Press.

Scott, W. R. 2001. *Institutions and Organizations.* Thousand Oaks, CA: Sage.

Senor, D., and S. Singer. 2009. *Start-Up Nation: The Story of Israel's Economic Miracle.* New York: Twelve.

Shafir, G., and Y. Peled. 2002. *Being Israeli: The Dynamics of Multiple Citizenship.* Cambridge: Cambridge University Press.

Shane, S. 2000. "Prior Knowledge and the Discovery of Entrepreneurial Opportunities." *Organization Science* 11 (4): 448–469.

———. 2001. "Technological Opportunities and New Firm Creation." *Management Science* 47 (2): 205–220.

Shane, S., and D. Cable. 2002. "Network Ties, Reputation, and the Financing of New Ventures." *Management Science* 48 (3): 364–381.

Shane, S., E. A. Locke, and C. J. Collins. 2003. "Entrepreneurial Motivation." *Human Resource Management Review* 13 (2): 257–279.

Shane, S., and T. Stuart. 2002. "Organizational Endowments and the Performance of University Start-Ups." *Management Science* 48 (1): 154–170.

Stahl-Rolf, S. R. 2000. "Descendance and Social Genealogies: Toward an Evolutionary Conception of Economic History." *Journal of Economic Issues* 34 (4): 891–908.

Stinchcombe, A. L. 1965. "Social Structure and Organization." In *Handbook of Organizations*, edited by J. G. March, 142–193. Chicago: Rand McNally.

———. 1968. *Constructing Social Theories.* New York: Harcourt Brace and World.

Stuart, T. E., H. Hoang, and R. Hybels. 1999. "Interorganizational Endorsements and the Performance of Entrepreneurial Ventures." *Administrative Science Quarterly* 44 (2): 315–349.

Suchman, M. C. Forthcoming. "Constructed Ecologies: Reproduction and Structuration in Emerging Organizational Communities." In *Remaking the Iron Cage: Institutional Dynamics and Processes*, edited by W. W. Powell and D. Jones. Chicago: University of Chicago Press.

Swaminathan, A. 1996. "Environmental Conditions at Founding and Organizational Mortality: A Trial-by-Fire Model." *Academy of Management Journal* 39 (5): 1350–1377.

Sydow, J., G. Schreyögg, and J. Koch. 2009. "Organizational Path Dependence: Opening the Black Box." *Academy of Management Review* 34 (4): 689–709.

Teubal, M. 1993. "The Innovation System of Israel: Description, Performance and Outstanding Issues." In *National Innovation Systems*, edited by R. Nelson, 476–502. Oxford: Oxford University Press.

———. 1996. "R&D and Technology Policy in NICs as Learning Processes." *World Development* 24 (3): 449–460.

———. 1997. "A Catalytic and Evolutionary Approach to Horizontal Technology Policies (HTPs)." *Research Policy* 25 (8): 1161–1188.

———. 2002. "What Is the Systems Perspective to Innovation and Technology Policy (ITP) and How Can We Apply It to Developing and Newly Industrialized Economies?" *Journal of Evolutionary Economics* 12 (1/2): 233–257.

Teubal, M., and E. Andersen. 2000. "Enterprise Restructuring and Embeddedness: A Policy and Systems Perspective." *Industrial and Corporate Change* 9 (1): 87–111.

Thompson, J. D. 1967. *Organizations in Action.* New York: McGraw-Hill.

Timor, E. 1997a. "It All Started in Boston." *Globes*, April 16.

———. 1997b. "What an Optical Illusion Can Do." *Globes*, April 16.

Trachtenberg, M. 2001. "Innovation in Israel 1968–1997: A Comparative Analysis Using Patent Data." *Research Policy* 30 (3): 363–389.

Tucker, D. J., J. V. Singh, and A. G. Meinhardt. 1990. "Founding Characteristics, Imprinting and Organizational Change." In *Organizational Evolution: New Direction*, edited by V. Singh, 182–200. Newbury Park, CA: Sage.

Tushman, M. L., and P. Anderson. 1986. "Technological Discontinuities and Organizational Environments." *Administrative Science Quarterly* 31 (3): 439–465.

Vergne, J., and R. Durand. 2010. "The Missing Link between the Theory and Empirics of Path Dependence: Conceptual Clarification, Testability Issue, and Methodological Implications." *Journal of Management Studies* 47 (4): 736–759.

Wasserman, N. 2012. *The Founder's Dilemmas: Anticipating and Avoiding the Pitfalls That Can Sink a Startup.* Princeton, NJ: Princeton University Press.

Weidenbaum, M., and S. Hughes. 1996. *The Bamboo Network.* New York: Free Press.

Wiewel, W., and A. Hunter. 1985. "The Inter-Organizational Network as a Resource: A Comparative Case Study on Organizational Genesis." *Administrative Science Quarterly* 30 (4): 482–496.

Winter, S. G. 1984. "Schumpeterian Competition in Alternative Technological Regimes." *Journal of Economic Behavior and Organization* 5 (3/4): 287–320.

Wylie, C. 2011 "Vision in Venture: Israel's High Tech Incubator Program." *Cell Cycle* 10 (6): 855–858.

Yaar-Yuchtman, E., and Y. Shavit. 2001. *Trends in the Israeli Society.* Tel Aviv: Open University.

Yerushalmi, S. 2002. "Incubators in Israel: Ten Years of Experience." *International Journal of Entrepreneurship and Innovation* 3 (4): 295–299.

Yona, A. 2006. *Mission with No Traces.* Englewood, NJ: Devora.

Zilber, T. 2006. "The Work of the Symbolic in Institutional Processes: Translations of Rational Myths in Israeli High-Tech." *Academy of Management Journal* 49 (2): 281–303.

———. 2007. "Stories and the Discursive Dynamics of Institutional Entrepreneurship: The Case of Israeli High-Tech after the Bubble." *Organization Studies* 28 (7): 1035–1054.

———. 2011. "Institutional Multiplicity in Practice: A Tale of Two High-Tech Conferences in Israel." *Organization Science* 22 (6): 1539–1559.

Index

Italic page numbers indicate material in tables or figures.